UNITED STATES OF SOCIALISM

ALSO BY DINESH D'SOUZA

Death of a Nation

The Big Lie

Hillary's America

Stealing America

America: Imagine a World without Her

Obama's America

Godforsaken

The Roots of Obama's Rage

Life after Death

What's So Great about Christianity

The Enemy at Home

Letters to a Young Conservative

What's So Great about America

The Virtue of Prosperity

Ronald Reagan

The End of Racism

Illiberal Education

UNITED STATES OF SOCIALISM

WHO'S BEHIND IT.

WHY IT'S EVIL.

HOW TO STOP IT.

DINESH D'SOUZA

ALL POINTS
BOOKS
NEW YORK

First published in the United States by All Points Books, an imprint of St. Martin's Publishing Group

UNITED STATES OF SOCIALISM. Copyright © 2020 by Dinesh D'Souza. All rights reserved. Printed in the United States of America. For information, address St. Martin's Publishing Group, 120 Broadway, New York, NY 10271.

www.allpointsbooks.com

Library of Congress Cataloging-in-Publication Data

Names: D'Souza, Dinesh, 1961- author.
Title: United States of socialism : Who's behind it. Why it's evil. How to stop it / Dinesh D'Souza.
Description: First Edition. | New York : All Points Books, 2020. | Includes bibliographical references and index.
Identifiers: LCCN 2020006770 | ISBN 9781250163783 (hardcover) | ISBN 9781250758309 (ebook)
Subjects: LCSH: Socialism—United States—History—21st century. | United States—Economic policy—21st century. | Socialism—Political aspects—United States. Socialist parties—United States.
Classification: LCC HX86 .D76 2020 | DDC 335.00973—dc23
LC record available at https://lccn.loc.gov/2020006770

Our books may be purchased in bulk for promotional, educational, or business use. Please contact your local bookseller or the Macmillan Corporate and Premium Sales Department at 1-800-221-7945, extension 5442, or by email at MacmillanSpecialMarkets@macmillan.com.

First Edition: June 2020

10   9   8   7   6   5   4   3   2   1

For Ed McVaney

I treasure our friendship,
which is rooted in a shared
sense of wonder and
love of the good.

TABLE OF CONTENTS

PREFACE

The Specter of Socialism

1

INTRODUCTION

Identity Socialism

11

1. THE INVENTION OF INVENTION

America and the Ideal of the Self-Made Man

33

2. THE DREAM AND THE NIGHTMARE

How Socialism Came to America

63

3. ALIEN NATION

Why Socialists Abandoned the Working Class

95

4. VENEZUELA, SI; SWEDEN, NO

Socialism and the Scandinavian Illusion

135

5. JUST DESERTS

The Moral Basis of Entrepreneurial Capitalism

173

6. THE ART OF WAR

Battle Plan to Defeat the Socialists

219

APPENDIX

257

NOTES

261

INDEX

281

UNITED STATES OF SOCIALISM

PREFACE

Here grows the cure of all, this fruit divine
Fair to the eye, inviting to the taste,
Of virtue to make wise; what hinders, then
To reach, and feed at once body and mind?[1]

—JOHN MILTON, *PARADISE LOST*

A specter is haunting America—the specter of socialism. Suddenly, almost out of nowhere, we encounter a mélange of strange socialist characters—Alexandria Ocasio-Cortez, Rashida Tlaib, Ilhan Omar, Bernie Sanders—and a whole political party that seems magnetically drawn toward the socialist camp. This development by itself is surpassingly strange, because socialism is arguably the most discredited idea in history.

True, many big ideas, and their corresponding ways of organizing society, have ended up on the ash heap of history. Monarchy, for instance, is gone, surviving today only in cosmetic—which is to say, constitutional—form. Feudalism exists in some form in backward countries, but for us in the West it can only be seen in history's rearview mirror.

Even so, monarchy and feudalism have never been fully discredited. From the beginning of time, there have been good kings and bad kings. At some point in history—dating to around the time of the American Revolution—most people in the West decided that they didn't want to live under kings, not even under good kings. They wanted to govern themselves, through some form of representative government. And

1

so monarchy was transcended without ever being completely refuted. Similarly, the feudal system was basically transcended by the capitalist system, as Marx himself recognized. Feudalism couldn't compete with capitalism, so feudalism was defeated without being discredited on its own terms. Feudal societies, like monarchies, "worked" for many centuries before their eventual demise.

None of this can be said about socialism. It is an utterly discredited system of ideas, like slavery, and it was discredited in a much shorter period. Slavery lasted for centuries—even millennia—before it was recognized as a thoroughly wicked and tyrannical regime of human exploitation. Socialism, which dates back to 1917, when Lenin founded the world's first socialist state, has had a much shorter shelf life. It too collapsed across the world because the people who lived under it considered it to be a form of slavery.

We see the connection between socialism and slavery in all the important works on socialism. Friedrich Hayek's critique of socialism is appropriately titled *The Road to Serfdom*. George Orwell depicted the tyrannical dimension of socialism in his two immortal novels, *Animal Farm* and *1984*. Using the techniques of both fiction and nonfiction, Alexandr Solzhenitsyn in a series of works—*The Gulag Archipelago, One Day in the Life of Ivan Denisovich*—depicted Soviet socialism as a vast network of slave camps stretching from Europe to the farthest reaches of Asia.

Slavery in its classic form has been abolished worldwide, although enslavement in other forms—sex trafficking for instance—continues as a gruesome relic of this barbaric practice. Even so, no serious person today could advocate the return of slavery. How ridiculous it would be to hear someone say, "The failures of slavery were all failures of implementation. This time we're really gonna make it work!" Yet here we have socialism in America attempting a comeback, and on precisely those terms: this time we're gonna get it right. Serious people advocate it; there is a sustained cultural push to apotheosize it; a major political party is pushing aggressively toward it. How is this possible? Apparently socialism means never having to say you're sorry.

Socialism has made everyday existence a living hell nearly everywhere it has been tried, all over the world. Let's not forget that within about a century since Marx wrote, and less than half a century since the Bolshevik Revolution, some 60 percent of the world's people were living under governments that embraced some form of socialism. At one time, Joshua Muravchik writes, "it was the most popular political idea ever invented, arguably the most popular idea of any kind about how life should be lived or society organized."[2]

The biggest socialist experiment was the Soviet bloc, an orbit of countries including the Soviet Union, Poland, Yugoslavia, Albania, Czechoslovakia, Hungary, Romania and East Germany. Prior to the Soviet occupation of its eastern region, Germany imposed its own distinct version of socialism, National Socialism or Nazism, from 1933 to 1945. In Asia, Vietnam, Laos, Cambodia, North Korea and China experimented with socialism. In South America, the governments of Cuba, Nicaragua, Bolivia and Venezuela tried it. Most of Africa went socialist in the aftermath of colonialism: Angola, Ghana, Tanzania, Benin, Mali, Mozambique, Zambia and Zimbabwe. I count here 25 experiments in socialism, all ending in unmitigated disaster.

The worst forms of socialism proved not only totalitarian but also murderous to an unprecedented degree. In the Soviet Union alone, socialist regimes killed some 20 million of their own citizens and enslaved tens of millions of others. The Chinese socialists, in the period known as Mao's Cultural Revolution, killed another 20–25 million. The Nazis murdered in comparable numbers, including Jews and gypsies and other occupied peoples, Poles, Russians, Eastern Europeans and others. Orwell's description of the future from *1984* seems appropriate to apply to socialism here: "A boot stamping on a human face."[3]

Socialists today disavow this historical record, insisting that these were authoritarian forms of socialism that they have no intention of copying. While socialism may have been the economic program of Communism and early fascism, modern socialists seek to dispense with the tyranny and merely keep the economic program. I'll examine the legitimacy of this selective borrowing later, but here it's worth stressing that socialism wasn't merely a political failure; it was also an economic failure.

Orwell somehow missed this. Interestingly, neither of his two novels offers an economic critique of socialism. There is no economic problem in *Animal Farm*; the only problem is that the pigs seize power. In *1984*, the ruling party creates poverty and scarcity to keep people in line. Great as he is, Orwell confines himself to a political critique; he exposes the totalitarian tendency of socialism. But he never shows *how* socialism creates this totalitarianism, and he leaves open the possibility of a more benign socialism that avoids it.[4]

In the real world, the political collapse of socialism was brought about by its economic failure. This was certainly true in the Soviet Union, where Gorbachev's rescue efforts—glasnost and perestroika—failed spectacularly, first bringing down the Soviet empire, then the Communist ruling party, and finally the socialist system itself. China too abandoned socialism due to its economic shortcomings. And look how poorly socialism is faring in Zimbabwe, Cuba and Venezuela today. So how can one adopt socialist ideas once again without considering the economic track record of socialist regimes?

TWO TEST CASES

Rarely in history is there a chance to actually compare social systems to see which one works better. One might compare the Plantagenet kings of England with the Tang Dynasty in China, but even if we line up the dates, we are talking about two completely different societies: different people, different cultures. Consequently, England's superiority and China's inferiority—or the other way around—can hardly be attributed to their rival systems of government, since so many other factors could be involved.

In the case of socialism, however, we have two perfect test cases: North and South Korea, and East and West Germany. The perfection of these examples comes from the fact that in each case we are dealing with the same people, same background, same culture, merely two rival economic systems. North Korea was socialist; South Korea, capitalist. East Germany was socialist; West Germany, capitalist.

When the results came in, they were decisive. At reunification, the per capita gross domestic product in socialist East Germany was just about one-third that of the capitalist West Germany, with other measures of economic performance displaying a similar chasm. Even the poorest part of West Germany, Schleswig-Holstein, was two and a half times as wealthy as the richest East German region, Saxony. Even now, the eastern part of Germany gets nearly 15 percent of its gross domestic product in net transfers from the western part of Germany.

The Korean example is even more telling, in part because the separation of the two societies has lasted longer and continues to this day. South Korea now is more than 20 times richer than North Korea, a difference manifested in virtually all indicators of human welfare. South Koreans are obviously freer than North Koreans; South Koreans are also taller, healthier and live about 12 years longer than North Koreans. Every year many thousands of North Koreans risk their lives seeking to escape to South Korea.[5]

I have my own lived experience to draw on to compare socialism and capitalism, both of which have been tried in my lifetime in my native country of India. The Indian leaders, some of whom studied Fabian socialism in England, adopted socialism complete with Soviet-style five-year plans when India became independent in 1947. I grew up under Indian socialism—which I remind you was democratic socialism—and experienced its signature institutions. One was everyday corruption; literally nothing could be done without paying some petty bureaucrat under the table. Another was the ration card, which specified the paltry amount of sugar or cooking oil that a family was permitted to purchase each month. A third was a seven-year waiting period to get a phone.

During this era, India was widely known as the begging bowl of the world. Americans told their children, "Eat your food because there are millions of starving people in India." Gandhi spoke wistfully about "wiping a tear from every Indian face." A whole generation of young Indians in the 1960s and 1970s saw no future for themselves and fled to work at sea, like my brother, or to Dubai to do manual labor, like some of my cousins, or to Australia, Canada and America, like me.

Today's young Indians plan no such mass exit, because there are now opportunities for them at home. I go back to India and see Indian families who used to endure the sweltering summer heat and wash their clothes in the sea now enjoying the full benefits of modern technology, including air conditioning and washing machines. India is doing measurably better, and there is a large and newly prosperous middle class. Even the country's global reputation has changed. Today Americans tell their children, "Study hard because there are millions of Indians waiting to take your jobs."

How did the change come about? It came about through economic liberalization, otherwise known as free market capitalism. And how did India decide to move in that direction? It was not inspired by the Indians reading Adam Smith. Rather, Indians looked across the Chinese border and saw that millions of once-impoverished peasants now lived in clean homes and nice apartments. The Chinese now shopped in well-stocked grocery stores. They drove new cars.

There was no question how the Chinese did it. The People's Republic of China was founded in 1949. Under Mao, the government nationalized factories and expropriated peasants' land. Mao targeted traders and businessmen—the "bourgeoisie"—attempting in his own words to "destroy the property-owning class by killing at least one landlord in every village via public execution."[6] Mao's Great Leap Forward, announced in 1958, accelerated the collectivization of farms; in fact, he banned all private farming. The result was the greatest man-made famine in history.

Then, in 1966, Mao launched his Cultural Revolution, an attempt to erase all remaining capitalist and traditional elements from Chinese society. The Communist Red Guard enforced a purge of all dissidents. Mao issued his famous book of quotations, *The Little Red Book*, that became a central part of the curriculum of every school. Chinese citizens were expected to have a copy of Mao's writings with them at all times. (This by the way is unobjectionable: I have similar expectations of my readers.) Even so, Maoist socialism represented a disastrous alloy of deprivation, starvation and tyranny.

The change came in the late 1970s, when China, under Deng Xiaoping, abandoned the socialism of Mao for its own brand of capitalism. In doing so, the Chinese inaugurated a new experiment in social organization: call it totalitarian capitalism. No one had attempted it before; as far as I can see, no one else is attempting it now, although President Trump seems to be urging North Korea to give it a try. The Chinese

did not relinquish their Communist dictatorship; rather, they married dictatorial political control to free market liberalization. Some say it was an awkward marriage, but it worked in economic terms.

So the Indians decided to follow the economic path the Chinese had marked out. While preserving a democratic political system, India largely jettisoned socialism and embraced technological capitalism. Large parts of the Indian economy are still regulated by the government, but the trend for three decades now has been moving away from that, toward privatization, deregulation and economic liberalization. And India too has seen spectacular results. Technological capitalism has realized Gandhi's dream by wiping millions of Indian tears. As for Indian socialism, the leftist writer Pankaj Mishra frets that it shows "no signs of revival."[7]

If socialism has produced a worldwide record of misery and tears, and if countries must flee socialism to experience prosperity, what then are American socialists up to? Why would they want to import misery and tears? They insist that they are not doing this. In a sense, they disavow history, both the political and the economic legacy of all professed socialist regimes. They insist that everyone else got it wrong. They emphasize that at least some of those depressing examples, maybe all of them, were not "real socialism."

How coherent is this idea of "real socialism"? If an economic idea fails once or twice or even three times, one can still assert it was a fine idea that was merely implemented poorly. But if an idea fails 25 times, all over the world, everywhere it has been tried, without even one counter-example of it working well, it strains credulity to think that there is still some undiscovered form of socialism, heretofore unattempted, that will finally prove its viability. Yet another go at socialism now feels like Elizabeth Taylor's eighth marriage, a triumph of hope over experience.

So why doesn't the failed track record of socialist regimes deter today's socialists? What keeps socialism alive for them? The answer is: the socialist dream! Yes, there is a socialist dream just as there is an American dream. And evidently, the socialist dream is one that survives all empirical refutation. No purely experiential argument—and no set of economic arguments—is sufficient to send socialism to its grave.

This is why conservative and libertarian critiques of socialism have

gotten nowhere. The conservatives and libertarians keep chanting, "Socialism doesn't work," and they produce charts and tables to prove it. The socialists glance over the charts and tables, and then they clamor for more socialism. They don't care about data, because no amount of data can refute a dream. The socialist mantra is, "We don't care if it hasn't worked. We will figure out a way to make it work." The critics are focused on yesterday, while the socialists are all about tomorrow. Owen Jones expresses this futuristic hope: "A socialist society . . . doesn't exist yet, but one day it must."[8]

I'm reminded of the early scene in John Bunyan's *The Pilgrim's Progress* where the pilgrim, Christian, is warned by the evangelist to pursue eternal life and "flee from the wrath to come." But how, Christian asks, do I do this? The evangelist points to a wide field. "Do you see yonder wicket gate?" No. "Do you see yonder shining light?" Christian looks hard; he can barely see it. He thinks he sees something. The evangelist is undeterred; he urges Christian to follow the light, and he will reach his desired destination.

When Christian's wife and children discover that he is about to leave on a quest, having no idea when, if ever, he will return, they summon the neighbors, and together the whole group rails against Christian, mocking and threatening him. They tell him that he is a fool, and that he is neglecting his responsibilities and pursuing an illusion. But none of this deters Christian, who, in Bunyan's words, "put his fingers in his ears and ran on, crying Life! Life! Eternal life!"[9]

So it is with the socialists. They are on a grand quest, and they refuse to look back. They insist that they are the champions of a moral ideal. The only way to refute them is to refute their moral ideal, to expose their dream as a nightmare, to pop their utopian balloon. Usually people try to defeat utopia by showing that it is a fantasy. But this approach is inadequate, because a fantasy continues to hold its appeal even when it is exposed as a fantasy. So my refutation is quite different. I will expose the socialist utopia not as an illusion but rather as a racket.

Sure, socialism presents a temptation, the same temptation that some cult leaders and TV evangelists hold out to their gullible audiences. They offer their followers the temptation of paradise, freedom from the

normal drudgery and travails of life, with manna from heaven dropping into their laps. This is pretty much what the socialists promise too. The main difference is that the televangelist promises these wonders in the next life; the socialist promises them in this one. The only thing you are expected to give up is your ownership of yourself, including your right to keep what is yours, your personal autonomy and dignity and your independence of mind.

In both cases, the enterprise is driven by lust for money and lust for power, the *libido dominandi* that Augustine warns about. In principle, no less than in practice, socialism is the ideology of thieves and tyrants. As for the people who fall for the temptation, they are connivers attracted by the rip-off scheme. But they end up as suckers, because the scheme is not designed to benefit them. This book is written not to persuade the thieves and tyrants but to show the conniving suckers a better way to get ahead and to demonstrate how the rest of us can finally defeat the socialists.

INTRODUCTION

IDENTITY SOCIALISM

The blue wave is African-American. It's white, it's Latino, it's Asian, Pacific Islander. It is disabled. It is differently abled. It is LGBTQ. . . . It is comprised of those who are documented and undocumented.[1]

—STACEY ABRAMS, SPEECH AT DEMOCRATIC
FUNDRAISER, 2018

Who are the socialists? Ever since its invention in the nineteenth century, socialism has been a coat of many colors. So what hue of socialism do our American socialists want? They insist that they are a new breed, with a new vision and a new agenda. While history and other countries may supply useful models, American socialists have introduced a unique element—identity politics—that Marx would have repudiated and other socialists assiduously avoided. Consequently, American socialism deserves its own name, and the name I propose is "identity socialism."

To understand identity socialism, we must begin with socialism itself, socialism in its original or classic sense. Here the most helpful definition does not come from Marx but from economist Joseph Schumpeter. In his classic work *Capitalism, Socialism and Democracy*, Schumpeter defined socialism as a system in which, "as a matter of principle, the economic affairs of society belong to the public and not to the private sphere."[2]

This strikes me as an excellent definition because it creates a spectrum. At one end is the free market society, which generates wealth and earnings in the private sphere, requiring little more to function than laws protecting property rights and enforcing contracts. At the other end is the socialist society, in which the wealth and earnings of the citizens are considered a common pool to be harnessed by the state or the public sphere and dispersed according to the government's objectives and priorities. Schumpeter's definition allows us to locate every type of socialism along this spectrum.

It also has the virtue of contemporary relevance; it is embraced by virtually all self-described socialists. It is not as precise as classical and historical definitions, but those don't seem to apply to our American situation. Consider Marx's definition of socialism—not original with him—as worker ownership of the means of production. In practice, this would mean that in America the workers at Amazon, Apple, Verizon and General Motors fully own their respective companies.

I'm sure we can find some incorrigible Marxist theorists at Bowdoin and Berkeley who are enthusiastic about this sort of thing. The socialist activist Matt Bruenig has proposed gradual worker takeover of companies based on a 1970s Swedish proposal that the Swedes themselves abandoned because they recognized how it would debilitate their economy.[3] While Elizabeth Warren and Bernie Sanders seek to give workers a stake in the companies they work for, I don't know any prominent socialist—certainly in Congress or running for president in the Democratic fold—who advocates a complete worker takeover of companies.

In fact, this type of socialism does not exist anywhere in the world. Never has.

Perhaps the most recognizable historical application of socialism is nationalization of industry. This understanding of socialism has the benefit of operational accuracy. Virtually all self-styled socialist societies have in fact nationalized industries. This is what professed socialist nations do. In full-scale socialist countries, the government owns or controls all major sectors of the economy, not only defense and infrastructure but also food and finance and even recreation. That was true of the old Soviet Union; it's true of Cuba today where the government controls the sugarcane crop and even the vacation resorts.

In India, a partly socialist country, the government took over some key sectors, such as the airlines and banks and later the coal and oil industries, while leaving others in private hands. Even capitalist societies have socialist domains that form part of their so-called welfare states; thus in England, the government nationalized the healthcare sector in the 1940s and now operates it directly by managing hospitals, paying doctors, and deciding what services to provide and who should get them.

Yet nationalization too has fallen out of favor with today's socialists. Under Obama, America saw an expansion of government power over healthcare, over banks, over car companies and over the energy sector. Yet this power is exercised through mandates, regulation and guarantees. Even under Obamacare we have private doctors, private hospitals and private insurance companies. The banking and finance industries remain private, though heavily regulated. The energy sector continues, in wildcatter fashion, to seek new places to drill, new markets to sell in and new ways to resist government intervention. While some Obama-era rules persist, the energy industry now has an ally in the Trump administration.

I have not been able to find a single socialist in America who advocates a government takeover of grocery stores, or retirement homes, or urgent care centers, even though all these industries provide the basics of food, shelter and medical care that are sometimes considered rights or entitlements. Nor can I find a single voice calling for the nationalization of, say, mail delivery or the phone companies or even space travel, even though all these sectors were once the exclusive province of the federal government. If someone were to insist today that the government, not the market, should nationalize computer companies and decide how many digital devices should be made next year, such a person would be considered an eccentric, a lunatic or a host on MSNBC.

What, then, is American socialism? Ask American socialists, and one word keeps coming up: *democracy*. "Stripped down to its essence, and returned to its roots," says Bhaskar Sunkara, the founder of the socialist magazine *Jacobin*, "socialism is an ideology of radical democracy." Even in Europe today, this is the preferred understanding. Writing on the occasion of Fidel Castro's death, Owen Jones put forward his definition: "That's socialism: the democratization of every aspect of society." And back in America, Ugo Okere, a self-styled democratic socialist who ran for Chicago City Council in 2019, insists that "democratic socialism . . . is about democratic control of every single facet of our life."[4]

The constitution of the Democratic Socialists of America—a group that counts at least two Democratic congresswomen, Alexandria Ocasio-Cortez and Rashida Tlaib, as members—states, "We are socialists because we share a vision of a humane social order based on popular control of resources and production, economic planning, equitable distribution, feminism, racial equality and non-oppressive relationships." Taking up this mantra, Congresswoman Ilhan Omar, a close ally of the group, tweets that "we must build a democratic economy that works for all of us." Ocasio-Cortez somewhat pithily terms it "putting democracy and society first."[5]

Here we have the central moral claim of American socialism: collective ownership. At least in principle, nothing is yours, nothing is mine, everything is ours. The people—that is to say, the democratic majority—control everything. They have final say. They have the right, and the power, to treat the wealth and earnings of the country as a common pool to be tapped by the state and dispersed through the democratic process. The majority also has the right to other forms of control: for example, subsidizing some lifestyles over others, limiting or confiscating guns and restricting citizens from exercising "hate speech."

Of course, the majority may not choose to exercise its full control. The majority might decide, for instance, that you should pay only a 50 or 70 or 90 percent marginal tax rate. This would, in the third case, allow you to keep 10 percent of your income on your last dollar earned. But the principle remains clear: even this residual portion is permitted to you at the behest of the majority. They could, if they wanted, take it and leave you with nothing.

I stress this because we should not miss the radicalism of the principle involved. As I will show in the next chapter, it seems to be a direct repudiation of the American founding. It transforms, if not overturns, the basic design of our constitutional system. If the socialist principle were adopted in this country, it would be a second American Revolution.

What redeems this vision, according to the socialists, is that it is an expression of the will of the people themselves. This freedom, however, is not exercised directly. What direct control do the people have over any socialist institution? What say do the British people have, for instance, over the National Health Service? What say do Americans have over the U.S. Post Office? None. The control is exercised indirectly, through elected representatives and the elaborate mechanism of government.

But, say the socialists, at least there is popular participation at some level. We can vote for our representatives, but we cannot vote for how private companies like Walmart or Amazon carry out their business. This is an issue I'll return to later. Here I emphasize that socialists view their program as continuous with the revolutionary principle of the founding. In other words, the founders established democracy, and socialism extends democracy to the sphere of economics and to society more generally.

Thus, to those who object that socialism involves a restraint on economic freedom and on individual freedom in general—meaning you no longer have the right to keep what you earn, or do what you want, or even say what you think—the socialist answer is that, in restricting your freedom, socialism advances a different type of freedom: the freedom of a people to govern themselves through democratic self-rule.

TRUTH IN LABELING

Labeling the socialists is a tricky matter, because many socialists move, amoeba-like, to elude labels. Even though democratic socialism is the name of the game, not all who seem to be in the socialist camp, or pushing a socialist agenda, admit that they are socialists at all. Consider some influential Democrats. Bernie Sanders has long embraced the socialist label. Other high-profile congresswomen like Alexandria Ocasio-Cortez, Ilhan Omar and Rashida Tlaib also call themselves socialists. There is a defiant honesty in these admissions.

Yet the country's leading Democrat, House Speaker Nancy Pelosi, told a CNN town hall audience, "We're capitalists, and that's just the way it is." On another occasion, Pelosi added, "I do reject socialism as an economic system. If people have that view, that's their view. That is not the view of the Democratic Party."[6]

Pelosi has taken steps to distance the House Democrats from the "squad"—the socialist wing identified with Omar, Tlaib and Ocasio-Cortez. She calls it a small faction with a big media presence. Yet this dismissal concedes that the socialists are the ones with the powerful media allies providing them with a megaphone to reach the American public. Pelosi also likens her differences with Ocasio-Cortez to differences among members of the same family. "Does your family always agree on everything?" she asked at a news conference when the issue of the squad came up.[7] Pelosi's point seems to be that while socialism has a place within the Democratic Party, it does not define the Democratic Party.

In this same vein, another aspiring presidential candidate, New Jersey senator Cory Booker, denies that he is a socialist. So do Kamala Harris, Democratic senator from California, and Elizabeth Warren, Democratic senator from Massachusetts. These disavowals seem odd because Booker's, Harris' and Warren's policy positions seem remarkably close to those of Sanders. Even so, Warren insists that "I believe in capitalism," and at one point she even said that she was "a capitalist to my bones." At the same time, Warren stresses that she does not favor unfettered capitalism; rather, she prefers "markets with rules," or, one may say, fettered capitalism.[8]

Meanwhile Joe Biden refuses to go near the socialist label, although he, like Warren and Pelosi, shares a good deal of Sanders' agenda. One of the minor candidates for the Democratic nomination, John Hickenlooper, warned against his party marching behind a socialist banner— "That's a tough hill to climb in Ohio, in Michigan, in North Carolina, in Pennsylvania, in Wisconsin"—although he too seemed to consider this prospect a problem of political marketing.[9] Hickenlooper doesn't repudiate socialist policies so much as he worries it will hurt Democrats politically if they allow those policies to be labeled as socialist.

My way of distinguishing these characters is to identify them with three broad types: the hard-core socialists, the quasi-socialists and the socialists lite. The hard-core group includes Sanders, Ocasio-Cortez, Tlaib and Omar and their innumerable allies in academia, Hollywood and the media. Among quasi-socialists I count Warren, Beto O'Rourke, Kamala Harris, Cory Booker and most of the other Democratic candidates, together with a large constellation of progressives who are largely on the socialist train but whose socialism doesn't go all the way, and who shrink from the socialist label. Finally, there are Biden and Hickenlooper, and also Tulsi Gabbard, who are socialists lite because they remain circumspect about socialist ideology and would move slower than other Democrats toward socialism.

While I have tried above to distinguish Democrats one from another, notice that they are all pulling in the socialist direction. Even Biden. Even Gabbard. Even Hickenlooper. Not one of them is pulling in the free market direction. When I listen to the Democratic debates, I am struck by the omnipresence of the collectivist pronoun "we." We must guarantee this, and we must ensure that. We are responsible for giving illegal immigrants free healthcare, or we are better than to allow young people to assume so much higher-education debt.

"We" in this context does not mean "us." If it did, then we might consider voluntary and private-sector solutions to healthcare and education. This is not what Democrats have in mind at all. "We" for them means the royal "we," which is to say, the whole society, acting through the coercive instrument of the federal government. Here is that familiar invocation of democracy to justify government confiscation of wealth or government seizure of some aspect of the free economy. Somewhat like the guy who contracted the tapeworm, the socialist's favorite term is "we."

Are there any prominent Democrats who resist this collectivist terminology? There are not. Some may term themselves progressive and others socialist, but they are all on the same side. One may say that progressivism differs from socialism as "push" differs from "shove." The progressives and the socialists are largely unified behind a Democratic Party agenda that can, notwithstanding Nancy Pelosi's caveat, accurately be termed socialist. It is socialist in that it involves expanded, if not total, government control of various sectors of economic and social life.

So what's the agenda—the model blueprint—of this socialist camp? The socialists have put forward a flurry of proposals. First, an expansion of Obamacare to a national healthcare system with the government as the single payer. This is being packaged as Medicare for All. This idea is so expansive that all the Democratic candidates, when asked whether it would provide healthcare to illegal aliens, raised their hand to indicate that yes, it would.

Second, an expansion of minimum wage, unemployment insurance and the earned income tax credit to provide all Americans with a Universal Basic Income. Silicon Valley entrepreneur Andrew Yang, one of the more obscure Democrats running for president, wants to give all adult Americans $1,000 a month to spend as they want. There are multiple universal income proposals floating around; some versions propose that all Americans would get a monthly check from the government, others limit the unrestricted money to Americans at or below a certain income level.

Third, free college. Things have moved well past Hillary Clinton's program to make college more affordable. It started when Bernie Sanders offered his own largely free college scheme. Then Elizabeth Warren sought to top him by adding a plan for the federal government to forgive a large portion of student debt. Bernie struck back by unfurling a plan for free college plus a cancellation of all student debt. No Democrat has yet topped that by offering a plan to pay students to go to college.

Fourth, the Green New Deal. This one comes in apocalyptic packaging—we have a mere 12 years left to reverse global warming and save the planet! The alarmism is absolutely necessary, because otherwise the whole thing would seem like a joke. Even though fracking has proven critical to America's energy independence, Elizabeth Warren pledges that, if elected, she will on day one sign an executive order banning fracking.[10]

Joe Biden goes further. "Look into my eyes," he said recently. "I guarantee you, we are going to end fossil fuel." Never to be outdone, Bernie Sanders says that America under his administration will stop using both coal and gasoline. If all of this seems like a comic version of can-you-top-this, the humorous element is heightened further by New

York mayor Bill de Blasio's recent boast: "We are going to introduce legislation to ban the glass and steel skyscrapers that have contributed so much to global warming. They have no place in our city or our Earth anymore."[11]

New York without skyscrapers? Is this a serious proposal? It was widely reported on television, and I didn't hear anyone laughing. I said to myself, "Can anyone talk New Yorkers into this? This would be like talking Venetians into getting rid of the canals, or Parisians into outlawing outdoor cafes." I realized that there is only one way to get the job done: warn that if you don't go along, the world will come to an end. And sure enough, de Blasio makes it sound like the world is coming to an end, and therefore his fellow New Yorkers must get behind his program to eliminate tall buildings of glass and steel.

The Green New Deal came to public attention when it was flashily proposed by Alexandria Ocasio-Cortez and an environmental group calling itself the Sunrise Movement. Not surprisingly, it was presented as a "save the earth" imperative. "I currently live in a place called Boston," says Sunrise cofounder Varshini Prakash, "and that's a place where, if we don't take action in the next couple of decades, will cease to exist and be lost to the seas forever."

No more Boston! This comes on the heels of Ocasio-Cortez's claim that Miami's days are numbered: apparently that city is projected to be underwater in "a few years." And Astra Taylor warns that the flooding of coastal cities and even inland towns and farms may force people to "escape to New Zealand, to the moon, or to Mars."[12]

But here's an anomaly. The Obamas recently acquired property in Martha's Vineyard for nearly $12 million.[13] Very interesting! The property, purchased from the owner of the Boston Celtics, doesn't merely have ocean views; it sits right on the Atlantic Ocean. The Obamas know about the literature on disappearing coastlines. Obama himself has repeatedly warned of rising sea levels engulfing coastal properties. And presumably everyone who lives on the coasts has access to this literature and has heard these dire warnings.

So if the climate change literature was persuasive, one would expect the price of coastal properties worldwide to plummet. This is called "putting your money where your mouth is." But, in fact, nothing like this has happened. This, by itself, suggests that sellers don't believe the climate change hysteria. Buyers don't believe it. Real estate agents don't believe it. Nobody believes it, including the Obamas—or else they wouldn't have put out $12 million for a rapidly depreciating asset.

Ostensibly with planetary preservation in mind, advocates of the Green New Deal unveiled a dizzying array of proposals, from eliminating fossil fuels to retrofitting every commercial building in the country to raising unemployment benefits and providing everyone with free daycare, free healthcare and a guaranteed family wage. "We're almost out of time," screeches Nathan Hultman in a Brookings Institution paper. The progressive economist Joseph Stiglitz insists that nothing less is required than "a mobilization of resources—the kind we saw during the New Deal and the Second World War."[14]

Much of this seems suspiciously unrelated to climate change. Something else seems to be going on, and something else is. A conversation recently surfaced between Ocasio-Cortez's chief of staff, Saikat Chakrabarti—who has since resigned—and the environmental policy advisers of Governor Jay Inslee of the state of Washington. In the meeting, Chakrabarti frankly admitted that from the beginning the Green New Deal was conceived with broader ends. "Do you think of it as a climate thing?" he chuckled. "Because we really think of it as a how-do-you-change-the-entire-economy thing."[15] In short, climate change is the ruse to get the public to go for full socialism.

MONEY IN THE WRONG HANDS

When the socialist camp advances its proposals, the media Left—itself residing in the socialist camp—inevitably goes into an orgy of celebration, moderated only by some ceremonial fretting over how much all this is going to cost. Sure enough, the conservative groups say that socialism will bankrupt the country. Predictably, the progressive think tanks attach absurdly modest price tags, some even insisting that programs like Medicare for All will end up saving the taxpayer money.

I'll get into some of this later, but addressing it now risks falling for the usual rhetorical ping-pong and missing the larger picture. The larger picture is that the socialist camp wants high, even confiscatory, income tax rates, complemented by additional levies on wealth and, in some cases, even compulsory worker control of large industries—which gets us closer to the classic, never-before-achieved Marxian conception of socialism.

The top marginal rate of federal income tax is currently 37 percent. Few of the leading Democrats have specified precisely how high they want this to go. Presidential candidate Pete Buttigieg, mayor of South Bend, Indiana, has proposed a rate of 49.99 percent. Economist Joseph Stiglitz calls for a top rate of "around 70 percent."[16]

Bernie Sanders never tires of reminding us that the top marginal rate in the late 1940s and early 1950s was over 90 percent, and those rates were accompanied by an era of postwar prosperity. True, but the rates themselves were the legacy of World War II; yet Sanders implies that we need something like those rates now, even though there is no world war going on.

It was a Democrat, John F. Kennedy, who lowered the top marginal rate to 70 percent, and a former Democrat, Ronald Reagan, who brought it down to 28 percent. The rate has crept up slowly to the high thirties since then. What term other than "confiscatory" can we use to describe a tax hike from a 37 percent marginal rate to a rate of 50, 70 or 90 percent?

Moreover, Democrats in the socialist camp also want wealth taxes. Some, like Buttigieg, say they support the concept but won't say how much. Elizabeth Warren wants wealthy families with a net worth exceeding $50 million to pay 2 percent of that every year to the government. The rate would rise to 6 percent for billionaire households. This "structural change," as Warren calls it, is necessary to get us out of America's second Gilded Age.[17]

Warren and Sanders—once again, separated by labels but working in ideological tandem—have both proposed further schemes for worker ownership of large businesses. Sanders would require large companies to contribute a portion of their stocks to a fund controlled by employees that would pay regular dividends to workers. The idea is to give employees gradual but increasing control of their companies.

Warren seeks an Accountable Capitalism Act that would require the government to charter all companies with more than $1 billion in annual revenue. The charter would be revoked if the company doesn't follow government rules. The government would require companies to include the interests of workers, customers, communities and society as a whole before making major decisions. The government would oversee this process, using the charter as a leash. As part of this deal, workers would elect at least 40 percent of board directors of all companies.[18]

There's a revealing mentality here. Part of it is the entitlement mentality, evident in Ocasio-Cortez's recent claim that "You have a right to a job, a right to an education, a right to a dignified home, a right to a dignified retirement, and a right to healthcare."[19] Since modern socialism travels behind the banner of such entitlements—a right to this, that and the other—it's worth exploring in this book where such rights come from and what obligations they impose on other people who are compelled to deliver on these putative rights.

Something of the same mentality is evident in Bill de Blasio's recent declaration: "There's the truth, brothers and sisters, there's plenty of money in the world. Plenty of money in this city. It's just in the wrong hands." For anyone tempted to dismiss this as idle rhetoric, de Blasio framed it in the context of a plan to seize the buildings of private landlords who mistreated tenants by making their homes "unlivable." De Blasio pledged, "We will seize the buildings, and we will put them in the hands of a community nonprofit that will treat tenants with the respect they deserve."

Earlier in 2016, de Blasio spelled out the logic of democratic socialism: "I think people all over this city, of every background, would like to have the city government be able to determine which building goes where, how high it will be, who gets to live in it, what the rent will be. Look, if I had my druthers, the city government would determine every single plot of land, how development should proceed. And there would be very stringent requirements around income levels and rents."[20]

Set aside de Blasio's flagrant disregard for property rights and his arrogant presumption that the city—he!—should oversee all property development like a landed monarch. Let's focus on his earlier statement in the context of three New Yorkers: the doorman at a hotel making $30,000 a year, an editor at a publishing house making $85,000 and a hedge fund executive making $750,000. De Blasio is not paying any of these people; who is he to say who is making too much or too little?

One cannot expect de Blasio's socialist allies at *The New York Times* to ask him such a question; they wouldn't want to go there. The blithering nitwits at the New York *Daily News* are not likely to think of it. But if someone bothered to ask, de Blasio's answer would likely be: "I get to decide because I am the elected mayor. The people of New York deputized me to make such decisions. In my view, the whole income pie in the city is best allocated not by employers and boards of directors—not even by shareholders who bear the cost of these decisions—but by me."

That's democratic socialism in a nutshell! The "people" decide nothing. De Blasio decides.

What we see, unmistakably, in these remarks by Ocasio-Cortez and de Blasio is a deep, almost pathological hostility to free market capitalism. This is the other side of the socialist coin—blissful talk about rights and entitlements and solemn paeans to the public good are inevitably accompanied by vicious assaults on capitalism.

Of course we hear the usual kvetching about how capitalism produces scandalous inequality, how it is motivated by selfishness and greed and how it rewards corpulent, do-nothing bosses while cheating the workers who actually make the products out of their due share of the rewards and profits. Between the 1950s and 1970s, the familiar leftist narrative goes, the tide of capitalism lifted all boats, producing relatively broadly distributed benefits. But since then, capitalism has allocated virtually all its rewards to the very rich, the "top 1 percent." Consequently, we must cure this market failure and adopt socialist schemes to redistribute the rewards. I'll address all these issues in subsequent chapters.

Here, however, I want to focus on an issue that has gained an urgent contemporary relevance. Writing three-quarters of a century ago, Schumpeter predicted that capitalism would sow the seeds of its own destruction, and socialism then becomes its "heir apparent."[21] Schumpeter meant that capitalism undermines traditional institutions and fosters values hostile and antithetical to capitalism. If Schumpeter were alive today, he might look at all those Bernie's boys, waking up at 10:00 a.m. in their moms' basements and putting on their protester costumes to go fight capitalism, as a vindication of his insight.

But Schumpeter might also prove right in a sense he didn't intend. We can examine this through a statement made by Ocasio-Cortez at the South by Southwest conference in Austin, Texas. There the talk was about how rapid developments in technology and automation, including artificial intelligence, might eliminate 800 million jobs worldwide and tens of millions in the United States.

Alexandria Ocasio-Cortez raised the subject of "the end of work." That happens to be the title of a book written by the socialist-leaning activist Jeremy Rifkin. Rifkin recognized of course that automation is nothing new. Automation on farms displaced millions of farmers. But, Rifkin pointed out, the displaced people moved to the manufacturing sector. When technology invaded that sector, there were still jobs to be had in the service sector. But what happens, Rifkin asked, when technology fully occupies the service sector? A recent article in *The Atlantic* makes the case that that day is not far off.[22]

Here's how Ocasio-Cortez responded to the prospect of the widespread obsolescence of human jobs: "We should not be haunted by the specter of being automated out of work. We should not feel nervous about the tollbooth collector not having to collect tolls. We should be excited by that." Our only reason to fear, she argued, is because we think we need jobs to survive. But we don't. "We should be working the least amount we've ever worked, if we were paid based on how much wealth we're producing, but we're not. We're paid by how little we're desperate enough to accept. And the rest is skimmed off and given to a billionaire."[23]

I'll take the liberty of putting AOC's argument a little differently, which is to say, more coherently. Her point is that we now live in a society where only a handful of creative people are needed to create mass comfort and mass prosperity. AOC doesn't like to emphasize the creative elite, so she pretends that "we"—the masses themselves—have produced the wealth and the billionaires did nothing more than appropriate it. We'll explore later whether this is actually so.

But the conclusion remains the same. Most people, in AOC's vision, no longer need to work. Or, to put it differently, they don't need to work as producers. They merely need to enjoy their lives, which is to say, to work only as consumers. Their "work" is to shop around and buy things. In doing so, they generate valuable information for markets and for the creative elite to know what to produce. And in exchange for this "work," AOC believes that people should be entitled to free healthcare, free education, a guaranteed monthly income and a comfortable provision for old age.

I want to emphasize that this isn't some exhilarating—or depressing—futuristic fantasy. Millions of Americans live like this now. Their only "work" is consumption. They rely on others, and on the state, to provide for them. And even more remarkable, they are convinced that this is a good and right way for them to live. America owes them a living.

Here is the way that I think Schumpeter's prophecy might come true. Capitalism might sow the seeds of its undoing, not by creating scarcity or inequality but by creating mass abundance that eliminates the need for most people to work. They can now rely on socialist measures—on the government—to redistribute the nation's wealth and guarantee them a secure and comfortable life. In that case, not Marx but rather the greatest of today's technologists and entrepreneurs will have fostered the end of American capitalism and the rise of American socialism.

STRANGERS IN OUR OWN LAND

So far we have focused on the economic agenda of the socialists, yet any conversation with them, or visit to a socialist conference, shows that the vision of these activists is not merely economic. They are equally energized, if not more so, by cultural issues. This is especially true of socialists on campus. They are not in the workforce, so economic issues are distant to them. They are young and healthy—what do they care about retirement plans or Medicare for All? But they do care about their moral self-image, and they also care about their race, their gender and their sex organs.

These are the identity socialists. It's a little hard to figure them out because some of them are genuinely wacky. Asked by an interviewer for the website PragerU to define her brand of socialism, a female student said it would really hard to do because socialism had so many dimensions. For example, "You're socializing with me right now. Socialism!" If this seems laughable, it's not. A Gallup survey, released in May 2019, found that 6 percent of respondents defined socialism as "being social, social media, talking to people."[24]

A writer for *New York* magazine attended a socialist confab called Red Party, hosted by the left-wing publishing house Verso, in a handsome loft overlooking the East River. There the young socialists talked about sex, white privilege and open borders. Mindy Isser, a young activist, whined that "socialist men don't date socialist women and it really bothers me." Another activist warned that socialists need better slogans. "The beauty of ABOLISH ICE," he said, was its sheer simplicity. It mirrored right-wing slogans. "BUILD THE WALL. LOCK HER UP. They're all perfect for shouting."[25]

Jarrett Stepman, a writer for the Daily Signal who attended the Socialism 2019 conference, sponsored by Jacobin and Democratic Socialists of America, captured the mood of identity socialism nicely. He went expecting to hear mostly about topics like minimum wage, student debt and the Green New Deal. Instead he found, somewhat to his puzzlement, that "transgenderism, gender nonconformity and abolishing traditional family structures were huge issues."

Typical of the speakers was Corrie Westing, a self-described "queer socialist feminist activist" based in Chicago who works as a "home birth midwife." Westing insisted that the traditional family is an instrument of capitalist oppression, and the transgender movement is critical to achieving "reproductive justice." Economics, she said, is based on "heteronormativity," and pregnancy is a tool of oppression to remove women from the workforce, thus reinforcing a "gender binary."

The solution, she said, was to reorganize society around what she termed "queer social reproduction." The traditional family would have to go. No more parents having and raising their own children. Rather, women and men would seek out one or more partners, of whatever gender, with whom to raise children, and then they might seek out a third party to carry the child. The third party, after giving birth, might or might not be involved in raising the child. Drawing on a term coined by the feminist writer Sophie Lewis, Westing called this "open-sourced, fully collaborative gestation."[26]

Yes, there's a weirdo element here, but the identity socialists are quite serious about seeking a transformation not merely of economic norms but of cultural and moral norms as well. Moreover, leading Democrats are on board with some or much of this agenda. Recently Senate Minority Leader Chuck Schumer announced his support for a bill sponsored by Cory Booker and Democratic representative Sheila Jackson Lee to study the issue of reparations for slavery. And Peter Hasson of the Daily Caller points out that all the leading Democrats—Biden, Warren, Harris, Sanders, Booker and Buttigieg—support the Equality Act that would prohibit discrimination based on "gender identity" and thus mandate that biological males who considered themselves females could not be denied participation in women's sports.[27]

Marx, I'm sure, would be baffled by all this. Certainly Marx also despised the traditional family and expected it to disappear under communism. Yet Marx insisted that society is divided into just two classes, workers and capitalists—in other words, the exploited and the exploiters. The working class, Marx wrote in his *Critique of Hegel's "Philosophy of Right,"* represents "the dissolution of all classes." It is "a sphere of society which has a universal character because its sufferings are universal, and which does not claim a particular redress because the wrong which is done to it is not a particular wrong but a wrong in general."[28]

Marx considered other forms of social division—white versus black, men versus women—to be sneaky techniques on the part of the capitalist class to divide and rule the working class. Marx would have opposed reparations because he held that feudal and capitalist arrangements that included slavery were part of the necessary forward march of history. In other words, without feudalism we would not have capitalism, and even capitalism is a required stage on the road to socialism. For Marx, to attempt to repudiate or to "correct for" these inevitabilities is to misunderstand the inexorable development of human history.

Bernie Sanders seems to be the only leading Democrat still holding to this tradition. He indignantly rejects the idea that because he is a white male he should step aside and make room for women and minority candidates. "We've got to look at candidates," he told Vermont Public Radio, "not by the color of their skin, not by their sexual orientation or their gender and not by their age." Rather, people should be judged "based on their abilities, based on what they stand for."[29]

Whoa! This is now heretical talk in the Democratic Party. Bernie, moreover, is skeptical of illegal immigration because he believes, as Marx would, that it is a tool of employers to drive down the wages of native workers. While identity socialists have put Bernie on the defensive for these positions and forced him to retreat in his antipathy to illegal immigration, he has not fully backed down.

In this respect, however, Sanders is not the mainstream—not even among card-carrying socialists. American socialism is now imbued with issues of "intersectionality," a term that refers to the crosscurrents of race, gender, sexual orientation and class. What Marx considered a divisive ploy is now the avowed strategy of progressives and Democrats: to turn black and brown against white, female against male, gay and lesbian and transgender people against "heteronormativity." In 2020, Democrats intend to use these multiple lines of division to create the majority coalition that will implement their new form of identity socialism across the economic and cultural landscape.

This broader agenda for identity socialism includes getting rid of ICE and flooding the country with illegals. They want sanctuary cities that shelter illegals and prevent the enforcement of the law. They seek to force citizens to pay for the healthcare of illegals. They support firing and ostracizing Americans for criticizing "Islamic terrorism" and for other forms of alleged Islamophobia. They revel in the digital censorship of views they regard as promoting "hate." They back lawsuits forcing churches to shut down for refusing to hold a gay wedding, as well as those compelling women in salons to shave the testicles of biological men who claim to be women.

What's the goal here? It goes beyond economic confiscation; I believe it is nothing less than to make traditional Americans feel like foreigners in their own country. The identity socialists seek an overturning of norms—a redefinition of the American dream—that would convert foreigners into natives, and natives into foreigners. An old Marxist concept, "alienation," is quite appropriate here. They seek to create a new form of belonging and, in the process, a way to alienate us from our own society.

This is why, for many progressives and socialists, an illegal American is now the model American. Part of their plan is to change the national DNA, and to do this they intend to import illegals who bring—in a quite literal sense—new DNA. They seek a "remaking of America," to use Obama's phrase, that would make the country unrecognizable to those who created it and to many of us who love it and call it our own.

And what do these socialists intend to do with dissenters like me who object to their transformation? Some of them, at least, intend to "reeducate us" if necessary, to put us into gulags. I'm not kidding. Project Veritas secretly recorded two Bernie Sanders staffers saying precisely this. "There's a reason Joseph Stalin had gulags, right?" said Kyle Jurek. Even uncooperative liberals should be forced to undergo this reeducation, Jurek said. Such extremes were required, he added, "because we're going to have to teach you not to be a f*ck*ng Nazi." A second Sanders field staffer, Martin Weissgerber, said he's ready to "guillotine the rich" and "send Republicans to reeducation camps."[30]

For me, I confess, a socialist transformation of America along these lines would be traumatic. I left India and came here to "become American," and I have. Becoming American is not an easy process for an outsider; it is like walking on a tightrope between two buildings, and for much of that time you feel a kind of vertigo. You are in no-man's land, belonging neither here nor there. But eventually I arrived at my destination, which is to say, I assimilated. Since then I have felt at home in America, and I have inevitably become isolated from India; in other words, I am now a foreigner in my native country.

But now these people want to destroy my American dream and make me an alien in my adopted country. I, for one, am not going to stand for it.

THE SOCIALIST TEMPTATION

My agenda for this book is twofold: first, to make the moral argument against identity socialism, and second, to make the moral argument for free market capitalism. I will debunk the socialist dream and affirm the American dream. These arguments are not a simple matter of ideological refutation. The refutation is dependent on directly confronting the root question: Who owns what? What are we entitled to? I'll explore these questions toward the middle of the book, after I've laid the necessary groundwork.

My refutation also requires me to expose the socialist temptation. After all, if socialism is such a bad idea, why do so many people go for it? Why do powerful figures in culture and politics so aggressively promote it? The socialist temptation is widely described by conservatives as the temptation to live off "free stuff." But this is not so—the temptation is actually more complex. It is the temptation to annihilate one's conscience by feeling justified in living off other people's work.

Think about it this way: most people would not dream of going into their neighbor's house, eating from his refrigerator and helping themselves to his wallet. It's just not right. So the only way to involve honest people in a theft scheme is to convince them that their neighbors have been stealing from them. Their neighbor has filled his refrigerator with provisions that belong to you. His wallet is filled with your money. Therefore, you should feel perfectly entitled to raid his refrigerator and his wallet because, in doing so, you are merely recovering stolen goods.

This is the apple that the serpent is offering to Adam and Eve. This is the false narrative that needs to be deconstructed and exposed.

The second part of the socialist temptation involves the serpents—I mean the socialists—themselves. This is a class of people that has no idea how to create wealth. Pretty much the only thing they know how to create is words. This does not mean, however, that they are untalented. They are actually very talented, just not at making iPhones or warehouse delivery systems or getting oil out of the ground. Resentful of those who can do these things, the socialists proclaim them "selfish" and "greedy" and imply that such vices are responsible for their notable prosperity and success.

What the socialist class is good at, however, is creating envy and entitlement. This is their peculiar talent. And even though they won't admit it, they are engaged in a desperate battle for social control. What they seek is a displacement of power in society in which they, not entrepreneurs, direct the great apparatus of American industry, indeed direct the lives of the people themselves.

They cannot, of course, admit this publicly, or even to themselves. If they admitted it, they would have to concede that the very labels that they apply to the entrepreneurs—namely greed and selfishness—would more accurately apply to them. So they insist that society is in need of a neutral, administrative class. Someone to run things fairly, to iron out the inequities, to take care of the needy, to check and penalize the bad guys, to regulate "hate" and "intolerance," to always keep the public good in mind.

They then anoint themselves to carry out this necessary task. They profess to undertake it on behalf of the people, in the name of the people, yet the people are scarcely involved at all. The people aren't even persuaded. They have to be cajoled, propagandized and bullied. This is the first task of aspiring socialists. This is what they are doing now. And they do it ruthlessly, relentlessly, keeping their eye on the prize they are seeking. They want to be Plato's guardians, the "people of gold" who rule by right over the lower orders, the "people of silver" and the "people of bronze."

Their entitlement and their virtue are, in reality, ignoble lies. In fact, they are motivated by the same ambition and desire for power and gain as anyone else. They love money and sex and all forms of perversion as much as anyone else, and they are just as reluctant as the next guy to share what they have with others. In fact, they are the least compassionate, most uncharitable group in society. This, then, is the temptation of the socialists: they are tempted to annihilate their consciences to conceal the ugly truth about themselves.

One fact they cannot face is that the only difference between them and capitalist entrepreneurs is that they seek unearned power, power without genuine accountability. As I will show, entrepreneurs are genuinely accountable to their customers, who exercise direct democracy: they vote every day with their purchases for the products that entrepreneurs supply. The socialists wish to answer to nobody. They are driven, as Nietzsche pointed out more than a century ago, by a nasty, vengeful "will to power."

Will capitalism undo itself and submit to the governance of this vile kakistocracy? It's a genuine danger. But I'll show that this fate is not inevitable. The socialists are, in the end, a corrupt gang. They conceal their crookedness behind a mask of virtue, and they appeal to crooked people by giving them reasons to steal from others. Thievery masked in this way can thrive for a while, but thievery unmasked cannot. Once the socialist morality play is exposed as a theft scheme, as I'll do in this book, they are done.

We need to reaffirm capitalism, not back away from it. Capitalism is what has brought us to where we are, and it's only just getting started. So what about "the end of work"? Capitalism can even meet this, its final challenge. Even in sowing the winds of "creative destruction" (Schumpeter's term), which displaces old industries and old institutions, the free market can and will create new opportunities for humans to thrive. It can help us rise above the muck and mire of routine labor to the exhilarating creativity and rewarding new forms of labor uniquely suited to human intelligence and aspiration, and to which man was from the beginning called by his Creator.

1

THE INVENTION OF INVENTION

AMERICA AND THE IDEAL OF THE SELF-MADE MAN

> Destiny is not a matter of chance; it is a matter of choice; it is
> not a thing to be waited for, it is a thing to be achieved.[1]
> —WILLIAM JENNINGS BRYAN

America was founded and built on principles antithetical to socialism. Strangely enough, two people who recognized this were Marx
and Engels. Marx called America a "bourgeois society" and later
noted that capitalism had developed in America "more rapidly and more
shamelessly than in any other country." Engels stressed the distinctive-
ness of America, and while he insisted that "there cannot be any doubt"
of the ultimate triumph of the working class, he admitted "the peculiar
difficulties for a steady development of a workers party" in the United
States.[2] Only their doctrinaire faith in the inevitability of socialism convinced Marx and Engels that socialism would come to America at all.

In 1906 the economist Werner Sombart published a book titled *Why
Is There No Socialism in the United States?* Sombart knew that socialism
had been all the rage in Europe. There were socialist movements, socialist parties, ultimately socialist governments. In other words, socialism
was in the political mainstream. But not in America. Sure, America had
socialists, and soon it would have a socialist candidate, Eugene Debs,
running for president. Yet Sombart recognized, as Marx and Engels

did, that socialism would have trouble gaining an enduring foothold in mainstream American politics. Sombart's explanation for this was that the American workingman has it too good. His stomach is too full for him to become a socialist agitator. In America, in Sombart's words, "all socialist utopias have come to grief on roast beef and apple pie."[3]

Another man who seems convinced that socialism isn't coming to America is Donald Trump. In his 2019 State of the Union, Trump resoundingly affirmed that "America will never be a socialist country." He echoed the same theme in his 2020 address. It has now become a standard line at his rallies, guaranteed to evoke whoops and cheers. For Trump—unlike for Marx, Engels and Sombart—this is not a matter of sociological analysis or historical prophecy. Trump's point is that he and other Americans must fight hard to prevent socialism from being established here.

It's obvious what Trump is against, but what is he actually for? And the same question can be asked more broadly of the Trump movement, of the Republican Party and of conservatives. What do conservatives want to conserve? We can answer this question by examining Trump's official 2016 campaign slogan, "Make America Great Again." Or his unofficial 2020 campaign theme, "Keep America Great." For me, all of this raises a prior question: How did America become great in the first place? It would seem that this quality—the spirit that built America—is what we are trying to conserve and revive.

As an immigrant, I became interested early on in this question of the building of America. When I arrived in Arizona in 1978 as an exchange student from India, I was simply stunned by the opulence of ordinary American life. Not the life of the "rich and famous" but the lives of everyday Americans. Like those of my host parents: a small-town postmaster and his wife; the local pastor and his wife; a rancher and his second wife; two public schoolteachers. These were ordinary people, yet they lived so well—a second car, a kitchen "island," a nice backyard—and they were all such characters who lived unique and interesting lives.

Shortly after I was settled in the small town of Patagonia, Arizona, just sixty miles from the Mexican border, my host family proposed to take me on a sightseeing trip. "We'll take you to the Grand Canyon," they said. "We'll take you to Tombstone, the site of the gunfight at the

O.K. Corral." "Oh wow," I said. "That sounds fantastic." But what I really had in mind was a different kind of sightseeing.

I wanted to see the local supermarket where I could survey the endless varieties of cheese and ice cream, or the hardware store where I could check out the countless contraptions, or a local farm where I could watch one guy on a tractor plow and fertilize hundreds of acres, or the mall in Tucson where I could ride the escalators and investigate innumerable objects of wizardry, from electric typewriters to reclining furniture to microwave ovens to toys that sang and talked.

Years later, I marveled at one of the most ingenious contraptions of all time: roll-on luggage. Such an obvious idea! Take mankind's oldest invention, the wheel, and attach four of them to a suitcase. Voilà! Yet people had been traveling for eons before anyone did that. Think of all that huffing and puffing, all those pulled shoulders and bad backs! Our lives are so much easier now because of roll-on luggage. Whoever thought of it is a genius. I wish I could meet the guy and thank him, but I don't even know his name.

Most Americans take the basic amenities of modern life for granted. What's the big deal? Growing up in a country that lacked all these basic things, however, I have a special appreciation for them. I know what life is like without them. I also know that not so long ago, Americans didn't have them either. In fact, America was one of the poor, backward countries. It was still largely rural and agricultural at the time of its founding.

Then, in relatively short order, America became the most productive and prosperous nation in the world. America doubled its gross domestic output in the middle of the nineteenth century, then doubled it again in the late nineteenth century. One by one, the United States surpassed all the advanced European countries, even overtaking its mother country England at the dawn of the twentieth century. That has been termed "the American century"—the century of unquestioned American dominance—and America remains to this day the world's most innovative and prosperous society.

So how did all this happen? This is the transformation that has produced not only American prosperity but also the contemporary American lifestyle, the American dream, the American experience of being the architect of your own destiny. So who made the goose that lays the golden eggs? I mean this quite literally: Who are the people who did this? What are their names? I'm interested in these people, and I'm also interested in the creation of a system that produces one marvel after another, giving each generation opportunities and experiences that even the wealthiest members of earlier generations completely lacked.

That's the topic of this chapter. I want to show the secret of American success, how America became rich, not just through inventing this or that but by creating a mechanism for innovation and growth, "the invention of invention." This is the genius of the American Revolution and of the American founding. It also creates a paradox for conservatism, a term ordinarily identified with stasis and stability. But not in America. In America, conservatism means conserving the principles of the American Revolution. This means that we are heirs to a revolutionary tradition, and rebellion, change and making our own destiny are all in our political DNA.

Implied here, and in the founding, is something more than a framework for prosperity and success. The founding also created the framework for a new type of human being, what both Abraham Lincoln and the runaway slave Frederick Douglass would later term "the self-made man." We will meet some self-made men in this chapter. Thus, America is responsible for the greatest of all inventions, one that makes Americans recognizably distinct everywhere in the world, and one that gives a thrilling immediacy to each American life: the idea of self-invention.

HISTORY FROM BELOW

The roots of American prosperity and of American self-invention could scarcely be more important, yet oddly enough they are completely ignored in the curriculums and classrooms of American schools and in the media. I learned little or nothing about them at Dartmouth, and now, a generation later, young people are comparably clueless about them. Why is this the case? Because the history that I learned then, and they learn now, is progressive history, history from the progressive viewpoint. This viewpoint is striking both for what it includes and for what it leaves out.

What it includes is what progressives call "history from below." Typical of this approach is Howard Zinn's classic work, *A People's History of the United States*. Zinn purports to show the discovery of America from the viewpoint of the Arawaks, the Constitution from the standpoint of the slaves, the Civil War as seen by the New York Irish, the Mexican War from the angle of deserting servicemen, the rise of industrialism as experienced by women working in the Lowell textile mills, the two world wars as seen by socialists and pacifists and postwar America's role in the world as seen by peons in Latin America.[4]

Essentially Zinn uses the victim's perspective to generate an anti-American narrative, one that is not confined to the academic sphere but has now spread virus-like through the culture. Precisely that same animus is behind New York governor Andrew Cuomo's recent assertion: "We're not going to make America great again, it was never that great." Along the same lines, Eric Holder asked, "When did you think America was great?" That remembered past, he said, "never in fact existed."[5]

This is the voice not just of socialism but of identity socialism. This is the perspective I was inundated with in college, and which is the dominant narrative taught to young people today. This victimology has now reached the point of parody. How can Einstein's equations be viewed from the perspective of the illiterate? How did Patton's military conquests appear from the viewpoint of a crow? My reaction then, as now, to this whole approach of identity politics was, to some degree, one of indifference. The founders, as we'll see, shared my lack of concern.

At first, this may seem like gross insensitivity, but it's not. Mexican migrants and Arawaks don't spend their time thinking about me; why should I spend my time thinking about them? Several years ago in a debate on race, my faculty opponent said to me, "Why are you so obsessed with African Americans?" To which I replied, "Obsessed? I don't particularly care about African Americans. I'm not African American. So my concern is only to the extent that I affirm the universality of the principles of the Declaration of Independence. Beyond that, I have no interest."

The truth is that no ethnic group—not even the groups that Zinn invokes—cares very much about any other ethnic group. Nor do immigrants, in general, care about the perspective of indigenous minorities. They are part of a familiar imploring mass that we're all too familiar with in our native countries. We're far more interested in the America that we left our countries to become part of. We're moderately interested in how American prosperity became more widely distributed, since that expansion now includes us, but we're much more interested in how it came about in the first instance.

Here progressive history lapses into silence. This is the great subject it leaves out. Progressive history tends to take America's wealth for granted and merely focuses on the issues of who has it, who doesn't and how lavishly it is spent. Typical of this approach is historian Charles Beard, whose famous work is called *An Economic Interpretation of the Constitution of the United States.* As part of his investigation, he might be expected to examine whether the founders were responsible for creating a system to produce the great explosion of wealth that took America from the back ranks to the most affluent society in the world.

Beard deftly skips over this. He doesn't affirm it or deny it; he merely ignores it. Instead, he generates an "economic biography" of the estimated 160,000 men involved in the framing and adoption of the Constitution. He seeks to portray them as members of a wealthy merchant class of moneylenders, traders and financiers. According to Beard, they were merely trying, through the new constitutional system they set up, to protect their class interests.

Beard tries to show that the delegates to the constitutional convention voted as economic interest groups. This guy was a whiskey producer, and that guy was a grain producer, and that's why they wanted protective tariffs! Beard's theories were resoundingly affirmed by other progressives who shared his ideological hostility to the founders. As a consequence, they held sway for a generation without anyone actually checking his facts.

Eventually historians like Forrest McDonald and Robert Brown did, and they found that Beard had spun his data. Convention delegates did not, in fact, vote as interest groups. There were merchants on one side of the debate who favored tariffs, but there were others in the same trades on the other side who opposed tariffs. Beard's quasi-Marxist theory of the founding as an institutional manifestation of class oppression doesn't hold up.[6] Yet progressive historians still promulgate Beard's discredited theories, losing no opportunity to portray the founders as dirty, rotten scoundrels.

Another classic of progressive scholarship is Thorstein Veblen's *The Theory of the Leisure Class*, first published in 1899, which deplores the excesses of the Gilded Age. Veblen focuses specifically on how American tycoons lavishly display their wealth. He devotes considerable attention to their coddled pets, cap-and-gown graduations, card games and walking sticks, all indications of their vacuous idleness. He surveys their ostentatious mansions, making particular note of the curved driveways. Why would anyone want a curved driveway? Veblen's theory is that it exists to demonstrate wasted space. Curved driveways show that their owners are so rich that they can afford to waste their own land by having driveways meander pointlessly before reaching the main house.[7]

All of this is clever enough—what savory intellectual hors d'oeuvres for the faculty cocktail circuit!—but I read Veblen wondering how those guys got those mansions. What did they do that Veblen didn't know how to do, since Veblen never had a mansion?

I've read a lot about those robber barons and about the vulgarity of the Gilded Age. Here is Jack Schwartz in the Daily Beast: "The Gilded Age produced an unbridled capitalism and a culture of excess that led to financial panics impoverishing millions at the hands of corporate profiteers professing the sanctity of property."[8] Here are all the familiar clichés reflecting the sour taste of progressive prejudice: "unbridled capitalism," "culture of excess," "sanctity of property." Each of those terms warrants critical unpacking.

We can pick up the same conventional wisdom from a recent article in the American Interest that says, "The Gilded Age economy was lopsided and dysfunctional, producing untenable extremes of vulgar opulence and abject poverty."[9] Once again, questions abound: Lopsided how? Dysfunctional in what way? Untenable for whom? Vulgar by whose standard? Abject compared to what? Surely not to how those poor people lived before, or else they would not have moved from the rural areas to the cities.

In the same vein, the *Encyclopedia Britannica* characterizes the Gilded Age as one of "gross materialism" dominated by "greedy industrialists."

Not a word about what those greedy industrialists did. What we do learn is that Mark Twain coined the term, and that the period produced "the novel as a vehicle of social protest, a trend that grew in the late nineteenth and early twentieth centuries with the works of the muckrakers and culminated in the proletarian novelists."[10] Yes, this is progressive history in which the inevitable upward path is to the progressives themselves!

In *1984*, Orwell warns of the socialist project of cleansing history where "the past is erased, the erasure was forgotten, the lie became the truth."[11] That has almost happened in this case. Fortunately, we can still excavate the truths that lie buried under the progressive palimpsest in order to save our history and, in the end, ourselves.

THE GENIUS AND THE BUM

It is tempting to begin our examination of the American founding with documents, but I'd like to begin with the founders, and one in particular, Benjamin Franklin. The founders, let's recall, were not career politicians or mere "men of letters." They were scientists, inventors, entrepreneurs and builders—in other words, practical men of varied talents.

President John F. Kennedy captured the spirit of the founders when he said at a dinner honoring Nobel Prize winners, "This is the most extraordinary collection of talent, of human knowledge, that has ever been gathered together at the White House, with the possible exception of when Thomas Jefferson dined alone."[12] George Washington was a farmer, whiskey entrepreneur, military leader and statesman. Franklin was a publisher, inventor, diplomat, philanthropist and author.

Through the founding, I believe, the founders sought to perpetuate Renaissance men like themselves. This is the grain of truth in Beard's indictment. The founders weren't advancing their economic interest, but they were, in a broad sense, replicating their own human types. That's why Franklin's *Autobiography* is so interesting. It captures a distinctive American mold that I'll call "capitalist man."

The first thing that strikes me on reading the book is the sheer variety and breadth of Franklin's pursuits. He edits and prints a newspaper, publishes *Poor Richard's Almanack*, organizes a fire company and later a defensive militia, establishes the American Philosophical Society, helps finance a hospital, founds a subscription library, invents a new type of stove, conducts electrical experiments and promotes the paving and lighting of Philadelphia's streets. This is not an exhaustive list! And while Franklin is not averse to serving his nation as a diplomat in France, he expends virtually all his energies in the private, entrepreneurial and civic sectors.

Second, Franklin is endlessly curious. His is not the idle form of curiosity that proverbially killed the cat. Rather, it is a practical curiosity. He sees construction workers with axes building a fort and times them to see how long it takes. He inquires into the art by which native Indians conceal their fires. He investigates the cultural and matrimonial practices of the Moravians. He conducts experiments and publishes his observations on electricity, and when a French pedant challenges him—partly based on incredulity that such work could come from America—Franklin refuses to reply, insisting that his time is better engaged "in making new Experiments, than in Disputing about those already made."

Third, Franklin is eloquent on self-fashioning and self-improvement. He doesn't take himself the way he is; he seeks to make himself into what he aspires to be. He admits that he has been profligate in his youth, granting his participation in "that hard-to-be-govern'd Passion of Youth," which I take to be cavorting with prostitutes. Franklin terms this one of his "great Errata," but not entirely because of moral compunction; in retrospect he regrets the expense, distraction from worthier pursuits and risks to his health.

Franklin makes a list of what he terms the seven virtues—temperance, frugality, sincerity and so on—and then enumerates them in a single column down the left-hand side of a page. At the top he lists the seven days of the week. His plan is to take the first virtue and practice it for one week straight. No Errata! He notes his progress each day with a check mark. His idea is that if he can practice a virtue for seven days, he will have internalized it. It will become part of his character. The following week he can take up the second virtue, and in this way he continues for seven weeks in a remarkable—and amusingly systematic—project of character improvement.

One final note about Franklin: he seems just as concerned with the appearance of virtue as with virtue itself. For instance, once he becomes prosperous through his business ventures, he is eager to show that he is still industrious and frugal. He took care, he says, "not only to be in *Reality* industrious and frugal, but to avoid all *Appearances* of the Contrary." So to demonstrate he was not above menial labor, Franklin "sometimes brought home the Paper purchas'd at the Stores, thro' the Streets on a Wheelbarrow."[13]

Franklin's *Autobiography* is itself a bit of a wheelbarrow ride. The book camouflages as much as it reveals. Still, it reveals plenty. One cannot help chuckling at Franklin, this picaresque fellow who always puts himself first but also never forgets to look out for others. I admire him for his creative genius and his perseverance, and I like him, despite his energetic self-promotion. He knows he's vain, so he tries to make himself less vain while admitting to some vainness about his advances in modesty. He's an American original and yet an American type; I have met a number of Americans who remind me of Franklin, and I intend the comparison as a compliment.

Yet the Franklin type is hardly the norm in America, and now we find other, less impressive types. Today in this country we have "capitalist man," but we also have "socialist man," and my case study here is Bernie Sanders. I recognize, of course, that Sanders and Franklin are separated by a chasm of two centuries. Even so, it's worth contrasting them because the Sanders type is recognizable all over the world—I had a close relative in India who was just like Sanders—while the Franklin type is uniquely and recognizably American.

Sanders too is the product of self-fashioning. Sanders, like Franklin, has made something of himself. But what has he made? Sanders is now well into his seventies, yet until he became a politician, well into his middle age, he never had a steady job. His main output to that point was a child produced out of wedlock with a woman named Susan Campbell Mott. In college he was a poor student, by his own admission, majoring in a topic that would become his career: political science. Most of his time seems to have been spent with the Young People's Socialist League.

His young life seems to have been devoted to agitating for two causes: socialism and sexual freedom. In his college years and in his twenties, he emphasized the latter. He editorialized about how sexual repression leads to cancer—"The manner in which you bring up your daughter with regard to sexual attitudes may very well determine whether or not she will develop breast cancer"—an idiotic theory he seems to have adopted from the crackpot theorist Wilhelm Reich. (Reich was imprisoned for selling bogus sexual treatments, and died in prison in 1957.)

Sanders also published rape fantasies—"A woman enjoys intercourse with her man as she fantasizes being raped by 3 men simultaneously"— that he now tries to explain away on the grounds that he was merely sounding an early version of *Fifty Shades of Grey* and seeking to explore and challenge conventional sex roles in America.

Occasionally he pivoted from sexual to social activism, as he does in his essay "The Revolution is Life Versus Death," in which he envisioned jobs in a capitalist system this way: "The years come and go. Suicide, nervous breakdown, cancer, sexual deadness, heart attack, alcoholism, senility at 50. Slow death, fast death. DEATH." There is more, quite a bit more, in this vein; basically, it's the kind of talk that one would expect to hear from a crank.

To foment an actual revolution, Sanders teamed up with a fellow socialist named Peter Diamondstone. They became friends because they "knew all the same Communists," according to Diamondstone. "When I was on the road," Diamondstone says, "I would stop at his house and I'd sleep downstairs, and we'd yell at each other all night long, and sometime around 3 o'clock in the morning, we'd say, 'We gotta stop this,' so we could get some sleep. Five minutes later we'd be yelling at each other again."

In 1971 Sanders showed up at a commune in Vermont called Myrtle Farm, a hippie outfit dedicated to self-sufficient living. Yet Bernie showed no interest in doing any kind of labor there. While others toiled to grow food and do repairs, Bernie engaged in what commune members held to be "endless political discussion." Recognizing this, the commune expelled Bernie for laziness, for failing to contribute to sustaining the commune. I'm trying to imagine what Ben Franklin would have made of a guy like Sanders.

Although Sanders for many years listed his occupation as "journalist," he published only a few articles over that entire period, mostly in small-circulation socialist and hippie rags that paid little or nothing. So there is no way he could have supported himself through writing. He seems to have done so through collecting unemployment from the government and leeching off his friends. One of them, an artist who lived next door, said Sanders "would take extension cords and run down to the basement and plug them into the landlord's outlet."

When Sanders was evicted from his house on Maple Street in Burlington for nonpayment of rent, he moved in with a friend, Richard Sugarman, and slept on his couch. This seems to have lasted for several months. Sanders' main contribution to his roommate during this period seems to have been late-night diatribes about how to save society from the evils of capitalism. Since Sanders didn't work, he could hardly claim that capitalism was exploiting him. Evidently, he was convinced that it was exploiting others, and his mission was to seek justice for them while finally getting a nice regular salary for himself.

After multiple failed tries, Sanders finally won elective office, as mayor of Burlington, and now he is a U.S. senator, drawing a handsome salary from the government. Public service has been good to him; Sanders now owns three homes, making him a multimillionaire.[14]

Unlike Franklin, Sanders does not focus on self-improvement. In fact, Sanders is basically the same person in his seventies that he was in his twenties. He seems at ease with his lack of curiosity, his unproductivity, his self-serving sycophancy and his parasitism on the largesse of capitalism to pay his salary through taxpayer outlays. Socialist man, you see, is dependent on capitalist man to keep him in business. Franklin types don't need Bernie types, but Bernie types need Franklin types. Yet Bernie shows no appreciation. He's hostile and indignant toward the Franklins of today, even while shamelessly leeching off them. Bernie, like Franklin, may indeed have invented himself. If he ever tells us this, we should accept it as an apology.

PASSIONS AND INTERESTS

Democratic socialists like Sanders are not fans of the American founding. That's because they recognize the founding as a free market revolution.

Consequently, it was antisocialist even though the term "socialist" had not been coined yet. Moreover—and this is a more controversial point—it was also antidemocratic. By this I mean that the founding rejected democracy in its original meaning and adopted a specialized form of democracy called a "constitutional republic." The constitutional republic erected numerous barriers to direct popular rule.

The most influential socialist publication in America is *Jacobin*. Get it? These guys want to identify with the French Revolution, not the American, and they don't hesitate to identify with the most radical faction of that revolution—the one associated with the guillotine and the Terror. The socialist historian Eric Foner urges Bernie Sanders not to look so much to Europe as to "the rich tradition of American radicalism." But this tradition as Foner sees it begins with Thomas Paine—an Englishman sympathetic to the American Revolution—and continues with the abolitionists, Frederick Douglass, and on to Eugene Debs and Franklin Roosevelt.[15]

Even here Foner is stretching things: Paine was a champion of free markets and property rights, and Douglass championed the "self-made man" who is anathema to modern socialism. What I want to stress here, however, is that Foner makes no identification with the American founders. As far as he's concerned, radicalism in America means moving to amend, transform and perhaps even overturn the principles of the founding.

We find the same antipathy to the founding in socialist Astra Taylor's recent paean to socialism in *The New Republic*. Taylor identifies the American founding with classical liberalism, but this liberalism, she says, with its staggered elections, free press, religious liberty, judicial review, separation of powers and federalism, is "not strong enough to survive, let alone constrain concentrated economic power." Liberalism, in her view, has been vanquished by capitalism, specifically by "unaccountable plutocrats who have rigged the rules of the game." Some form of socialism that overturns the structure of this constitutional republic is the only remedy.[16]

In October 2019, *Harper's* sponsored a symposium on the Constitution, raising the question, "Has America's founding document become the nation's undoing?" The progressive legal scholars who made up the panel mostly answered yes. For Rosa Brooks, relying on the Constitution today was akin to a neurosurgeon using the world's oldest neurosurgery guide, "or if NASA used the world's oldest astronomical chart." Mary Anne Franks averred, "We have not, as a county, fully confronted the fraudulent nature of the Constitution and the founding itself." And Louis Michael Seidman said that courts and law schools should dispense with the Constitution. "We need to forget about constitutionalism entirely."[17]

Let's see what the socialists find so troubling about America's founding principles and how they have played out in this country. I'll begin with Abraham Lincoln's 1859 lecture on discoveries and inventions, in which Lincoln attributed much of the economic success of his country to Article 1, section 8 of the Constitution. Among the few express powers granted to Congress, the framers charged it "to promote the Progress of Science and useful Arts by securing for limited Times to Authors and Inventors the exclusive Right to their respective Writings and Discoveries."

This, let us note, is the only time the word "right" appears in the original Constitution, prior to the later addition of the Bill of Rights. Before the advent of the patent system, Lincoln says, "any man might instantly use what another had invented." So the patent system "secured to the inventor, for a limited time, the exclusive use of his invention, and thereby added the fuel of interest to the fire of genius, in the discovery and production of new and useful things."[18]

This is Lincoln doing his best Adam Smith imitation, which is significant because Adam Smith is a "visible hand" behind the American founding. The founders, we know, were familiar with his work. Franklin knew Smith personally, having initially met him through their mutual friend, the philosopher David Hume. Smith's *The Wealth of Nations* was published in 1776, the same year that the Declaration of Independence was adopted.

Lincoln takes up Smith's point that entrepreneurs and inventors need to be motivated—in economic terms, they need incentives—and moreover they need a regime dedicated to the protection of patents, property rights and contracts. Historically wealth was mainly land, but Lincoln now identifies wealth with new ideas and new human production. Underlying Lincoln's philosophy is the message that "the hand that makes the corn has the right to put the corn into its own mouth"—in other words, that people have the right to keep the fruit of their labor.

We can situate Lincoln's argument better by putting it in the context of Albert Hirschman's important book *The Passions and the Interests*. Hirschman argues that from ancient times, wealth was considered a zero-sum game. If you have more, I have less. And the only way for me to get more is to get some of yours. Hirschman reminds me of when I'd go to elementary school with ten marbles in my pocket. I realized that the only way for me to get more marbles was to take some from others. There was no other way to increase my collection of marbles.

Wealth in ancient times, Hirschman contends, was obtained mainly by seizure. Conquest, theft and looting were the preferred mechanisms for acquisition. Recall the famous story of Alexander the Great, who summoned a pirate and asked him, "What is your idea of raiding other ships and seizing their possessions?" The pirate replied, "The same idea as yours, except that you do it with a larger fleet and are therefore called a great emperor, while I do it with my small boat and am therefore called a pirate."

Hirschman identifies the powerful human impulse to raid and seize and conquer with the passions. For centuries, he says, humans turned to religious and moral exhortation to temper and regulate the passions, but with limited success. One may say that the lower side of human nature tends to predominate. So the early modern philosophers came up with a rival human proclivity that they considered just as powerful. This was "interest"—specifically interest in capitalist accumulation.

Passion is sudden, tempestuous, violent; interest is steady, calm, rational. The desire to accumulate, Adam Smith tells us, "though calm and dispassionate, comes with us from the womb, and never leaves us till we go into the grave."[19] So in the long run, interest can overcome passion. Why go on a raiding spree when you can make steady improvements to your house and yard? Moreover, through a system built on interest, we discover that wealth is not zero-sum after all. It does not have to be seized; it can be created. Who wants to take someone else's marbles by force when there is a way of trading for them, or better still, making marbles of your own?

This is what Lincoln was getting at in his praise of the patent laws. Notice that for Lincoln, as for Adam Smith, self-interest is not a bad thing. His concern is not to suppress it but to motivate it. More self-interest means more wealth legitimately gained; it also means less passion and less seizure by unlawful force. Hirschman sums up his argument with a telling quotation from Montesquieu's *Spirit of the Laws*: "It is fortunate for men to be in a situation in which, though their passions may prompt them to be wicked, they have nevertheless an interest in not being so."[20]

These are the principles that shaped the American Revolution—or perhaps I should say both American revolutions, the Revolution of 1776 and the Revolution of 1789. The first was the War of Independence, provoked by the Declaration of Independence; the second was the framing and adoption of the Constitution and the Bill of Rights. Most people focus on the second and ignore the first, even though the first laid the foundation for and actually provides valuable clues about what motivated the second.

HANDS IN OUR POCKETS

What motivated the first American Revolution? George Washington put it well in 1774: "Great Britain hath no more right to put their hands into my pocket without my consent than I have to put my hands into yours for money." This helps us to understand that the right to property was the first principle at issue in the American Revolution. "Can there be any liberty," wrote James Otis in 1763, "where property is taken without consent?"[21]

Consider how John Dickinson, in an influential pamphlet, responded to the Stamp Act, which aimed at bringing in revenue to the British Treasury. "If the Parliament succeeds in this attempt, other statutes will impose other duties . . . and thus the Parliament will levy upon us such sums of money as they choose to take, without any other limitation than their pleasure."[22] Strikingly, American resistance here is not over the amount of taxation, which was quite modest, but the process by which the British Parliament imposed these taxes.

The British repealed the tax, but then in the Declaratory Act of 1766 they rejected the American insistence on "no taxation without representation." England retained full power to make law for the colonies "in all cases whatsoever." Then came the Townshend Acts imposing import duties on essential goods, including paper, glass, lead and tea. Some of these were also repealed, leaving in place—to italicize a point of privilege—the tax on tea. All these measures were, in Jefferson's words, "a series of oppressions" that "plainly prove a deliberate and systematical plan of reducing us to slavery."[23]

This theme of asserting economic freedom from government confiscation continues to undergird the Constitution, as explicated in its magnificent apologia, *The Federalist*. "The first object of government," Madison writes in the tenth book of *The Federalist*, is "the protection of different and unequal faculties of acquiring property." Note that this is not one of the goals of the new regime created by the Constitution; it is the primary goal.

Hamilton in the twelfth book of *The Federalist* continues this theme. He notes that all statesmen now recognize "a prosperous commerce" to be "a primary object of their political cares." Consequently, "by multiplying the means of gratification," the new government can ensure that "the assiduous merchant, the laborious husbandman, the active mechanic, and the industrious manufacturer . . . all orders of men, look forward with eager expectation, and growing alacrity, to this pleasing reward of their toils."[24]

Even though he was Hamilton's political rival, Jefferson agreed with Hamilton that government should not seek to redistribute the gains of private enterprise. "To take from one, because it is thought his own industry and that of his fathers has acquired too much, in order to spare others, who, or whose fathers, have not exercised equal industry and skill, is to violate arbitrarily the first principle of association, the guarantee to everyone the free exercise of his industry and the fruits acquired by it."[25]

For the founders, this principle was about more than assuring growth and prosperity. It was about the cultivation of human personality itself. This point was made much later, by the psychologist William James, but in a way that the founders would have affirmed. "It is clear," James wrote, "that between what a man calls me and what he simply calls mine, the line is difficult to draw. . . . Our fame, our children, the work of our hands may be as dear to us as our bodies are, and arouse the same feelings and the same acts of reprisal if attacked. . . . A man's self is the sum total of all that he can call his . . . his reputation and work, his land and houses and yacht and bank account. All these things give him the same emotions. If they wax or prosper, he feels triumphant; if they dwindle and die away, he feels cast down."[26]

The importance of this passage is its emphasis that economic rights are no less fundamental than civil rights and civil liberties. It makes no sense to say that I own my religious and political opinions and have a right to them but I don't own my labor and have a right to the fruits of it. As James explains, we are equally attached to what we possess as to who we are—in fact, we define ourselves in extended form to include the home we have built, the cars we drive, the clothes we wear, the books we have written and the things we have made. James' point resonates with me as it would have with the American founders; I know I feel this way.

So the founding is a socialist nightmare. It's a nightmare because it affirms as the possession of citizens what the socialists would like to take away through the agency of government. In order to take away your wealth and earnings and possessions, the socialists must insist that those things don't really belong to you. You somehow stole or appropriated them. You seized for yourself what belongs to the commonweal of society. A majority of citizens, agitating through the democratic process, have every right to seize some or all of what belongs to you to cover the wants or demands or "entitlements" of others.

For socialists, this is what democracy means: the collective right to appropriate. What gives this right the force of justice, and of law, is that it is supposedly an expression of the "will of the people." But the founders did not agree with this. They did not agree that there is some "will of the people" that can directly govern a society. And even if there were, they rejected the premise that the people have the right to gang up in a majority and seize the property and earnings of their fellow citizens whose only crime is to be in the political minority.

TYRANNY OF THE MAJORITY

Let's begin by considering the very definition of democracy: rule by the *demos*, or the people. Yet the people don't directly rule in any existing society. Even in ancient Athens, where there was direct democracy, only a few thousand people actually showed up at the agora to vote and decide issues. This is the same democracy that routinely violated life and liberty, as evidenced by its practice of mass-scale slavery and its decision to put Socrates to death just for philosophizing on the streets of Athens.

For Madison, writing in the tenth book of *The Federalist*, democracy is mob rule. "Democracies have ever been spectacles of turbulence and contention; have ever been found incompatible with personal security or the rights of property; and have, in general, been as short in their lives as they have been violent in their deaths."[27] Ancient Athens, for all its glory, fits this tragic description.

The central principle of democracy is majority rule. We're so accustomed to hearing progressives and democratic socialists sing the praises of majority rule that it's worth pondering why majorities have a right to rule in the first place. Consider this: Should the citizens of a large country dominate those of a smaller country because they are more numerous? Certainly not. Why then should the majority of a society hold sway over the whole society, making decisions not merely for itself but also for the minority?

Let's say the majority makes rules that discriminate in its favor and against minorities. Should this be allowed? Let's say we have a society of 100 people, and 51 of them decide to confiscate the property or earnings of the other 49 for their own use. Or to force the other 49 to build their houses in a certain way, or to pay for the majority's children to attend college, or to purchase healthcare at prices set by the majority itself. How about if the majority passes a law to seize the lawfully acquired wealth of a single citizen—say Bill Gates? Are these things just or permissible?

If these seem like fanciful examples, they are not. I get them from the proposals of progressives and democratic socialists who never run short of ideas for appropriating other people's wealth or controlling their lives. Moreover, there is historical precedent for majorities acting oppressively. Lincoln confronted precisely such a doctrine from his Democratic rival Stephen A. Douglas. Douglas advocated "popular sovereignty," a system in which majority rule in each state and territory would decide on allowing or forbidding slavery.

For Lincoln, this was morally unacceptable. First, a majority cannot "choose" to enslave others, because this is a choice exercised in order to deny choice to someone else. No majority, Lincoln insisted, has the right to steal the bread that is made by the sweat of other men. In Lincoln's words, popular sovereignty amounted to saying that if one man chooses to enslave another, no third man is allowed to object. Thus majority rule in this context amounted to a legitimation of tyranny.

Lincoln understood the socialist impulse and rejected it. Responding to both slavery apologists and socialists who condemned what they called capitalist wage slavery, Lincoln said, "The man who labored for another last year, this year labors for himself, and next year he will hire others to labor for him." Cautioning against socialist wealth confiscation schemes, Lincoln told a delegation of workingmen during the Civil War, "Let not him who is houseless pull down the house of another, but let him labor diligently and build one of his own."[28]

Jefferson and Madison would have agreed: even democratic majorities have no business seizing the property or earnings of citizens. "An elective despotism," Jefferson wrote in *Notes on the State of Virginia*, "was not the government we fought for." In his famous discussion of faction, Madison identified two types: minority factions and majority factions. How do they arise? "The most common and durable source of factions," he writes, "has been the various and unequal distribution of property."[29]

Minority and majority factions, says Madison, pose a danger to the public welfare because they both enviously eye the belongings of others. Yet of the two types of factions, Madison considers majority factions to be more dangerous. Why? Because minority factions can be curbed by the power of the majority. But how, Madison asked, can majority factions be curtailed? Nowhere does Madison assume that majorities have an unlimited right to do their will. On the contrary, he seeks mechanisms to regulate and control the will of the majority.

These observations lead to a startling conclusion. The American founders held that unrestricted majority rule is the principle of modern tyranny, just as unrestricted one-man rule is the principle of ancient tyranny. As historian Gordon Wood points out, they broke with their British predecessors in this respect. "So convinced were the English, in the decades following 1689, that tyranny could come only from a single ruler that they could hardly conceive of the people tyrannizing themselves."[30] The American founders, by contrast, sought to avoid dual forms of tyranny: tyranny of the monarch, and tyranny of the people as expressed through majority faction.

Of course the founders, like Lincoln, did submit to the principle of majority rule. But they did so in highly qualified terms. Majorities are not inherently wiser than minorities. So why should they rule over them? Lincoln spelled out the logic in his first inaugural address. Ideally society would be ruled by unanimous consent. Since unanimous consent is practically impossible, there are two alternatives: majority rule or minority rule. Obviously minority rule over the majority would be unjust, so majority rule is the only remaining alternative.

But how to prevent majority rule from being unjust? This was the fundamental problem that the founders, through the constitutional structure, sought to solve. The founders did so through several block-and-tackle measures designed to limit, frustrate and in some cases thwart majority rule. I count at least eight.

First, they adopted a written Constitution—again a departure from Great Britain, which has a common law but no such constitution—that operates as a supreme charter, overriding the will of the majority. The Constitution creates a framework for limited government—which is to say, the authority of the federal government covers enumerated areas but no others. Outside that purview, the government has no authority.

Second, the Bill of Rights. Later added to the Constitution—ironically at the insistence of its Anti-Federalist opponents—this roster contains a series of limitations on government that typically begin, "Congress shall make no law." Congress shall make no law restricting speech, or the press, or the free exercise of religion. Citizens have the right to assemble, and to own firearms, and to enjoy due process of law, and to be protected against unreasonable search and seizure. In his famous commentary on the Constitution, Justice Joseph Story noted how a bill of rights places strict limits on majority rule. "A bill of rights is an important protection against unjust and oppressive conduct on the part of the people themselves."[31]

Admittedly, the Constitution can be amended, but the process is so onerous that it requires something approaching unanimity for this to occur. The authority to compare federal laws to the Constitution and to strike down those that contravene constitutional provisions is given to the Supreme Court. So this is our third block-and-tackle mechanism, judicial review. The Supreme Court has independent authority to enforce the Constitution and protect the rights of citizens against the will of the majority.

Fourth, representative government. What this means is that the people do not rule directly; they rule by electing representatives who govern in their stead. Madison counted this practice—a radical departure from the direct democracy of the ancient Athenians—as the distinguishing mark between a "democracy" and a "republic." A large and extended society, in Madison's words, can function effectively only as a republic.

Fifth, separation of powers. Here power is divided between an elected legislature charged with making laws, an elected executive charged with enforcing them and an appointed judiciary empowered with arbitrating and resolving legal disputes. Sixth, federalism, which divides power between the national government and the states, so that some powers are exercised at the national level, others at the state and local level.

Seventh, checks and balances. This means that in addition to dividing power, there is mutual oversight. Congress has the power to make laws, but the president can veto them, and vetoes can be overridden only by congressional supermajorities. The president and his executive branch enforce the laws, but there is congressional and judicial oversight. The

judiciary interprets the Constitution and the laws, but judges are nominated by the president and confirmed by the Senate.

Finally, the Electoral College and the two branches of the legislature,
the House and the Senate. While the president, members of Congress
and senators are all elected by the people, the distribution of power is
weighted to give representation to small and large states. The Electoral
College ensures that a few large states cannot by themselves decide the
presidency. Small states have fewer congressional representatives than
large ones, in proportion to size, but all states, small and large, have
two senators apiece, creating a parity among states in that branch of the
legislature.

What does all this mean? It means that America was designed to foster a spirit of freedom and enterprise among its people, and to thwart
majority rule from tyrannizing over that spirit. In sum, America is a free
market society whose founding principles, as long as they remain intact,
provide a powerful bulwark against socialism of every stripe, including
democratic socialism.

SELF-MADE MAN

It may seem surprising that, in this account of the American founding,
I have given so little emphasis to what the founders thought about race,
gender and sexual orientation. In other words, I seem to have neglected
the "identity" issues altogether. For progressive historiography, this is
something of a scandal. Progressive scholars across a range of disciplines
talk of little else. They write as if the founders cared about little else.

Yet the truth is that the founders gave little attention to the politics
of race, even less to the politics of sex and none whatever to the politics
of sexual orientation. Why? Not because the founders were racists and
sexists. Rather, they were concerned with the norms of society, and in
constructing these, they emphasized the typical or normal case. They
were not unfamiliar with the anomaly of race. They understood that
their wives and daughters were part of their *novus ordo seclorum*. I would
be shocked if Franklin and Jefferson—in Europe if not in America—
had not encountered the phenomenon of the homosexual or the trans-
vestite.

So why not build a society keeping minorities and outliers foremost in mind? For the same reason that every group in the world organizes its society without giving primary consideration to the outsiders who might wish to emigrate to that society. For the same reason that a dinner host organizes a party keeping the general tenor of the guests in mind. The basic principles are those of normalcy and inclusion. Most people eat meat, so there will be meat on the menu. A few are vegetarian, so let's make sure that there is enough for them also.

Now imagine that one of the invitees is a dwarf. I don't pick this example at random. Identity politics includes physical handicap; this is one of its recognized categories. So here we have our dwarf, and he is annoyed to discover that the chairs are too high for him to climb into. Moreover, his view is consistently blocked by the taller people around him. The dwarf also notices that no one is paying special attention to him. Becoming angrier by the minute, he finally shuts off the music and screams at the top of his lungs, "You people are bigots! You are all obsessed with height!"

It's very hard for the dwarf to understand that the guests are actually indifferent to height. This is not a party organized by dwarves or for dwarves. The good news is that there is a principle of inclusion. The organizers have made room for him to be part of the festivities like everyone else. But the operating principle is one of universality, not of difference. This is the aspect of the American founding that identity socialists hate.

Frederick Douglass, the runaway slave, hated it too. At first he viewed the American founding purely from the point of view of the slave. Why didn't the founders outlaw slavery at the outset? Douglass couldn't see what Lincoln saw: the founders could not do this and still make a union. Slavery prior to the founding was legal in all the states; many—and certainly the southern states—would refuse to join a union that forbade slavery at the outset.

So the founders chose, in Lincoln's words, to create a union that tolerated slavery. They hoped and even expected that slavery would continue to lose political power in such a union. Even Jefferson—one of the largest slaveholders among them—anticipated a total emancipation. The founders really believed all men are created equal. They simply couldn't make good on that belief in their own time. So, in Lincoln's phrase, they chose to declare the rights whose enforcement would follow as soon as the circumstances permitted.

When he heard this argument, Douglass' reaction was that this was very easy for a white man to say. Douglass carried his animus over to Lincoln. Lincoln, he charged, was the white man's president. Blacks were at best the accidental beneficiaries of his actions. After all, Lincoln didn't campaign in 1860 to get rid of slavery; he campaigned merely to arrest the spread of slavery. Even that, Douglass bitterly noted, was framed in the Republican platform in terms of opening up the new territories to white settlement.

Until he met Lincoln, Douglass never considered the question from Lincoln's side. Lincoln was white; why should he give priority to blacks? Douglass, after all, considered it right and natural for him to give priority to his own race. Douglass saw that Lincoln treated him not as a black man but simply as a man. And that, Douglass realized, was enough. He didn't need Lincoln to see difference; he only needed Lincoln to recognize their common humanity.

Over time, Douglass reconsidered his longtime hatred for the founders. He came to see that the founders too articulated universal norms and rights that included him even while not recognizing his blackness. Douglass termed slavery the mere "scaffolding" to be removed when the American edifice was completed. And Douglass also championed women's rights and women's suffrage in the understanding that these too were an application of the equality principle of the Declaration of Independence. "All men" was a phrase that was, from the beginning, intended to include women.

Speaking to the Massachusetts Anti-Slavery Society just days after the Civil War ended, Douglass raised the question, "What must be done for the slaves?" His answer: "Do nothing with us! Your doing with us has already played the mischief with us. Do nothing with us. . . . If the Negro cannot stand on his own legs, let him fall. All I ask is, give him a chance to stand on his own legs! Let him alone. . . . If you will only untie his hands and give him a chance, I think he will live."[32]

Douglass' most famous speech—the one he delivered most often—was in keeping with this philosophy of self-reliance. In fact, it went beyond self-reliance to stress the theme of self-invention. It was titled "Self-Made Men." America, Douglass argued, is the land of the self-made man, and in the fulfillment of its original principles it offers that prospect to the woman no less than to the man, to the black man no less than to the white man. Douglass himself, the self-taught former slave who became a publisher, an orator and a diplomat, was a walking embodiment of the self-made man.

As if addressing the identity socialist across the reach of time, Douglass noted that there are those who scorn the self-made man, crediting his achievement to privilege or luck. This criticism, he said, takes "no cognizance of the very different uses to which different men put their circumstances and chances. . . . It does not matter that the wind is fair and the tide is at its flood, if the mariner refuses to weigh his anchor and spread his canvas to the breeze." The self-made man is not a whiner; he makes full use of the opportunities that luck provides.

The self-made man is not perfect, Douglass admitted. He can be rough-hewn, he can be somewhat arrogant, attributing all his success to himself. Even so, Douglass said, the self-made man can take justifiable pride, because he is indebted to himself for himself. In Douglass' own phrase, he has made the road on which he has traveled. He has built his own ladder. "There is genuine heroism in his struggle, and something of sublimity and glory in his triumph."[33]

Douglass, who started life at the bottom, one might say as a dwarf, became what he could become only in America: a giant among men. He did so despite enduring the slings and arrows of racial prejudice, both in the North and in the South. He became a patriot and a stalwart of the Republican Party who insisted, at election time, that "the Republican Party is the ship—all else is the sea." Here, in the argument and person of Douglass, is the moral case for America and for the Republican Party, and a full and decisive refutation of the identity socialist's indictment of the American founding.

IN PRAISE OF ROBBER BARONS

I'd like to conclude this chapter by highlighting the achievements of some of the men of enterprise who embody the spirit of the American founding, the Franklin spirit. These are the very "robber barons" vilified in progressive and socialist historiography. I'll focus on three figures who pioneered America's industrial revolution and also the first communications revolution, defined by the steamship, the railroad and, later, the airplane.

The progressive narrative focuses on various government subsidies that were extended to pioneers in these industries. Naturally, there was a scramble for the loot, and corruption was commonplace. The left blames the corruption on the greed of the capitalist class. Yet for progressives, the positive lesson is that without government aid, the railroads and other key modes of transportation would not have been built. So history, in this version of the story, illuminates that the path to government direction of industry—the path toward socialism—is the right one.

The truth, however, is precisely the opposite. The great innovations examined here all occurred without government involvement; in fact, they were achieved in the face of obstacles erected by the government. The corruption in virtually every case involved a group that we may term the "political entrepreneurs"—namely businesses that sought to thrive not by prevailing in a free market but by accepting government subsidies and protection.

When Cornelius Vanderbilt began running steamboats on the Hudson River, the traffic was controlled by Robert Fulton's vessels. Fulton's monopoly had been granted to him by New York State. Under the monopoly arrangement, Fulton could charge higher prices, since customers did not have a choice. Fulton paid off the politicians, and the politicians returned the favor by giving Fulton exclusive control over the Hudson waterway. Under this cozy arrangement, Vanderbilt's boats were technically illegal. Yet Vanderbilt eluded the law and offered lower prices.

Fortunately for Vanderbilt, there was a public uproar. The uproar led to lawsuits, and the Supreme Court struck down the Fulton monopoly.

This was the landmark case of *Gibbons v. Ogden*. It opened up the Hudson River to competition, which attracted more steamship operators and drove down prices. Fulton could not compete and went out of business.

Vanderbilt offered the lowest prices, his business flourished and he expanded to routes all over New England. At one point, historian H. W. Brands notes, Vanderbilt cut his ticket price on the Albany line to a meager 10 cents; then, when a local association of steamboat operators tried to undercut him, he offered his service for free, covering his cost and making a profit solely based on selling food and drink to passengers.[34]

As steamers got bigger and began to make transatlantic crossings, the British line Cunard dominated, in large part through subsidies from the English Parliament. An American, Edward K. Collins, convinced the U.S. government to give him subsidies to compete with Cunard. Vanderbilt challenged Collins with no subsidies. Vanderbilt built better ships, conserved his costs, offered high-volume, low-cost fares and put Collins out of business once his subsidy ran out.

During the Civil War, Vanderbilt gave his 5,000-ton ship, somewhat immodestly named the *Vanderbilt*, as a gift to the U.S. Navy. He also offered to personally sink the Confederate ship *Merrimac*, requesting only that while he was doing it, the government should stay "out of the way." After the war, Vanderbilt moved his investments from steamships into railroads; he was instrumental in building the New York Central Railroad, which connected New York with Chicago and other Midwestern cities.

Progressives like to tell the story of the multiple railroad companies that built their cross-country lines with the help of government charters and subsidies. The two best known are the Union Pacific Railroad and the Central Pacific Railroad. Both desperately sought to fill their coffers with government cash as they raced to complete their projects. Meanwhile, Henry Villard's Northern Pacific attracted both investors and government subsidies with his promise to build a railroad across the Rockies up through the Pacific Northwest. The moral of the progressive story is that, without the government, it can't be done.

The problem with this narrative is that while the rush for subsidies was at full pitch—and this is where the corruption came from—James J.

Hill built a transcontinental line through the Northwest with no federal aid. Notwithstanding his government subsidies, Villard failed and went bankrupt; Hill, however, succeeded.

Why did Hill succeed and Villard fail? They both faced a daunting challenge because of the remoteness of the Northwest and the harsh climate. The difference came in their contrasting approaches to the task at hand. Villard, a political entrepreneur who came from New York, viewed the Northwest like a postcard; he built along the most scenic routes. It cost more, but so what? Villard was spending the government's money. Hill, a local man with more practical concerns, chose the shortest and most efficient routes. Hill was spending his own money.

Villard viewed the great Pacific Northwest as good for passing through; Hill encouraged the development of farming communities alongside his railroad. To make this happen, Hill imported cattle and gave them to settlers free of charge. He offered to transport people to the Northwest for just $10 if they would farm near his railroad. Hill expected that if these farming communities prospered, his railroad would too.

Unlike Villard and other railroad builders on government support, Hill was obsessed with efficiency. He had heard, from the expeditions of Lewis and Clark way back in 1805, that there was a crossing called the Marias Pass that shortened the distance through the Rockies. No one, however, could locate the pass. So Hill hired local adventurers to comb through western Montana to find it. They did, and Hill was able to cut his costs by cutting his distance by a hundred miles.[35]

Finally, we turn to airplane travel, where the story is nearly the same. The well-connected political entrepreneur Samuel Langley had pledged to build an airplane. He had the support of the Smithsonian, the most prominent scientific institution in America. He had hundreds of thousands of dollars in government subsidy. He received devotional press coverage as the man who would conquer the sky. Yet despite multiple attempts over a period of 10 years, Langley's airship project failed miserably.

Meanwhile, as historian David McCullough tells the story, two owners of a bicycle business, Wilbur and Orville Wright, used $1,000 in profits from their company to purchase building materials. They designed an airplane. They got their materials to Kitty Hawk, North Carolina. They paid their own way to get there. They built the makeshift airplane. They flew it. In doing so, they revolutionized the capacity of human beings to travel—now not just on land, like animals, or by sea, like fish, but also through the air, like birds.[36]

Vanderbilt, Hill, the Wright brothers—these are the American pioneers. They were self-made men who also helped make a new nation. What a transformation these men wrought, taking a country from the infancy of its development to a great and prosperous maturity. They spearheaded a communications revolution even more radical and life-changing than the one we are living through now. Ignored these entrepreneurs may be—vilified even—in progressive historiography. Yet who can deny that they embody the inventive, enterprising and—I hope—indestructible spirit of America?

2

THE DREAM AND THE NIGHTMARE

HOW SOCIALISM CAME TO AMERICA

You all did see that on the Lupercal,
I thrice presented him with a kingly crown,
Which he did thrice refuse. Was this ambition?[1]

—SHAKESPEARE, *JULIUS CAESAR*

In the scene above from *Julius Caesar*, Mark Antony poses a rhetorical question to the Roman mob. The rhetorical question has the presumed answer, "No." The crowd is supposed to arrive at this conclusion from the undisputed fact that Caesar made a triple disavowal of the offer to become a monarch. The crowd is struck dumb because ambition is part of human nature and a characteristic expected in a military and political leader. What normal human being refuses power in this way? The crowd is awed by Caesar's abstemious virtue. He is not a normal human being; he is something higher than that.

But Antony himself knows why Caesar disavowed the crown, and so does the skeptical aristocrat Casca, who is also in the audience. These men recognize that Caesar's refusal was not a suspension of ambition but an exercise of it. Caesar's action here can be contrasted with that of George Washington, who was offered the monarchy and refused it. Washington, however, genuinely didn't want that kind of power. He understood that the American Revolution was not merely a rejection of British monarchy; it was a rejection of monarchy itself. Washington intended to serve as president and then return to private life on his Virginia farm, which he did.

Caesar, however, had a more dissembling motive for an action that outwardly resembled Washington's. Caesar knew that ever since the Romans drove out the Tarquin kings, monarchy was detested by the people. For Caesar to show deference to this public sentiment was a political necessity. Caesar recognized that the best way to be an emperor was to exercise the powers of kingship without the title. In short, Caesar was a very good actor, Antony was his very capable public relations man and the crowd fell for it. The correct answer to Antony's question is, "Yes."

I offer these thoughts as prelude to the issue we will explore in this chapter, which is about how socialism came to America. By this I don't mean that America has become a socialist country. We are not the United States of Socialism, at least not yet. But the socialists are here, and their agenda is now part of the national discourse. If the discrediting of socialism was one of the biggest stories of the late twentieth century, the revival of the prospect of socialism in the United States must undoubtedly be one of the biggest stories of the early twenty-first century.

Surveys show that Americans take socialism more seriously than ever before. A Gallup survey from 2019 has 51 percent of U.S. adults saying socialism would be a bad thing for the country, but a respectable 43 percent say it would be a good thing. Not since World War II have the socialist numbers been so high. Indeed, according to Gallup, surveys from the post–World War II era recorded only 15 percent of Americans saying they wished to see the country "go more in the direction of socialism."[2]

The two groups most receptive to socialism? Young people and Democrats. It is not surprising, perhaps, for young people to be more disposed to socialist schemes than their elders, but what is striking today is how many young people—survey evidence suggests somewhere between half and two-thirds—espouse some form of socialism. And young people are joined in their socialist afflatus by Democrats, well over 50 percent of whom, according to Gallup, have a positive view of socialism.[3]

The activist group Democratic Socialists of America has grown from a few thousand to over 50,000 members, and a couple of its members can be found in the U.S. Congress. The socialists have their own publications, like *Jacobin*, and their own national conferences. More significant, much of the national media is sympathetic, and socialist ideas now dominate the Democratic Party and shape the nation's political agenda. Socialism may not prevail in America, but it has a greater respectability and a better chance to prevail now than at any previous time. "It's an encouraging time," writes Nathan Robinson in *Why You Should Be a Socialist*, "to be a socialist in America."

How did this happen? In a recent speech delivered at George Washington University, Bernie Sanders—who has done more than any single person to advance the socialist program in the past few years—gave his answer. It happened because of Franklin Roosevelt. "Let me define for you, simply and straightforwardly, what democratic socialism means to me. It builds on what Franklin Delano Roosevelt said when he fought for guaranteed economic rights for all Americans. . . . And, by the way, almost everything he proposed, almost every program, every idea, was called socialist." Sanders described his own socialist platform as "the unfinished business of the New Deal."[4]

Sanders stopped short of calling FDR and the New Deal socialist, but according to him, they paved the way for American socialism. And FDR's critics called him a socialist, Bernie implied, because they saw that he was heading in that direction. The point of Sanders' invocation was to anchor socialism within the American tradition and the American mainstream. He—Sanders—was not some sort of political weirdo; he was merely making additions to the building that FDR constructed way back in the 1930s.

Sanders' speech provoked some indignant pushback from leading progressives, because it contradicted the progressive narrative that is taught in schools and promulgated in the media. According to this narrative—amplified in countless textbooks and articles—FDR and the New Deal saved America from socialism. They also saved capitalism by creating a new, more humane form of capitalism that protected its victims: workers, the unemployed, the sick, the elderly and widows and orphans. Calling FDR socialist, fumed progressive economist Robert Reich, is to characterize him with a "scare word." The progressive historian Sean Wilentz blames such rhetoric on "right-wing name-calling." Writes left-wing columnist Jamelle Bouie, "Being attacked as a socialist doesn't make one a socialist, and neither FDR nor the New Deal was socialist."[5]

Wilentz insists that FDR was a progressive, not a socialist. The socialist leader Norman Thomas recognized this. Asked whether FDR had carried out the Socialist Party platform, Thomas quipped that he had not, "unless he carried it out on a stretcher." Wilentz stressed that while socialism is defined by public or state ownership of finance, industry and agriculture—all of which FDR rejected—progressivism refers to what FDR sought, a government that provides "security for all citizens in the essentials of life, including education, housing, employment and medical care."[6]

Yet it wasn't just right-wingers and Republicans who called FDR a socialist. So did Al Smith, the Democratic Party's presidential nominee in 1924. Smith had officially nominated FDR at the Democratic Convention in 1928. Incredibly, this Democratic stalwart broke with FDR and opposed his reelection. Smith knew that many of FDR's New Deal programs, including Social Security, unemployment insurance and agricultural price supports, had come from the socialists. The socialists today are fully aware of this. "The prescription may have had 'Democrat' on the label," writes Jack Schwartz in the Daily Beast, "but the inspiration often came from socialists."[7]

So who's right, Sanders or the progressives? Sanders! Even the progressives know this. Their protest against Bernie seems to be against his candor. Shut up, Bernie! We're supposed to be a team; stop blowing the whistle on us. The progressives know that even though FDR didn't nationalize industries or establish worker control, he tried. As we'll see, he tried and failed. FDR also attempted—with partial success—to destroy the independence of the Supreme Court. If he had prevailed completely, he would have become something close to a tyrant, and America would be much more of a socialist country.

Moreover, FDR vilified the rich in terms that Bernie and Alexandria Ocasio-Cortez would applaud. He laid both the rhetorical and policy foundations for the type of socialism that Bernie and others champion in America, a socialism rooted in public entitlements or "free stuff." This chapter will substantiate Bernie's contention that progressivism was the conveyor belt that brought socialism into the American mainstream.

SISTER IDEOLOGIES

Sanders, in fact, understated his case for FDR being the pioneer of American socialism. As the German sociologist Wolfgang Schivelbusch argues in a book tellingly titled *Three New Deals*, progressivism, Communism and National Socialism (also called fascism) were all sister ideologies, variations on a single theme, motivated by the same impulses, seeking to move society in a similar direction—away from free market capitalism and toward a collectivist society with the state as the instrument of the common good.

Consistent with this ideological kinship, FDR and American progressives admired socialist regimes: not just the "international socialism" of the Soviet Union but also National Socialism in Italy and Germany. Bernie could easily have pointed this out, and then added that he himself honeymooned in the Soviet Union and praised Soviet socialism, at one point even defending the great symbol of socialist shortages, namely, bread lines. Bernie, however, was as silent about all this as the progressive historians who write about FDR.

Yet all of it is there, undeniable, in the historical record. This exemplifies the phenomenon that political scientist Paul Hollander calls "political pilgrims," a term referring to leading leftists in America and Europe who visited socialist regimes, from the Soviet Union to Mao's China to Castro's Cuba and later even Nicaragua, only to return singing their praises. As Hollander shows, leading progressives praised the worst abuses of socialism—mass purges, liquidation of whole populations, show trials resulting in the execution of the innocent—as exemplary demonstrations of how socialism could create a model society.[8]

Why would they do it? More broadly, what motivates the progressives today who are pushing America in the direction of socialism? Here the standard conservative answer is: the dream! They are intoxicated by the socialist dream of the just society. They want, in the words of philosopher Eric Voegelin, to "immanentize the eschaton," or in plain English, to bring heaven down to earth. Captivated as they are by utopia, they are blinded to the facts on the ground.

Yes, but the facts were so obvious, even at the time, that it makes no sense to hold that otherwise intelligent people were simply deceived. If they were deceived, they wanted to be deceived. And why? Again, the standard conservative response is that they have to believe in theoretical socialism because actual socialism never works. And actual socialism never works because it is "against human nature." Since it is against human nature, all existing socialist regimes fail, and each generation of socialists has to harken back to the dream and promise a new type of socialism different from all the types that came before.

But what is it about socialism that is "against human nature"? Charles C. W. Cooke writes in *National Review* that "real socialism can't exist" because "selfishness is ineradicable" and "man isn't perfectible."[9] This is admittedly a part of early socialist rhetoric. Marx spoke in grandiose terms about transforming human nature. But this was in the context of the final stage of communism that would supposedly involve the abolition of the state itself. No socialist in the world wants that. No actual socialist has ever attempted that.

Anyone who thinks that socialists from Lenin to Nicolás Maduro to Bernie Sanders are genuinely trying to eradicate selfishness or human imperfection is living on Mars. Maduro, for instance, promises poor Venezuelans that he will make rich people vacate their land and homes; then he will distribute that wealth among the poor. Is this an eradication of selfishness? And what about the Bernie voters who want other people to pay for their college tuition and healthcare? Their behavior is hardly an eradication of selfishness; rather, it is a manifestation of it.

Even Soviet socialism didn't fail because it was against human nature. Well, you might say, Soviet socialism didn't work. That, however, depends on your definition of "work." It certainly worked for those who were running it, and that's why it lasted for more than 70 years. Venezuelan socialism today "works" for the Chavistas, who live high on the hog. The truth is that socialism is consistent with human nature; it draws on its worst impulses, which cannot be publicly acknowledged. This may be why the true motives of today's socialists are not easily recognized.

What's in it for them? One way to think about this question is to consider what politics is about in every society: Who holds the power? As I've suggested before, it makes no sense to reply, "The people." In every society, the people live in a fog. They are not directly involved. Absorbed in the hubbub of everyday life, they are only dimly aware of the larger world around them, and if you told them that they were in fact running society, they would have no idea what you were talking about. They no more run society than they run the National Football League!

Sure, they may vote every two or four years, but even that may not happen if it rains on Election Day. What this means is that the "will of the people" is not something given; rather, it is made. In Schumpeter's words, "The will of the people is the product and not the motive of the political process."[10] Progressives know this, and, as we will see, they devote tremendous resources and energy to forging a climate of public opinion favorable to their projects. But what are their projects? What is their actual dream?

THE ONES LEFT BEHIND

Is their actual dream about justice or about power? A strong case can be made for the latter. As historian Bernard Bailyn writes, it is well understood in political theory that "the ultimate explanation of every political controversy" is the "disposition of power." Affirming this point, John Adams used the term "dominion." Dominion means force, control by some human beings of others. And for Adams, the defining feature of dominion is aggression, its constant tendency to break loose of legitimate boundaries. Power is "grasping" and "tenacious," and it takes great vigilance on the part of those who love their freedom to protect against its "encroaching nature."[11]

The American founding, as we saw in the last chapter, was an elaborate mechanism to protect freedom and check the encroachment of irredentist power. But progressivism, as we will see, is akin to socialism in that it developed in opposition to the principle of the American founding. The progressives and socialists advanced their own dream in opposition to the American dream.

At first glance, this seems odd. The American Revolution was a successful revolution—in fact, the only successful revolution in world history. Even the subsequent modifications of the Constitution, in the wake of the Civil War, for instance, were nothing more than general applications of the principles of the Revolution themselves. The Thirteenth, Fourteenth and Fifteenth Amendments can be understood as a full implementation of a single provision of the Declaration of Independence.

Every revolution other than the American has proven to be a failure or a disaster. The French Revolution, for instance, began with the glorious affirmation of "liberty, equality and fraternity" and ended with Robespierre's Reign of Terror. What finally brought the Terror to an end was the ascent of Napoleon to the throne. Democracy itself was overthrown, only returning slowly, haltingly, over the subsequent century and a half. The Russian Revolution was an unmitigated disaster from the beginning, and at its nadir it reached depths of tyranny and depravity rivaled only by Mao and Hitler.

So why repudiate a successful revolution and embrace the ideals of failed revolutions? To understand this, we must recognize that every revolution has winners and losers. Even the American Revolution! Who were the losers? One might say they were the partisans of the British. And what happened to them? Some were killed; others made their peace with the new regime in America; still others fled to Canada.

But let's examine the question more broadly. Which was the class of people left behind by the American Revolution? That would be the aristocratic class, the ruling class of the ancien régime. America never had an ancien régime, but Europe did. And who were the members of this group? They were the courtiers who served at court, the barristers who advised the throne, the men of letters who received patronage at the hands of monarchs and aristocrats.

What did these people actually produce? Not much. Nothing, really. What they produced were mainly words. They prized wordsmithing, but hated doing other types of work, especially manual work. The philosophy of this group was summed up by Oscar Wilde. To do manual work like painting fences and sweeping floors is depressing enough, he quipped, but to take *pride* in doing such things is downright appalling.

These people were once at the helm of power. They were the old regime's ruling class. In Europe, such people watched angrily, resentfully, as the new entrepreneurial class rose in power to rival and then surpass them. In America, the situation was even worse. What the American Revolution did was to push such people to the side. And even today this class feels sidelined.

Certainly we have whole groups of people today—in academia, in media, in the legal and nonprofit sector—who produce nothing but words. I guess I have to admit that I'm in this group. But I'm not a typical member, in that I don't share the group's prejudices and resentments. What are these? Well, the people of words often do pretty well, but in their view they don't do well enough. They want to be the ruling class.

Viewing themselves as smart—the smartest people in society—they feel entitled to be the ones who exercise power, who tell others what to do. And they view with dismay an American Revolution and an American system that brings the entrepreneur to center stage, disburses to him the greatest rewards and places intellectuals and "courtiers" of every stripe in an ancillary, even subservient, role.

How, then, do the "people of words" rise up and displace the people who make and do things? The short answer is that they go into full thespian mode. They are good at this; it is the courtier stance, and for centuries it has been their natural métier. They indignantly portray the entrepreneurial class as wicked exploiters. Such exploiters, they argue, will be the ruin of society unless their interests are subordinated to the interests of the people.

Then, drawing themselves to full height, as if playing the role of Richard III, the people of words insist that they are cut from a finer cloth. They are not like the wicked entrepreneurs. What the people require—indeed demand—is a professional class of planners and administrators like the people of words, selflessly devoted to social justice and the common good. So this is what makes the progressives akin to Caesar. Their goal is a kind of Caesarism, to mobilize the resentment of the people against the innovators and wealth creators.

To do this, they have to conceal their ambition, conceal their envy and pretend, as Caesar himself did on the Lupercal, that they are entirely on the side of the masses and indifferent to power. Yet, like Caesar, they are actually the hungriest, most grasping seekers of power. The people are merely the vehicle for them to get it. And the power they seek is absolute enough to pose a genuine prospect of tyranny. What motivates progressivists and socialists in large part is their desire to exercise tyrannical power over others.

And yet, in the end I have to admit that power is not their sole motive. Ideology matters too. We can see this by doing a thought experiment. Let's say that we gave the progressives and socialists all the power they wanted. Now they can rule contentedly over all the great organs of American industry, and even more broadly over American culture. Would they be satisfied with just having the power? Or would they still push their ideological agenda?

It's quite obvious that they would still push their agenda. They would still inundate the country with illegals. They would still force female athletes to compete with biological males. They would still seek to demonize white males and push Christian symbols out of the public square. My conclusion, therefore, is that power is not their solitary motive; rather, they seek both power and an ideological transformation of American society.

HONEYMOON IN MOSCOW

The importation of socialism to America requires the art of historical forgetting. By analogy, consider a group of neo-Nazis who want America to go fascist. This is not a far-out example, because fascism, let's recall, is a species of socialism, and like socialism in general, it is one with a genocidal record. Yet that record endures in such slogans as "Never again!" So today's neo-Nazis would want to dissociate themselves from that record—that wasn't us!—and hope for a new sensibility that has "moved on" from the Holocaust. "Never again!" suddenly becomes "Why not?"

Historical forgetting is very much in vogue on the left these days. Alexandria Ocasio-Cortez insists that her brand of democratic socialism cannot be linked with the "McCarthyism Red Scare of a past era." Astra Taylor writes that "cold war fearmongering just doesn't work the way it used to" because "the horror of a defunct Soviet bloc" is now a "distant threat." Historian Maurice Isserman says that young people in particular are no longer afraid of the "Cold War bogeyman."[12]

In a recent article, "Trump Versus the Socialist Menace," Paul Krugman mocks Trump and other critics of socialism. Here is how he mimics their argument: "You say you want free college tuition? Think of all the people who died in the Ukraine famine!" Krugman distances American socialists from Stalinist Russia and Maoist China. All that, he pompously affirms, has nothing to do with us. It's not what we Americans are all about![13]

Yet American socialists and leftists were some of the most ardent devotees of Stalinist and Maoist socialism. They also embraced German national socialism, Italian national socialism, Cuban socialism, North Korean socialism and now Venezuelan socialism. We can see this devotion in contemporary progressives and socialists from Bill de Blasio to Bernie Sanders. We also see it in leading progressives and socialists of the past: Charles Beard, Herbert Croly, Corliss Lamont, W. E. B. Du Bois, Franklin Roosevelt and his New Deal "brain trust."

This history is largely suppressed in progressive accounts, so it bears a closer look. Echoing a standard refrain, Bernie Sanders says that he is not a Soviet-style socialist. In his words, Soviet authoritarianism is "not my thing." Yet as is often the case with socialists and the left, this denial camouflages as much as it reveals. The record shows that Sanders was very much an apologist for Soviet tyranny. And for Cuban tyranny. And Sandinista tyranny. In keeping with many American leftists, he now pretends an aversion to totalitarian socialism he once extolled.

In 1983, Bernie Sanders received a letter from Soviet Embassy first secretary Vadim Kuznetsov, congratulating him on his reelection as mayor and thanking Sanders for receiving him in Sanders' office. Kuznetsov came to Vermont to attend a conference on nuclear disarmament—a cause dear to Sanders' heart. What Sanders may not have known is that Kuznetsov was a top KGB officer posing as a diplomat to infiltrate American politics.

Sanders is one of the very few Americans who chose the Soviet Union as the place to go on his honeymoon. During his 10-day visit in 1988 with an American tour group, he professed an open-minded neutrality. "Let's take the strength of both systems," he said. "Let's learn from each other." Yet on Soviet soil, Sanders blasted U.S. foreign policy as recklessly interventionist, stunning other Americans in his tour group and causing some of them to walk out.

If it seems odd to have Sanders—at that time mayor of Burlington—opining on foreign policy, Sanders regarded it as appropriate to his position, because as mayor he insisted that the town of Burlington, with just 40,000 residents, have its own foreign policy. Feigning ignorance of the constitutional line between local and national jurisdiction, Sanders asked, "How could issues of war and peace not be a local issue?"

A year prior to his honeymoon trip, Sanders invited a Soviet choir to Vermont, part of a "sister city" arrangement between Burlington and Yaroslavl, a Russian city on the Volga River. When a Soviet choir of 30 young girls performed in Burlington for about 500 residents, Sanders took the stage and sarcastically riffed, "This is the enemy!"

Back in Vermont, Sanders held a news conference extolling Soviet transportation, housing and healthcare policies and blasting the cost of both in the United States. "Subway systems in Moscow cost 5 kopecs or 7 cents. Faster, cleaner, more attractive and more efficient than any in the U.S."

Soon after his Soviet visit, Sanders went to Cuba. While he failed in his hope to meet Castro, he returned effusive about Cuban socialism. "Under Castro, enormous progress has been made in improving the lives of poor people. I did not see a hungry child. I did not see any homeless people." Cuba, he added, "not only has free health care but very high-quality health care. The revolution there is far deeper and more profound than I understood it to be. It really is a revolution in terms of values." More recently, Sanders waxed rhapsodic about Cuba's literacy program.

When the Sandinistas established a socialist regime in Nicaragua, Sanders once again went into a familiar orgy of praise. He established a new "sister city" exchange between Burlington and Puerto Cabezas, Nicaragua. He wrote to the Sandinistas, telling them the U.S. media refused to report the "truth" about Nicaragua. To a skeptical CBS reporter—yes, there were skeptical CBS reporters in those days—Sanders shrieked his disdain for the press: "You are worms."

Sanders then visited Nicaragua, where he participated in anti-American protests featuring chants like, "Here, there, everywhere, the Yankee will die." Of the socialist government, he said, "The Sandinista government has more support among the Nicaraguan people than Ronald Reagan has among the American people." Sanders defended that staple of socialist economic failure, bread lines. "It's funny," he said at a news conference, "sometimes American journalists talk about how bad a country is because people are lining up for food. That's a good thing!"

One place Sanders did not visit—and it was right in his home state of Vermont—was the farm on which the world's most famous dissident, Alexandr Solzhenitsyn, lived. Solzhenitsyn, who spent eight years in a concentration camp for a letter criticizing the Soviet dictator Stalin and who wrote classic works like *The Gulag Archipelago*, could easily have educated Sanders on bread lines, forced labor camps, and much else in the socialist repertoire. But the rendezvous was not to be, and perhaps it was all for the best.

Sanders had no interest in learning anything from Solzhenitsyn, and I suspect Solzhenitsyn would have found Sanders the reductio ad absurdum of Western decadence. We'll never know; in 1994, after the collapse of the Soviet empire, Solzhenitsyn returned to Russia, where he died in 2008.[14]

WHAT DE BLASIO SAW—AND CHOSE NOT TO SEE

If Sanders' enthusiasm for a succession of tyrannical socialist regimes seems anomalous, it's not. Bill de Blasio got married in 1994, but he couldn't honeymoon in the Soviet Union, since by that time the Soviet Union did not exist. So he decided to honeymoon in Cuba. Recently asked about it on ABC's *The View*, de Blasio pretended his decision had nothing to do with politics. "I went on my honeymoon to a country that is part of this hemisphere and is a historically and culturally important place."

Yet on the presidential campaign trail in Miami, de Blasio stirred the ire of the Cuban American community when he quoted the Latin American socialist Che Guevara—who was also Castro's deputy during the Cuban revolution. "Hasta la victoria siempre," de Blasio said, meaning "ever onward to victory." Once again, de Blasio went into full denial. "I just didn't know the phrase was associated with Che Guevara, wouldn't have used it if I knew that."

In 1988, very much in the Sanders mode, de Blasio visited Nicaragua. According to a *New York Times* profile, he had become "an admirer of Nicaragua's ruling Sandinista party" and an "ardent supporter of the Nicaraguan revolutionaries." He raised funds for the Nicaraguan socialists, dispatching food, clothing and supplies to the regime. Twice he was arrested for disorderly behavior at rallies protesting U.S. support for the antisocialist contras. And he subscribed to the Sandinista party newspaper *Barricada* (Barricade).

"The Nicaraguan struggle is our struggle," read a poster at the Nicaragua Solidarity Network, where de Blasio volunteered. "My work was based on trying to create a more fair and inclusive world," de Blasio recently said. Earlier, in 1990, he said in an interview about the Sandinistas, "They gave a new definition to democracy. They built a democracy that was striving to be economic and political, that pervaded all levels of society." This sounds like something de Blasio might say today about his own platform. He admits his Nicaragua sojourn shaped him. "It was very affecting for me."

During his volunteer work at a health clinic in Masaya, de Blasio says, he saw doctors and social workers distributing immunization and hygiene information using maps that showed the precise location of every family in the region. Nicaragua inspired him about what could be achieved in America. "There was something I took away from that— how hands-on government has to be, how proactive, how connected to the people it must be."[15]

One would never know from de Blasio that Nicaragua was a socialist dictatorship whose goal, in the words of Pulitzer Prize–winning reporter Shirley Christian, was "to assure themselves the means to control nearly every aspect of Nicaraguan life, from beans and rice to religion." From harassing the Catholic Church to closing and later censoring the reform newspaper *La Prensa* to unleashing secret police to crush dissent, the Sandinistas operated out of the same socialist playbook as the Soviets and the Cubans.

Along the same lines, the aspiring Democratic presidential candidate Michael Bloomberg offered a rhapsodic account of the Chinese Communist Party, insisting in an interview with Margaret Hoover on *Firing Line* that the ruling regime in Beijing was democratically accountable to the Chinese people.

> BLOOMBERG: The Communist Party wants to stay in power in China. . . . Xi Jinping is not a dictator; he has to satisfy his constituents or he's not going to survive.
>
> HOOVER: He's not a dictator?
>
> BLOOMBERG: No, he has a constituency to answer to.
>
> HOOVER: He doesn't have a vote. He doesn't have a democracy. He's not held accountable by voters.
>
> BLOOMBERG: If his advisers gave him . . .
>
> HOOVER: Is the check on him just a revolution?
>
> BLOOMBERG: You're not going to have a revolution. No government survives without the will of a majority of its people.[16]

There is a deep historical pattern here, brilliantly chronicled in Paul Hollander's *Political Pilgrims*. Hollander shows how the Soviet apologist Walter Duranty, writer for *The New York Times*, suppressed the existence of famines and food shortages. Hollander depicts leading American progressives defending the liquidation of the kulaks or independent farmers, the murder of Trotsky and Stalin's show trials. George Orwell couldn't make this stuff up.

Then Hollander moves to China and Cuba and Nicaragua, and it's the same story. The American left is not removed from these horrors—it is complicit; it is implicated. My favorite example: the socialist philosopher Corliss Lamont insisted that the Chinese didn't have cars not because they couldn't build them under socialism but because they were not into the bric-a-brac of modern capitalism. In short, the Chinese people didn't really *want* cars.

Hollander's only blind spot: fascism. Hollander could have done a whole chapter on the enthusiasm of FDR and New Deal progressives for Mussolini's fascism. He has the leftist muckraker Ida Tarbell raving about the Soviet Union but misses her praising Mussolini. Most of all he misses how FDR and Mussolini formed a mutual admiration society, reviewing each other's books and praising each other as ideological soul mates.

I have written about this in an earlier book, so I won't go into it here. We can summarize FDR's position by quoting his own words: he viewed fascism from the outset as a "phenomenon somewhat parallel to the Communist experiment in Russia."[17] It's worth noting that the progressive historian Robert Dallek's 692-page biography of FDR contains not one word about any of this. Neither do most other progressive accounts. Fascism has become toxic and, in the manner depicted by Orwell in *1984*, FDR's early connection to it has been erased.

The eminent leftist scholar W. E. B. Du Bois is mainly known for cofounding the NAACP and authoring his autobiographical work *The Souls of Black Folk*. Yet Du Bois, who became a socialist, championed every socialist regime no matter how murderous. He praised Leninism, Stalinism, Maoism: if it carried the socialist label, he had nice things to say about it. Here's Du Bois on Soviet Russia. "If what I have seen with my eyes and heard with my ears in Russia is Bolshevism, I am a Bolshevik."

Here's Du Bois on Mao's Cultural Revolution: "Come to China . . . and look around. . . . Yonder old woman is working on the street. But she is happy. She has no fear. Her children are in school and a good school. If she is ill, there's a hospital where she is cared for free of charge. She has a vacation with pay each year. She can die and be buried without taxing her family to make some undertaker rich." The whole picture is a lie and an embarrassment. But Du Bois at the time had no hesitation about composing this propaganda brochure for Chinese socialism.

Du Bois was even, to a degree, a champion of Hitler. Du Bois visited Nazi Germany in the late 1930s and praised German National Socialism as an "absolutely necessary" scheme that "showed Germany the way out." As late as 1955—a decade after American troops liberated the concentration camps—he credited Hitler, who "built a magnificent system of roads and excellent public housing, controlled finance and wages, owned railroads, telegraphs and telephones."[18] At least the man got something right!

Hollander emphasizes what he calls "the techniques of hospitality." He highlights the Potemkin village aspect of this ideological tourism. He thinks the socialist regimes in Russia, China and Cuba bamboozled American progressives and socialists. I don't think so. They were smart enough to see, but they didn't want to see. They went to see what they wanted, and they saw what they wanted to see. Now that those regimes have proven unviable, they pretend that they never saw what they then professed to see.

What did they want to see? Their project was to protect and defend a system that they understood to be analogous and akin to what they were attempting here. In defending those regimes then, they were defending themselves, just as in denying their previous attachments now, they are also now defending themselves. This is how crime families behave. It's called deniability.

THE UNNECESSARY AUTOMOBILE

We're now going to track how socialism and progressivism first came to America. They came as cousins, quarreling cousins. The leading figure of socialism was a cranky charismatic figure, Eugene Debs. The leading figure of progressivism was the somber, pompous Woodrow Wilson. The former was, to use Obama's phrase, a "community organizer." The latter was the president of Princeton, later governor of New Jersey, then president of the United States.

The Wilson administration prosecuted Debs under the Sedition Act, and in 1918 he was imprisoned, facing a 10-year sentence. It took a Republican, Warren G. Harding, to commute his sentence in 1921. So Debs went into obscurity while Wilson served two terms. Debs lost and Wilson won. Yet, as we'll see, Wilson incorporated a good deal of Debs' platform into his progressive agenda. Using the hindsight of history, we can see that Wilson created a framework for implementing over time much of what Debs agitated for.

The important thing to know about Wilson—a fact neatly omitted from many of his progressive biographies—is that he opposed cars. The automobile, he said, was the "picture of arrogance and wealth." He warned that cars in America would lead to socialism! "Nothing has spread socialistic feeling more than the use of the automobile."[19] Notice that Wilson isn't merely expressing a personal aversion to driving a car. He doesn't think anyone should have a car. They are a rich man's toy. They exist only for ostentatious display. They create class resentment. Who really needs a car for personal transportation when we already have the horse and buggy?

True, Wilson made this statement in 1906, while he was at Princeton. True, the cars he observed on the streets of New York *were* rich men's toys. They were crafted by hand from custom-order parts, some of them imported from Europe. There were dozens of companies producing their own versions of the automobile. Each type was different, and in some cases, companies made cars to the individual specifications of a prospective wealthy buyer. And at the dawn of the twentieth century, cars weren't much faster than horses!

Wilson, however, lacked vision. His argument against the car may be termed the "argument from personal incredulity." I get this phrase from the biologist Richard Dawkins, who used it in a different context. Here is how the argument works. "What is the point of a car? Can I think of any good reason why anyone would want to own a car? Here, sitting in my office and twiddling my thumbs, I cannot. Clearly there is no good reason why anyone should want a car. Therefore, cars should not exist."

It may seem that I'm singling out Wilson for special abuse, but this is actually a common progressive mode of argument. To take a contemporary example. "Fracking is such a bad idea. Who knows what it is doing to the environment? It could be causing earthquakes for all we know. Here, sitting in my office and twiddling my thumbs, I cannot personally think of a single good reason for fracking. Fracking should not exist." This is the same progressive sensibility, operating in pretty much the same way, more than a century later.

Wilson saw the car only as it was, not as it could be. He viewed the entrepreneurs making cars as useless dabblers, catering to the pretentions of the upper class. Wilson viewed himself more as a man of the people, not one of them, certainly, but an objective administrator of the people's genuine interests. He knew what they wanted and, just as important, what they ought to want. He was there to show them how, under his leadership, their lives could be better. This was true democracy, democracy under adult supervision. Here is the familiar pose of the enlightened progressive intellectual.

It's helpful to contrast Wilson with one of the objects of his contempt, Henry Ford. It's tempting for me to say that Ford had a better understanding of what people wanted than Wilson, that Ford, in other words, recognized consumer demand, whereas Wilson didn't. But in reality there was no consumer demand for cars. Ford himself said that had he consulted the customers beforehand to ask them what they wanted, they would have told him they wanted a faster horse![20]

So Ford's genius was to envision a society in which not only the rich but nearly everybody would own and drive cars. He could see consumer demand, which didn't exist then but would develop later, after people saw what Ford had made for them. We customarily think of demand preceding supply, but with transforming innovations, like the car and the iPhone, it is typically the opposite: supply precedes demand. If we make it, they will come.

Ford knew he had to make it right. He didn't have a Princeton education, but he didn't think he needed one. Observation and practice were more important. "It's not possible to learn from books how everything is made. Machines are to a mechanic what books are to a writer. He gets ideas from them."[21] Before he started work on the automobile, Ford worked as an apprentice in a machine shop, then in the engine room of a shipbuilding firm, then at a power plant.

Ford built his cars using two important innovations: interchangeable parts and the moving assembly line. Interchangeable parts enabled Ford to make a standardized product. He didn't care about customization; later he would say that you could buy his Model T in any color you wanted "as long as it is black." Ford got his idea for a moving assembly line from what he observed in the giant slaughterhouses of the Chicago stockyards. By bringing this concept to the factory floor, Ford found a way to mass-produce cars. Then he added a marketing innovation, the car dealership, where cars could not only be purchased but also regularly serviced.

While cars were initially selling for around $3,000—a fortune in those days—Ford sold his first cars for under $1,000. He reinvested his profits to make a better, cheaper product. It's important to recognize here that Wilson's bogeymen, the rich show-offs who paid the higher initial price, ended up subsidizing the research and development that brought car prices lower. By 1916, Ford's Model T was selling for less than $400.

What started out as a rich man's toy became the aspiration of every working family in America, and then the world. Ford created the culture of the automobile that transformed American society. The prototypical entrepreneur had a much greater impact than the prototypical progressive statist. Moreover—and this is the crushing point—the car was perhaps the most democratizing force in history. Ford did far more to promote social mobility, social equality and social justice than his disdainful detractor. If the word "progress" has any meaning, Ford was the progressive, Wilson the regressive.

WISE MINORITY IN THE SADDLE

We'll return to Wilson, but first a word about how the socialists as a party simply couldn't get their act together. They somehow never reached the masses they purported to speak for. Their agenda was the talk of the nation in the pivotal year of 1912, yet two of the three leading candidates that year, Wilson and Teddy Roosevelt, called themselves progressives rather than socialists. In terms of reaching the corridors of power, the socialists were so near and yet so far. Why did the progressives succeed while the socialists failed?

Eugene Debs, who started the Socialist Party with a couple of other guys in 1901, is the founder of American socialism. Ocasio-Cortez probably hasn't heard of him, although the name might remind her of one of her superfans named Deb. Sanders knows Debs well. He still hangs a portrait of Debs in his office, and in 1979 he made a documentary film about him in which he delivers parts of Debs' speeches in a somewhat comical cadence, sounding, as *The New Yorker* put it, "more or less like Larry David."[22]

Debs was a socialist in the classic sense. He praised the Bolshevik Revolution in Russia and declared that, here in America, "we shall transfer the title deeds of the railroads, the telegraph lines, the mines, mills and great industries to the people in their collective capacity; we shall take possession of all these social utilities in the name of the people." Notice who takes possession: not the people but Debs and his buddies. They do it "in the name of the people." This is the voice of socialist tyranny, masking itself from the outset in the language of democracy.

Fortunately, the people weren't interested. Not that they rejected power; they rejected the idea of giving the power to Debs in their name. Debs ran for president five times: in 1900, 1904, 1908 and 1912. In 1920 he ran one last time, from jail. He attained his highest vote total in 1912, when he got almost a million votes. Yet that was just 6 percent of all votes cast. Debs reminds me of the toy soldier who walks into the wall—and keeps going.

After Debs, socialism produced just one other figure worth naming: Norman Thomas. Thomas ran for president six times. Another Debs! In 1932, during the depths of the Depression, Thomas too almost received a million votes, but in four subsequent presidential elections, he couldn't manage that number even cumulatively. In his recent book *The Socialist Manifesto*, Bhaskar Sunkara concedes that apart from a brief surge in 1912 and 1931, card-carrying socialists have never been "a serious force in national politics."[23] At least until now.

Parties calling themselves "progressive" have done much better. Running on a progressive ticket, Henry Wallace got over a million votes in 1948. A couple of decades earlier, in 1924, Wisconsin senator Robert La Follette, who was backed by the socialists, got nearly 5 million votes. But the most successful progressive candidacy was in 1912. Teddy Roosevelt quit the Republican Party to run as a progressive. He split the vote with Taft to give Woodrow Wilson the presidency.

Wilson was the other progressive running, but he ran on the Democratic ticket. His ideas mirrored those of Teddy Roosevelt. So what were those ideas? Modern progressive scholarship makes it sound like the progressives were all about "reform." They fought against the political bosses. They exposed the trusts and the meatpacking industry. They fought for more democracy through ballots and referendums. They were for women's rights and generally for the little guy.

This is the way that modern propaganda emphasizes the "shiny" achievements of the progressives while covering up their deeper agenda. To understand this deeper agenda, we must listen to what the progressives themselves said at the time. Wilson was the first president to attack the founding. In words every previous president would have considered heretical, Wilson said, "We are not bound to adhere to the doctrines held by the signers of the Declaration of Independence."[24]

Let's recall that even during the Civil War, when the divisions in American politics were the sharpest, both sides emphasized that they were the true exponents of founding principles. Wilson, however, made no effort to camouflage that progressivism represented a sharp break with the founding. Wilson outlined his doctrine in a 1913 speech titled "What Is Progress?" The speech contrasted what Wilson termed the Newtonian principle of the founding with the Darwinian approach of progressive Democrats.

The founders, according to Wilson, erroneously thought politics was a "variety of mechanics." They used terms like "checks and balances." "The trouble with this theory," Wilson said, "is that government is not a machine but a living thing. It falls not under the theory of the universe, but under the theory of organic life. It is accountable to Darwin, not to Newton." Wilson concluded, "Society is a living organism and must obey the laws of life, not of mechanics. It must develop."[25]

What sense can we make of this gobbledygook? Wilson is making the case for society to be run by enlightened planners, not through some sort of spontaneous operation of natural laws of the kind that Newton described in his *Principia* or Adam Smith in his *The Wealth of Nations*. This for Wilson is what "progressive" means. It means progress away from the founding, progress according to a Darwinian principle of adaptation. Wilson's actual analogy, of course, makes no sense. In fact, it conveys the very opposite of what Wilson intends to convey.

Let's reflect on what Darwinian evolution is about. It's about creatures struggling to survive in a competitive environment. Some live, and others perish. The ones that live pass on their adaptive traits to successive generations. That's how species evolve; that's what Darwin means by "progress." The key point—Darwin was very insistent about this—is that evolution operates without the need for supervisory planning or design. Order is spontaneously generated through adaptive behavior at the local level in varying competitive environments.

Now this sounds a lot like how free markets operate. The only difference is that for Darwin, the transmission of favorable traits is biological while for markets it is cultural. The biologist Jean-Baptiste Lamarck, a contemporary of Darwin, mistakenly thought that we can acquire favorable traits and somehow pass them on to our offspring. Biologically, we can't. But culturally, we can. Free markets can be considered a form of Lamarckian or cultural adaptation and evolution. Yet in both cases, what survives and works is what gets replicated, with no need for a central planning authority. Wilson's whole argument collapses.

Wilson's speech remains interesting, however, not for its logic—a null set—but rather for what it shows about progressive psychology. Wilson exhibits the typical profile of the progressives. He despises the founding and the kind of people the founders cherished. He considers himself better than them, more enlightened. He seeks to reorganize society in a way that puts this better kind of person, a person like himself, in the driver's seat—or perhaps I should say, in deference to Wilson's view of cars, in the saddle!

We can hear this same self-aggrandizement in most of the progressive literature of the early part of the twentieth century. This is what all the leading progressives, from Herbert Croly to Edward Alsworth Ross to John Dewey, were about. Here's Ross, from his book aptly titled *Social Control*: "The state is an organization that puts the wise minority in the saddle." Ross has no illusions about the state being run by the majority. He envisions not the people but a "wise minority" guiding the people and thus winning their grateful allegiance.

If this seems an unfair or harsh description, listen to more from Ross: "The state aims more steadily at a rational safeguarding of the collective welfare than any organ society has yet employed." While in theory the state is supposed to be democratically run by the society, Ross candidly states that "as a matter of fact the state, when it becomes paternal and develops on the administrative side, is able in a measure to guide the society it professes to obey." It becomes, in a sense, "an independent center of social power."[26]

During the Wilson years, the progressives made some key changes to establish the power of the centralized state. They introduced the graduated or "progressive" income tax. This required a constitutional amendment. Previously the U.S. government raised most of its revenue through customs duties and excise taxes on tobacco and alcohol. Later the progressives added corporate and inheritance taxes. Now the mechanism to fund the centralized state was in place.

Progressives also created the Federal Reserve Board to regulate money, banking and credit, and the Federal Trade Commission to oversee industry. By themselves these agencies did not amount to much, but they were the beginning of the administrative state, a kind of "fourth branch of government." In his second term, Wilson also recognized the Bolshevik regime in the Soviet Union just days after the czar abdicated. The United States was the first government in the world to do so, establishing a dishonorable tradition of progressive endorsement of socialist tyranny.

Well, actually Wilson did more. He had his own version of identity politics. As I've shown in my earlier books, he introduced racial segregation to the federal government, which had not been segregated prior to his administration. He helped to revive the Ku Klux Klan. He supported eugenic measures that would later inspire the Nazis, who used them as a model for the Nuremberg Laws. "During the Wilson years," Ira Katznelson writes, "the composite of racism and progressive liberalism came to dominate the Democratic Party."[27]

We'll see this pattern of using white nationalism to build an effective political coalition continue with the Democrats through the middle of the century. It may seem contradictory that the party of white supremacy then is now the party that rails against it. I'll explain this contradiction later; actually, it is not a contradiction, merely a change of tactics. The party of identity politics in one direction remains the party of identity politics in the opposite direction.

But this inventory of the "accomplishments" of the progressive Democrats does them an injustice. To see how much more they accomplished, let's take a quick look at the Socialist Party platform—not the Democratic platform but the Socialist platform—in 1912. It called for an eight-hour workday at a guaranteed wage. It called for public works programs for the unemployed. It advocated old-age pensions, unemployment insurance, a graduated or progressive income tax, an inheritance tax, getting rid of the Electoral College and a convention to revise the Constitution.

Some of this is unobjectionable. I myself agree with certain goals—and many other conservatives would also. Other aspects, like revising our constitutional system, are not conservative goals. My point is not to dispute the agenda of the early socialists but simply to show how closely it tracks the agenda of the political left and the Democratic Party. So in the end, that's what progressives did: they steadily took on board the socialist program. They made it their own, they carried out some of it and, over time, they brought all of it into the political mainstream.

This is Wilson's true and lasting legacy: creeping socialism. He was too much of a pompous academic to get it done himself. It would take a man less cerebral but more cunning to largely enact this program lifted from the socialists. In Wilson's time, that man was a young navy secretary. He rarely invoked Wilson, whose popularity dimmed before he left office, but he never swerved from Wilson's priorities. Elected in 1932, he found himself in the midst of a national emergency—the Great Depression. He knew long before Rahm Emanuel said it that a Democrat should never let a crisis go to waste. He seized on the crisis to do what Wilson never had the savvy or the chance to do. He, not Wilson, is the man who "remade America" by pushing it in the socialist direction.

A SECOND BILL OF RIGHTS

What is socialism, in the sense now meaningful in American politics? In his George Washington University speech, Bernie Sanders said it is "the right to quality healthcare, the right to as much education as one needs to succeed in our society, the right to a good job that pays a living wage, the right to affordable housing, the right to a secure retirement, and the right to live in a clean environment." Alexandria Ocasio-Cortez's definition, delivered in the context of explaining the Green New Deal, is virtually identical.

All these rights! Yet where do they come from? We have a Bill of Rights in the Constitution, and it doesn't mention even one of these rights. Rather, it mentions other rights—the right to free speech and religious expression, the right to own a gun, the right to freely assemble, the right against unreasonable search and seizure.

Not only does the Constitution enumerate a very different set of rights, it is also based on a very different philosophy of rights. This can be seen in the standard formulation "Congress shall make no law." Congress shall make no law restricting speech or the press. Congress shall make no law establishing religion or prohibiting the free exercise of it. And so on. The basic idea here is that rights are asserted against the government. The state is the basic enemy of my rights. We remain free by limiting the power of the state over our lives.

By contrast, Bernie and Ocasio-Cortez view the state not as the adversary of rights but as the deliverer of them. In this perspective, the state is the friend of my rights. Government makes available to me things like education, healthcare, home ownership and retirement benefits. It does so by seizing the earnings and resources of a minority of the successful, those disparagingly termed "the 1 percent." My rights, in this formula, rely on the government acting on my behalf to put its hand into someone else's pocket.

Where did this crazy socialist idea come from? It came from one man, Franklin Delano Roosevelt, who spelled it out in an important speech delivered late in his presidency on January 11, 1944. Roosevelt declared that it was time for America to adopt what he termed a Second Bill of Rights. Every American, he insisted, is entitled to a "useful and remunerative job"; the opportunity to "earn enough" to provide adequate food, clothing and recreation; to a "decent home" for his family; to "adequate medical care"; to a "good education"; and finally to "adequate protection" in old age and retirement.

There it is! Every right listed by Bernie and AOC is on the FDR list. When it comes to outlining the socialist agenda—and let's be clear, this is not my interpretation of the socialist agenda, it is the socialists' interpretation of a socialist agenda—we can say that FDR got there first. No wonder Bernie is so enthusiastic about this guy. No wonder the Green New Deal evokes FDR's original New Deal. No wonder that today's socialists like Bernie, AOC, Omar, Tlaib and the rest aren't in a socialist party—they comfortably inhabit the Democratic Party. FDR made the Democratic Party a natural fit for them.

The legal scholar Cass Sunstein, in his book *The Second Bill of Rights*, terms FDR's speech "the greatest of the twentieth century."[28] Greater than the speeches of Churchill! What makes Sunstein, a leftist legal scholar, so enthusiastic is that FDR didn't merely spell out all these new rights, he offered a rationale that basically flips the founders' idea of rights on its head. In a sense, it redefines what America is all about and what it means to be an American.

FDR argued that human beings in an age of scarcity find themselves pressed by something he called "necessity." This is the basic struggle to survive and to thrive in the world. Life requires certain necessities like food, clothing and shelter. Now—and this is the key move—FDR insisted that "necessitous men are not free men." He said that to give citizens true freedom, the government must insure them against deprivation, against the loss of a job, against illness and against impoverished old age.

What people need, in other words, is what FDR frankly and without irony called "freedom from fear."[29] Yes, freedom from fear. We have a right not to be afraid. And who can deliver that right? For FDR, there was only one answer to this question: the federal government. So in FDR's vision, the government, previously viewed by the founders as inimical to rights, now becomes the friend and the guarantor of rights. As Sunstein recognized, this is truly an intellectual revolution.

It is a revolution away from the entrepreneurial society the founders created and toward the socialist society that FDR envisioned but dared not name.

FRANKLIN DELANO PONZI

I want to conclude this chapter by highlighting three things—all destructive—that FDR did to advance his socialist agenda. First, he passed the Ponzi scheme called Social Security. Now I recognize that Social Security is very popular with seniors. I also recognize it would be political suicide to try to get rid of it. I'm not saying that FDR was wrong to pursue some form of retirement insurance as part of a government-guaranteed "safety net." I am saying that he set up a bad program in a bad way, and he knew full well what he was doing.

Let's start with how Social Security was sold to the American public. The government basically said, "We're going to set up an account in your name. Then through tax withholdings you will make contributions to that account. The contributions will earn interest and grow over a long period of time. By the time you retire, you'll have a nice nest egg that you can count on to live comfortably in your later years."

Except that this was a form of false advertising. FDR had no intention of setting up accounts in anyone's name. He didn't even have any intention of pooling contributions into a single fund and then conserving and investing it so as to grow at a compounded rate. Rather, FDR's goal from the outset was to use current contributions to pay out to currently retiring seniors. In other words, he planned to deplete the money as soon as it came in. Then, as the current generation of payees grew older, he would count on a new generation of working people to fund their Social Security payouts.

This is why it's a Ponzi scheme. Charles Ponzi raised investment from people by promising to pay them handsome returns. Rather than invest the money, however, he spent it. He then sucked in new investors whose money he used to pay interest to the old investors. And when the new investors wanted their money back, Ponzi sought still more investors whose money he could draw on to repay the second tier of investors. And so on! Ponzi went to jail for this racket.

Yet FDR's racket has been going for nearly a century now, with no end in sight. Sure, there is now a diminishing pool of earners who must bear the burden of supporting a widening pool of seniors. This is bad for both groups! Yet it must be said that FDR wanted it this way. He was warned about the economic risks of his program. He replied, "I guess you're right on the economics, but those taxes were never a problem of economics. They are politics all the way through. With those taxes in there, no damn politician can ever scrap my social security program."[30]

Let me translate. FDR didn't care who got screwed financially. His goal was to set up a retirement scheme that would be under government—which is to say his—control. He also wanted to fool people into thinking that they had earned their Social Security benefits. They had paid into the system, and now they were just getting their own money back plus interest. Any attempt to get rid of Social Security would provoke the fury of people as if their personal bank accounts were being raided. FDR understood the political benefit of creating an entitlement mentality.

I find it interesting that, even in the Depression era, FDR had to be so deceitful about what he was doing. He couldn't sell Social Security as a "right," despite all his big talk about a Second Bill of Rights. And he had to use the whole deceptive vocabulary of "contributions" to make people think they were "contributing" to their own future welfare. Even today we hear the same mind-numbing language in reports and articles on the Social Security program.

But Social Security taxes are not "contributions." Let's say that I decline to make those "contributions." I inform the government, "I'm delighted you have made such excellent provision for my future. But as an emancipated American, I say thanks but no thanks. Let me provide for my own retirement. When I'm old, if I cannot do it, I'll rely on family or private charity. Failing that, I'll take my chances."

Would the government go along with this? Absolutely not! Why? Because they need my "contributions" to pay retirees right now. So they would demand that I pay. Let's say I decline. They would then put a lien on my house and property. Let's say I refuse to turn them over. They would send armed police to seize it. Let's say that I attempt to defend my home and possessions. They would then shoot me and if necessary kill me. All because I declined to make a "contribution."

FDR's second destructive act was confiscatory taxation. FDR raised the top marginal rate of the federal income tax to more than 80 percent, while it had previously been only 25 percent. One might think it ridiculous to ask people to forfeit four-fifths of their last dollar earned to the government while keeping only one-fifth. Yet FDR wanted all income more than $100,000 to be taxed at 99.5 percent. At one point he recommended a 100 percent tax rate, but Congress shot that one down, no doubt realizing that no one would work if they got to keep nothing of their earnings.[31]

What did FDR want all that money for? Most of it was for his work programs, or perhaps I should say "make-work" programs. Did all those workers FDR hired build the nation's highway system? They did not; that occurred under Eisenhower in the 1950s. So what did they do? Some of them dug ditches and filled them up again. FDR hired 40,000 artists and painters to produce music and theater, paintings and murals, local travel guides and surveys of state records.

While the British economist John Maynard Keynes had approved make-work under carefully restricted conditions, FDR saw it as a way to "create jobs" while (and this was never far from his mind) at the same time creating loyal voters for the Democratic Party.

It's obviously a good thing for people to have jobs by which they can support themselves, but couldn't the money be put to better use? Alexander Forbes, a Harvard classmate of FDR who went on to be a professor at Harvard Medical School, wrote FDR to say, "Look at the sorry spectacle presented by long rows of beneficiaries of the boondoggle, leaning on their shovels by the hour, at futile projects, and contrast it with the great universities, museums and research laboratories which have come from the wise and generous giving of such as J. P. Morgan, and then consider which is the major constructive force in building a stable civilization."

Ouch! Forbes was raising a profound question. Yes, it is good for the rich to support the culture, but who knows better how to use the money, the people who have made it or the government that treats it with the fabled indifference of anyone who is spending someone else's money? FDR's response was to brand Forbes "one of the worst anarchists in the United States."[32] Here we get a window into FDR's deep arrogance. Moreover, it arose out of his conviction that he, and only he, was the "people's" man, while private entrepreneurs were greedy selfish bastards out only for themselves.

Finally, we turn to FDR's unscrupulous willingness to use the "race card." We are familiar today with the race card being played against whites, but like Wilson, FDR played it against blacks. He was a practitioner of white identity politics. This is important because when Democrats today say they are fighting the racism of the past, they omit to mention that they are the ones who practiced that racism. The Democrats are the ones who poisoned the wells, and now they show up pretending to be the water commissioner.

Historian Ira Katznelson shows in his book *Fear Itself* how FDR cut deals with racist Democrats to exclude blacks from New Deal programs. The legislation creating Social Security was deliberately crafted to exclude domestic workers and farmworkers, the two occupations in which blacks were most heavily concentrated. (Not until 1954, when Republicans controlled Congress and the presidency, were these exclusions lifted.) FDR blocked anti-lynching legislation to appease this group.

FDR also named Hugo Black to the Supreme Court, a man with deep and longtime ties to the Ku Klux Klan. When a Pittsburgh newspaper exposed Black's lifetime Klan membership, FDR feigned surprise. Yet the progressive historian Robert Dallek, who gives a highly truncated account of these events, doing his best to protect his subject, nevertheless admits that "there seems little question that Roosevelt was aware of his Klan membership."

Later Black wrote in a 1968 memo that he had informed FDR about his background. "President Roosevelt told me there was no reason for my worrying about having been a member of the Ku Klux Klan. He said some of his best friends and supporters were strong members of that organization. He never in any way, by word or attitude, indicated any doubt about my having been in the Klan nor did he indicate any criticism of me for having been a member of that organization."[33]

I'm not suggesting that FDR himself had Klan sympathies. I am suggesting that he wanted to stack the Supreme Court with loyal New Dealers, and Black's nomination was part of this scheme. Around the same time, FDR attempted to "pack" the Court by increasing the number of justices from 9 to 14. This scheme—rebuffed by Congress—mirrors progressive proposals today to increase the number of justices in order to prevent a conservative majority on the Court.

Recently, Democratic presidential candidate Pete Buttigieg called for expanding the Supreme Court from 9 to 15 justices, and Beto O'Rourke has said that this is "an idea we should explore." Kamala Harris, Kirsten Gillibrand and Elizabeth Warren have all said that they are open to adding judges to the Supreme Court. Remarkably, several Senate Democrats recently filed a brief warning the justices to "heal" the Court or face restructuring. Even leftist justice Ruth Bader Ginsburg pushed back against these schemes, wryly observing that "nine seems to be a good number" for the Court because "it's been that way for a long time."[34]

Stacking and packing the Court—this is what FDR cared about. He knew Black was an ardent New Deal man and would vote his way—to suppress economic liberties. That Black was closely linked with a group that lynched blacks in "Negro barbecues" attended by families that ate hamburgers and applauded the grisly proceedings was a matter of relative indifference to American progressivism's most hallowed president. Identity politics is a dirty business, and FDR was willing to get his hands dirty in order to move America, slowly but surely, in the direction of socialism.

3

ALIEN NATION

WHY SOCIALISTS ABANDONED THE WORKING CLASS

"The time has come," the Walrus said,
"To talk of many things:
Of shoes—and ships—and sealing wax—
Of cabbages—and kings—
And why the sea is boiling hot—
And whether pigs have wings."[1]

—LEWIS CARROLL, "THE WALRUS
AND THE CARPENTER"

Socialism, a system for raising up the working class, has now largely abandoned the working class. A program for raising the condition of ordinary citizens and workers has turned into a coordinated effort to make those very citizens and workers feel unwelcome and demonized in their own country. Socialism in America today has turned black against white, female against male, homosexual and transsexual against heterosexual and illegals against legal immigrants and American citizens. The typical socialist today is not a union guy who wants higher wages; it is a transsexual ecofeminist who marches in Antifa and Black Lives Matter rallies and throws cement blocks at her political opponents.

If FDR were alive today, he would not recognize the modern Democratic Party he created. Nor would he recognize the progressivism and socialism that formed the ideological pillars of his party. For FDR, as for Marx, socialism was primarily a matter of class. It was the rich versus the poor. Its political base was the working class—specifically the white working class that to this day forms the majority of working-class people in America. While the socialist left still employs the old rhetoric of class warfare, it seems something of a relic. Contemporary socialism is no longer rooted in class, and moreover, its oldest allies—working-class white males—are now its villains and enemies.

If FDR had attended the 2016 primary debates among Democratic Party contenders, he would have heard Hillary Clinton jibe at Bernie, "If we broke up the big banks tomorrow, would that end racism?" Recently he would have encountered this outlandish tweet from Elizabeth Warren: "Thank you @BlackWomxnFor! Black trans and cis women, gender-nonconforming, and nonbinary people are the backbone of our democracy." Warren has also pledged that, if elected in 2020, she will fill half her cabinet with "women and non-binary people."[2]

FDR would probably have no idea what she was talking about. Who are these people and how could they be the "backbone of our democracy"? They certainly seem to be the backbone of the socialist left. At a recent meeting of the Democratic Socialists, FDR would have encountered a strange menagerie of activists calling themselves ecosocialists, Afro-socialists, Islamo-socialists, Chicano socialists, sanctuary socialists, #MeToo socialists, disability socialists, queer socialists and transgender socialists.[3]

Typical of the new type of socialist is Stacey Abrams, the Democrat who narrowly lost the governor's race in Georgia. "My campaign," she says, "championed reforms to eliminate police shootings of African Americans, protect the LGBTQ community against ersatz religious freedom legislation, expand Medicaid to save rural hospitals, and reaffirm that undocumented immigrants deserve legal protections."[4] Only one of these four planks—the one about saving rural hospitals—would be even remotely recognizable to FDR as part of the progressive agenda.

Consider the identity politics of the crop of Democratic candidates for 2020. One, Beto O'Rourke, is a white guy posing as a Mexican by taking on a Hispanic name, something I was tempted to do when I was in federal confinement. (My Latina wife—whom I was dating at the time—suggested Diego De Sosa.) Elizabeth Warren spent most of her career posing as a Native American; a law review article in the 1990s even described her as Harvard Law's "first woman of color." Warren was busted after taking a DNA test; yet seemingly continuing to "identify" as a Native American, she somewhat comically released a special plan to aid her people.[5]

Another, Cory Booker, makes a big deal out of his blackness, although he has nothing on Kamala Harris, whose main claim to fame is that she is both African American and a woman. Pete Buttgieg appears on talk shows bashing Christians for taking seriously the biblical passages disputing homosexuality and joking playfully about how his partner would become, following Buttigieg's election, the "first man" in the White House.

Kirsten Gillibrand, a white woman, insists that as president she would be a kind of missionary to white people, seeking to cure them of their white privilege.[6] Meanwhile, Marianne Williamson has made racial reparations a centerpiece of her campaign. In this contest of historical victimhood, poor Bernie and Joe Biden seem somewhat out of place. As white males, what do they have to offer, except perhaps some apologies? In the left and in the Democratic Party, it's all about identity politics now.

Recently, the left-wing filmmaker Michael Moore addressed Democratic strategists who fret about winning back working-class whites. "News alert!" Moore said on MSNBC. "They're not coming." Moore pointed out that Democrats from Bill Clinton to Obama won the presidency without the white vote. In 2016, the white working class voted for Trump. Moore's message was simple: Forget about the whites. In fact, let's mobilize against them! "Let's get out the Democratic base of women, young people and people of color."[7]

The implications of this go beyond party politics; they involve how the left views the country itself. For FDR, America was an "imagined community." I get this term from sociologist Benedict Anderson. Anderson points out that a nation is imagined because it is made up of people who have never met and don't know each other. Yet each nation seeks to create a "deep horizontal comradeship" in which its people identify with others they've never heard of. They are their "fellow citizens."

This identification is critical because without it, who would be willing to die for his or her country? Anderson points out that no one is willing to die for the Labor Party, the American Medical Association or the United Way.[8] Not only soldiers but even cops and firemen who risk their lives for "strangers" must have an imagined comradeship with those strangers. Lincoln understood this. Memorial Day was created immediately following the Civil War, and it was during that era that the American flag became a symbol of quasi-religious national devotion.

Even socialist redistribution within a country relies on some sense of solidarity among the citizens; otherwise why should my hard-earned money go to pay the medical expenses of someone I could care less about? In India, I learned a proverb that may seem somewhat heartless: "The tears of strangers are only water." It means we are obligated to help only our own; if others have a problem, we wish them well, but it's their problem.

For FDR, the New Deal was a patriotic project. He routinely defended his programs in terms of "the greater good of the greater number." Moreover, he appealed to this same patriotic solidarity during World War II. Martin Luther King Jr. also spoke in terms of restoring the "beloved community." Their assumption was that America is a good country, based on noble ideals. The political task is to fully integrate and assimilate everyone—blacks, women, immigrants—into that America.

Today's socialist Left, however, wants an America that integrates the groups seen as previously excluded while excluding the group that was previously included. "If you are white, male, heterosexual, and religiously or socially conservative," writes author and editor Rod Dreher, "there's no place for you" on the progressive left. On the contrary, it should now be expected that in society "people like you are going to have to lose their jobs and influence."[9]

In other words, for identity socialists and for the left more generally, blacks and Latinos are in, whites are out. Women are in, men are out. Gays, bisexuals, pansexuals and transsexuals, together with other, more exotic types, are in; heterosexuals are out. Illegals are in, native-born citizens are out. One might think this is all part of the politics of inclusion, but to think that is to see only half the picture. The point, for the left, is not merely to include but also to exclude, to estrange their opponents from their native land.

Consider how normalcy has been defined in America. Because whites were a clear majority, whiteness was the norm. Since the structure of society was, however loosely, patriarchal, maleness was also seen as normative. And of course the same applied to heterosexuality, since most people were and are heterosexual. For the socialist left, it's vital to overturn this hierarchy not by leveling the playing field but by creating an inverse hierarchy. Whiteness, maleness and heterosexuality are now viewed as pathological, as forms of oppression. In this way, the left by design seeks to demonize white male heterosexuals and thus make a large body of Americans feel like aliens in their own country.

How did we get here? This, I believe, is the story of the 1960s, because that was when this great shift occurred. The 1960s was the decisive decade that gave us the Democratic left that we have today. Yet we don't typically understand the 1960s in this way. In college, for example, I learned how the progressive baton passed from FDR to Lyndon B. Johnson. LBJ modeled himself on FDR; notice how he used a three-letter abbreviation just as FDR did. And FDR's New Deal found its fuller realization in LBJ's Great Society.

What I didn't learn—what I found out later—is that LBJ was also a lifelong bigot in the FDR tradition, which is to say that both men were not above manipulating white supremacy for political ends. Just as FDR used his behind-the-scenes influence to block lynching legislation, LBJ was calling blacks the N-word even after he signed the Civil Rights Act of 1964. As I've previously shown, LBJ's embrace of civil rights was cynically motivated to preserve the Democratic plantation and guarantee a reliable African American dependency on the Democratic Party. Progressive scholarship says very little about all this.

LBJ's programs like Medicare and Medicaid built on top of FDR's programs like Social Security and unemployment insurance. The main difference is that while FDR's socialist schemes were passed in an era of depression, LBJ's schemes were passed in an era of affluence. One influential document here is economist John Kenneth Galbraith's *The Affluent Society*, a book I first read as a teenager in India. Earlier, FDR had argued for federal programs on the grounds that the country was in a depression. The situation was desperate. So it was morally imperative to act!

Galbraith made the opposite argument. He argued for an expansion of federal programs on the grounds that America was now a rich country and could afford them. How scandalous to have need in the midst of plenty. So once again it was morally imperative to act! We see here the cunning mode of the progressive argument. Both scarcity and abundance lead to the same conclusion: we must expand the reach of the federal government. Heads I win, tails you lose.

This is all very interesting, but even more interesting is the story of how America went from class socialism to identity socialism. That happened during the same period, but who made that happen? I'll show that one man, whose name few people know, was the prophet of the change. He is the one who posed the big questions: How do you get socialism when the people who are supposed to want it the most don't want it? How do you create a proletariat when the original proletariat opts out? And where do you find the replacements? To answer these questions is to discover the roots of the socialist left that defines and directs the Democratic Party.

MARCUSE'S MARXIST CONUNDRUM

To understand identity socialism, we must go back to the 1960s and meet the man who figured out how to bring its various strands together: Herbert Marcuse. A German philosopher partly of Jewish descent, Marcuse studied under the philosopher Martin Heidegger before escaping Germany prior to the Nazi ascent. After stints at Columbia, Harvard and Brandeis, Marcuse moved to California, where he joined the University of San Diego and became the guru of the New Left in the sixties.

Marcuse influenced a whole generation of young radicals, from Weather Underground cofounder Bill Ayers to Yippie activist Abbie Hoffman to Tom Hayden, president of the activist group Students for a Democratic Society (SDS). Angela Davis, who later joined the Black

Panthers and also ran for vice president on the Communist Party ticket, was a student of Marcuse and also one of his protégées. It was Marcuse, Davis said, who "taught me that it is possible to be an academic, an activist, a scholar and a revolutionary."[10]

Marcuse egged on the activists of the 1960s to seize buildings and overthrow the hierarchy of the university, as a kind of first step to fomenting socialist revolution in America. Interestingly, it was Ronald Reagan—then governor of California—who got Marcuse fired. Still, Marcuse retained his celebrity and influence over the radicals of the time. He did not, of course, create the forces of identity socialism, but he saw, perhaps earlier than anyone else, how they could form the basis for a new and viable socialism in America. That's the socialism we are dealing with now.

To understand the problem Marcuse confronted, we have to go back to Marx. Marx saw himself as the prophet, not the instigator, of the advent of socialism. We think of Marx as some sort of activist, seeking to organize a workers' revolution, but Marx emphasized from the outset that the socialist revolution would come inevitably; nothing had to be done to cause it. The Marxist view is nicely summed up by one of Marx's German followers, Karl Kautsky, who wrote, "Our task is not to organize the revolution but to organize ourselves for the revolution; it is not to make the revolution, but to take advantage of it."[11]

But what happens when the working class is too secure and contented to revolt? Marx didn't anticipate this; in fact, the absence of a single worker revolt of the kind Marx predicted, anywhere in the world, is a full and decisive refutation of "scientific" Marxism. In the early twentieth century, Marxists across the world—from Lenin to Mussolini—were fully aware of this problem. Fascism or national socialism represented one way to respond to it; Leninism represented another.

I'll focus on Lenin, because his was the approach that influenced Marcuse and the New Left in the 1960s. Basically Lenin argued that the working class was never going to revolt; they might join trade unions, but that was about it. In Lenin's diagnosis, workers could develop "trade union consciousness" but not "revolutionary consciousness." So then what? In his famous work *What Is To Be Done?* Lenin insisted that the socialist revolution would not be done by the working class; it would have to be done for them.

In other words, a professional class of activists and fighters would be required to serve as a revolutionary vanguard. Lenin assembled a varied group of landless farmers, professional soldiers, activist intellectuals and attorneys and criminals to collaborate with him in overthrowing the czar and introducing Bolshevik socialism to Russia. Although Lenin presented his approach as continuous with Marxism, it represented, as socialists around the world recognized, a radical break from and revision of Marxism.

Around the same time, in the early 1920s, the Italian Communist Antonio Gramsci made his own revision of socialist theory by introducing the theme of culture. "Hegemony" was Gramsci's key concept. He insisted that the capitalists did not rule society solely on the basis of economic power. Rather, they ruled through "bourgeois values" that permeated the cultural, educational and psychological realm of society. Economics, Gramsci insisted, is a subset of culture.

For Gramsci, socialist revolution under conditions at the time was impossible because the working class had internalized bourgeois values. The ordinary worker had no intention of toppling his employers; his aspiration was to become like them. Gramsci's solution was for socialist activists to figure out a way to break this hegemony and to establish a hegemony of their own. To do this they would have to take over the universities, the art world and the culture more generally. In this way, they could combat bourgeois culture "from within."

Lenin and Gramsci provided Marcuse with a starting point. He agreed with both of them that the working class had become a conservative, counterrevolutionary force. But his greatest early influence was a third man, Heidegger. Marcuse read Heidegger's magnum opus, *Being and Time*, and it inspired him so much that he apprenticed himself to Heidegger, becoming first Heidegger's student and then his faculty assistant at the University of Freiburg. Marcuse found in Heidegger a way to ground socialism in something more profound than better salaries and working conditions, in something that transcended Marx's materialism itself.

The basic idea of Heidegger's *Being and Time* is that we are finite beings, "thrown," as Heidegger puts it, into the world with no knowledge of where we came from, what we are here for or where we are going. We live in a present, yet we are constantly aware of multiple future possibilities in which we must choose even though we can know only in retrospect whether we chose wisely and well. This radical uncertainty about our situation, Heidegger argued, produces in us anxiety—anxiety that is heightened by our knowledge of death. "Being," in other words, is bracketed by "time." Humans are perishable beings that for the time being exist.

Yet how should we "be"? That, for Heidegger, was the big question. Not "What is it good to do?" but "How is it good to be?" Typically, we have no answer to this question; we are barely even aware of it as a question. We go through life like a twig in a current, steered by a tide of sociability and conformity. Thus we lose ourselves; we cease to be "authentic." Authenticity, for Heidegger, means coming to terms with our mortality and living the only life we get on our own terms. We cannot rely on God to show us the way; we are alone in the world, and have to find a way for ourselves. When Frank Sinatra sings, "I did it my way," he expresses a distinct Heideggerian consciousness.

Marcuse eventually broke with Heidegger when he heard that Heidegger had joined the Nazi Party and become an apologist for Hitler. Marcuse seems to have had no objection to Heidegger's—or Hitler's—national socialism, although, being partly Jewish, he was naturally less enthusiastic about the accompanying anti-Semitism. Even so, Marcuse continued to draw from Heidegger's philosophy to illuminate the political problems he was dealing with.

Essentially his problem was the same as the one Lenin faced: if the working class isn't up for socialism, where do you find a new proletariat to bring it about? Marcuse knew that modern industrialized countries like America couldn't assemble the types of landless peasants and professional soldiers—the flotsam and jetsam of a backward feudal society—that Lenin relied on. So who could serve in the substitute proletariat that would be needed to agitate for socialism in America?

Marcuse looked around to identify which groups had a natural antipathy to capitalism. Marcuse knew he could count on the bohemian artists and intellectuals who had long hated industrial civilization, in part because they considered themselves superior to businessmen and shopkeepers. In Germany, this group distinguished "culture"—by which they meant art—from "civilization"—by which they meant industry— and they were decidedly on the side of culture. In fact, they used art and culture to rail against bourgeois capitalism.

These were the roots of bohemianism and the avant-garde. "Bohemia," wrote Henri Murger, "leads either to the Academy, the Hospital or the Morgue." Elizabeth Wilson in her book *Bohemians* concurs: "Bohemia offered a refuge to psychological casualties too disturbed to undertake formal employment or conform to the rules of conventional society. It was a sanctuary for individuals who were so eccentric or suffered from such personal difficulties or outright psychological disorder that they could hardly have existed outside a psychiatric institution other than in Bohemia."[12]

These self-styled "outcasts" were natural recruits for what Marcuse termed the Great Refusal—the visceral repudiation of free market society. The problem, however, was that these bohemians were confined to small sectors of Western society: the Schwabing section of Munich, the Left Bank of Paris, Greenwich Village in New York and a handful of university campuses. By themselves, they were scarcely enough to hold a demonstration, let alone make a revolution.

A NEW PROLETARIAT

So Marcuse had to search further. He had to think of a way to take bohemian culture mainstream, to normalize the outcasts and to turn normal people into outcasts. He started with an unlikely group of proles: the young people of the 1960s. Here, finally, was a group that could make up a mass movement. Yet what a group! Fortunately, Marx wasn't around to see it; he would have burst out laughing. Abbie Hoffman? Jerry Rubin? Mario Savio? Joan Baez? Bob Dylan? How could people of this sorry stripe, these slack, spoiled products of postwar prosperity, these parodies of humanity, these horny slothful loafers completely divorced from real-world problems, neurotically focused on themselves, their drugs and sex lives and mind-numbing music, serve as the shock troops of revolution?

Marcuse's insight was Heideggerian: by teaching them a new way to be "authentic." By "raising their consciousness." The students were already somewhat alienated from the larger society. They lived in these socialist communes called universities. They took for granted their amenities. Ungrateful slugs that they were, they despised rather than cherished their parents for the sacrifices made on their behalf. They sought "something more," a form of self-fulfillment that went beyond material fulfillment.

Here, Marcuse recognized, was the very raw material out of which socialism is made in a rich, successful society. Perhaps there was a way to instruct them in oppression, to convert their spiritual anomie into political discontent. Marcuse was confident that an activist group of professors could raise the consciousness of a whole generation of students so that they could feel subjectively oppressed even if there were no objective forces oppressing them. Then they would become activists to fight not someone else's oppression, but their own.

Of course it would take some work to make selfish, navel-gazing students into socially conscious activists. But to Marcuse's incredible good fortune, the sixties was the decade of the Vietnam War. Students were facing the prospect of being drafted. Thus, they had selfish reasons to oppose the war. Yet this selfishness could be harnessed by teaching the students that they weren't draft-dodging cowards; rather, they were noble resisters who were part of a global struggle for social justice. In this way, bad conscience itself could be recruited on behalf of left-wing activism.

Marcuse portrayed Ho Chi Minh and the Vietcong as a kind of Third World proletariat, fighting to free itself from American hegemony. This represented a transposition of Marxist categories. The new working class were the Vietnamese "freedom fighters." The evil capitalists were American soldiers serving on behalf of the American government. Marcuse's genius was to tell leftist students in the 1960s that the Vietnamese "freedom fighters" could not succeed without them.

"Only the internal weakening of the superpower," Marcuse wrote in

An Essay on Liberation, "can finally stop the financing and equipping of suppression in the backward countries." In his vision, the students were the "freedom fighters" within the belly of the capitalist beast. Together, the revolutionaries at home and abroad would collaborate in the Great Refusal. They would jointly end the war and redeem both Vietnam and America. And what would this redemption look like? In Marcuse's words, "Collective ownership, collective control and planning of the means of production and distribution."[13] In other words, classical socialism.

Okay, so now we got the young people. Who else? Marcuse looked around America for more prospective proles, and he found, in addition to the students, three groups ripe for the taking. The first was the Black Power movement, which was adjunct to the civil rights movement. The beauty of this group, from Marcuse's point of view, is that it would not have to be instructed in the art of grievance; blacks had grievances that dated back centuries.

Consequently, here was a group that could be mobilized against the status quo, and if the status quo could be identified with capitalism, here was a group that should be open to socialism. Through a kind of Marxist transposition, "blacks" would become the working class, "whites" the capitalist class. Race, in this analysis, takes the place of class. This is how we get Afro-socialism, and from here it is a short step to Latino socialism and every other type of ethnic socialism.

Another emerging source of disgruntlement was the feminists. Marcuse recognized that with effective consciousness raising, they too could be taught to see themselves as an oppressed proletariat. This of course would require another Marxist transposition: "women" would now be viewed as the working class and "men" the capitalist class; the class category would now be shifted to gender.

"The movement becomes radical," Marcuse wrote, "to the degree to which it aims, not only at equality within the job and value structure of the established society . . . but rather at a change in the structure itself."[14] Marcuse's target wasn't just the patriarchy; it was the monogamous family. In Gramscian terms, Marcuse viewed the heterosexual family itself as an expression of bourgeois culture, so in his view the abolition of the family would help hasten the advent of socialism.

Marcuse didn't write specifically about homosexual or transgender people, but he was more than aware of exotic and outlandish forms of sexual behavior, and the logic of identity socialism can easily be extended to all these groups. Once again, we need some creative Marxist transposition. Gays and transgenders become the newest proletariat, and heterosexuals—even black and female heterosexuals—become their oppressors.

We see here the roots of "intersectionality." As the left now holds, one form of oppression is good but two is better and three or more is best. The true exemplar of identity socialism is a black or brown male with a Third World background transitioning to be a woman, who is trying illegally to get into this country because his—oops, her—own country has allegedly been wiped off the map by climate change.

These latest developments go beyond Marcuse. He didn't know about intersectionality, but he did recognize the emerging environmental movement as an opportunity to restrict and regulate capitalism. The goal, he emphasized, was "to drive ecology to the point where it is no longer containable within the capitalist framework," although he recognized that this "means first extending the drive within the capitalist framework."[15]

Marcuse also inverted Freud to advocate the liberation of eros. Freud had argued that primitive man is single-mindedly devoted to "the pleasure principle," but as civilization advances, the pleasure principle must be subordinated to what Freud termed "the reality principle." In other words, civilization is the product of the subordination of instinct to reason. Repression, Freud argued, is the necessary price we must pay for civilization.

Marcuse argued that at some point, however, civilization reaches a point where humans can go the other way. They can release the very natural instincts that have been suppressed for so long and subordinate the reality principle to the pleasure principle. This would involve a release of what Marcuse termed "polymorphous sexuality" and the "reactivation of all erotogenic zones."[16] We are a short distance here from the whole range of bizarre contemporary preoccupations: unisexuality—people falling in love with themselves—group sexuality, pansexuality—people who do not confine their sexuality to their species—and people who attempt to have sex with trees.

Marcuse recognized that mobilizing all these groups—the students, the environmentalists, the blacks, the feminists, the gays—would take time and require a great deal of consciousness raising or reeducation. He saw the university as the ideal venue for carrying out this project, which is why he devoted his own life to teaching and training a generation of socialist and left-wing activists. Over time, Marcuse believed, the university could produce a new type of culture, and that culture would then metastasize into the larger society to infect the media, the movies, even the lifestyle of the titans of the capitalist class itself.

Marcuse, in other words, foresaw an America in which bourgeois culture would be replaced by avant-garde culture. He foresaw a society in which billionaires would support socialist schemes that take away a part of their wealth in exchange for social recognition conferred by cultural institutions dominated by the socialists. Bill Gates, Warren Buffett and Mark Zuckerberg are three such billionaires; they don't seem to mind paying higher taxes if they can now hobnob with comedians, rock stars and Hollywood celebrities. Why only be rich when you can also be rich and cool?

Marcuse's project—the takeover of the American university, to make it a tool of socialist indoctrination—did not succeed in his lifetime. In fact, as mentioned above, he got the boot when Governor Reagan pressured the regents of the university system not to renew Marcuse's contract. In time, however, Marcuse succeeded as the activist generation of the 1960s gradually took over the elite universities. Today, socialist indoctrination is the norm on the American campus, and Marcuse's dream has been realized.

Marcuse is also the philosopher of Antifa. He argued, in a famous essay called "Repressive Tolerance," that tolerance is not a norm or right that should be extended to all people. Yes, tolerance is good, but not when it comes to people who are intolerant. It is perfectly fine to be intolerant against them, to the point of disrupting them, shutting down their events and even preventing them from speaking.

Marcuse didn't use the term "hater," but he invented the argument that it is legitimate to be hateful against haters—meaning those who might disagree with the socialist agenda. For Marcuse, there were no limits to what could be done to discredit and ruin such people; he wanted the left to defeat them "by any means necessary." Marcuse even approved of certain forms of domestic terrorism, such as the Weather Underground bombing of the Pentagon, on the grounds that the perpetrators were attempting to stop the greater violence that U.S. forces inflict on people in Vietnam and other countries.

Our world is quite different now from what it was in the 1960s, and yet there is so much that seems eerily familiar. When it comes to identity socialism, we are still living with Marcuse's legacy.

HOW THE PLANET CAUGHT A FEVER

Now let's explore the never-never land of identity socialism that Marcuse helped create. The most ambitious proposal to achieve socialist ends is, oddly enough, the Green New Deal. Backed by a group called the Sunrise Movement, Alexandria Ocasio-Cortez introduced the Green New Deal in apocalyptic terms. The planet has a fever! Humans have only 12 years to avert climate catastrophe! We must do these things to avert extinction! Leading Democrats—Elizabeth Warren, Kamala Harris, Bernie Sanders, Cory Booker and Kirsten Gillibrand—have climbed aboard.

Democratic senator Ed Markey, lead sponsor of the legislation, ridiculed opponents of the Green New Deal. "They call the Green New Deal pie in the sky," he yelled into a crowd of environmentalists and progressive activists. "They call it socialism." At this point, the crowd burst into approving applause. Markey seemed startled! The crowd itself was vindicating what the critics said. A befuddled Markey shook his head.[17]

Here we have to defer to the "wisdom of crowds." They saw something that Markey pretended not to see. The Green New Deal is socialism—the most expansive socialist agenda since the Nazi 25-point platform of 1920. It calls not only for getting rid of fossil fuels and transitioning to a full renewable-energy economy but also for a new power grid for the country, an upgrading and retrofitting of every home and industrial building, job guarantees for all working-age citizens at a "living wage," an assured basic income even for those "unwilling to work," universal rights to housing and education and a universal single-payer healthcare system.

Set aside the Himalayan price tab, which could go as high as $90 trillion over a 10-year period. That figure comes from a study directed by Douglas Holtz-Eakin, former director of the nonpartisan Congressional Budget Office.[18] It works out to $600,000 per American household, a prohibitive sum. But advocates of the Green New Deal respond to such sober calculations with tantrums and hysteria. We cannot, they say, afford not to do it! Our lives depend on it! The world will explode if we don't embrace this socialist agenda.

Conservative critics of the Green New Deal have focused on some of its ridiculous elements. Could farting cows—identified as environmental culprits—really pose a mortal threat to the planet? Was it practical, as Ocasio-Cortez suggested in a promotional video, for workers to get rid of oil pipelines and instead plant mangroves "with the same salary and benefits"? The original Green New Deal proposal quixotically implied that high-speed rail travel might enable us to get rid of yachts and airplanes.

Yet on this point even the climate change activists do not seem to be "on board." Recently a group of celebrities, including Google honchos Sergey Brin, Larry Page and Eric Schmidt, designer Diane von Furstenberg and Hollywood billionaire David Geffen, converged in Sicily to discuss the dangers of fossil fuels. More than 100 came by private jet. Others came by helicopter and luxury yacht.[19] As with the Pharisees of old, no one seemed conscious of the hypocrisy on display.

A bigger problem is that a significant part of the Green New Deal— its guaranteed living wage, incomes for those unwilling to work, state guarantees for housing and education, government-run universal healthcare—has little or nothing to do with the climate. This seems to be socialism hiding behind an environmentalist banner. And this is of course why socialists like AOC and Bernie love it. They neither know nor care if the planet is getting hotter or colder. They like the diagnosis of the earth's terminal condition because they like the socialist preventive medicine that is recommended to save it.

Is socialism actually mandated by oceans rising, glaciers melting and penguins coughing? I get these images from Al Gore's film *An Inconvenient Truth*. The film provides a vivid contrast between dramatic staged scenes of the end of civilization as we know it and Al Gore's flat, soporific narration. How contemptuously Marx would have guffawed had he seen the film. Marx insisted that the vehicle to bring about socialism was the rage of the working class. The proletariat—not the average temperature of the earth—was the driving force of history. Marx thought that a proletarian uprising was the only way to have socialism and then communism. Marx advanced his theory as "scientific."

Green New Deal advocates insist that their program too is "scientific"—backed, they say, by 97 percent of all climate scientists. Given this scientific consensus, critics are dismissed as climate "deniers." The analogy here is to Holocaust deniers, fanatics who simply refuse to accept empirical reality. But the Holocaust is an event that already happened. The Green New Deal is a projection of something that is in no way supported by experience—after all, most of us recognize that the climate is not recognizably different from what it was when we were kids—and is an event that will supposedly occur in the future. Denying things that may or may not come to pass is not the same as denying what has already occurred.

Where is the proof that 97 percent of climate scientists support the Green New Deal? There is none. What the scientists agree on is the greenhouse effect—that releasing carbon dioxide traps heat in the atmosphere and thereby warms the planet—and this agreement is then invoked to imply that there is an equal measure of support for the whole feverish climate change doctrine. This would be similar to arguing that because people gradually grow older, the human race is therefore facing imminent extinction.

There is also consensus on how much the earth has warmed: about 1 degree Celsius (less than 1.5 degrees Fahrenheit) in the past 100 years.

This number is usually downplayed by Green New Deal activists because of its whoop-de-do effect. The earth has seen that rate of increase many times in its history. Can humans who have been around for more than 100,000 years really not survive a one- or even two-degree uptick in the climate? Those of us who live in uncomfortably cold regions might even welcome a little warming, especially during those frigid winter months.

Scientists, however, do not agree on whether humans or other factors produced that warming. They do not agree on what precise risks are posed by that warming. They do not agree on what, if anything, we should do about climate change. They don't even agree on whether climate change is a real science. Yes, we have climate change "scientists" and they use scientific "models." But the test of a model is to predict climate in advance.

Right now, the models can't do that. When climate takes a rapid warming turn, we hear, "Wow, there is clear evidence of climate change." When climate takes a rapid cooling turn, we hear, "Wow, that's more proof of climate change." No wonder the environmentalist left had to change the name from "global warming" to "climate change." Global warming is subject to empirical refutation with accumulated evidence of cooling. The beauty of climate change is that it is essentially irrefutable, because somewhere, in some way, the climate is always changing.

Consider a classic example of Green New Deal reasoning. The glaciers are melting, and therefore if this keeps up there won't be any glaciers left. But now I turn on the television to hear that the Jakobshavn Glacier in Greenland—the very one that was supposed to be melting—is growing again. The data is from NASA's Jet Propulsion Laboratory, published in a reputable scientific journal. "That was kind of a surprise," said Jason Box, a climate scientist at the Geological Survey of Denmark and Greenland.

Box points out that Jakobshavn is "arguably the most important Greenland glacier because it discharges the most ice in the northern hemisphere." Six years ago, it had retreated 1.8 miles and was losing 130 feet annually. But for the past two years, it has been growing at the same rate, which means it could soon be back to its original size. "At first we didn't believe it," said Ala Khazendar of the NASA lab. "We had pretty much assumed Jakobshavn would just keep going on as it had over the past 20 years."[20]

Not so. And if Greenland seems like an anomaly, let's move over to Iceland, where I read, "Largest Glaciers in Iceland Growing for the First Time in Decades." In previous years, Iceland's glaciers Vatnajökull and Langjökull lost about 1.5 meters a year. Now both have stopped losing mass. Meanwhile Hofsjökull has grown slightly, and Mýrdalsjökull has grown substantially. These are the four largest glaciers in Iceland. None of them are currently shrinking. Many roads in Iceland, the article notes, are "difficult to pass or even closed to traffic due to record amounts of snow."[21]

What about the polar bears? Climate activists warn that as sea ice shrinks, the polar bear population will thin out to extinction, because polar bears need sea ice to hunt seals. Once again, we can test this hypothesis by counting polar bears. This isn't easy to do—they live on barren, windswept terrain relatively inhospitable to human counters. But a recent survey by Susan Crockford, an expert on polar bears, puts the current polar bear population in the range of 22,000–31,000. That means there are four times as many of them as there were in 1960, and the polar bear population is now at a 50-year high.[22] The bears are doing fine.

Poor Alexandria Ocasio-Cortez! Every time there is a hurricane or a heat wave, she shrieks: global warming! So apparently extreme weather supports the theory. Yet when there is record cold, AOC's minions are on hand to shriek, with equal venom, "Weather does not equal climate!" Somehow, the distinction between weather and climate applies only when the weather pattern can be invoked to undermine the theory, but it does not apply when the weather pattern can be invoked to illustrate the theory.

Even AOC's prediction that, absent concerted human action, the earth has just a dozen years to go has fallen on hard times. The 12-year number actually comes from a UN climate change panel, so it would appear to have some reputable backing. Even so, when AOC was challenged, she tweeted out, "This is a technique of the GOP, to take dry humor + sarcasm literally and 'fact check' it. Like the 'world ending in

12 years' thing, you'd have to have the social intelligence of a sea sponge to think it's literal."

So it's not literal, and we all missed the joke. But then, just a few days later, AOC was back on the 12-year timetable. She released a climate change video, which she promoted with the following tweet: "Climate change is here + we got a deadline: 12 years left to cut emissions in half."[23] A dozen years from now, when the earth is pretty much the same as it is now, I'm sure she'll go back to calling her prediction humorous and sarcastic.

Now let's turn to the predictions of James Hansen, widely considered the world's leading authority on the subject. In 1986, Hansen predicted that average global temperatures would rise by half a degree to one degree Fahrenheit from 1990 to 2000, and another two to four degrees between 2000 and 2010. In fact, using Hansen's own measurements, these predictions turned out to be wrong. The warming in the 1990s was very slight, much lower than predicted.[24] The average temperature now is about the same as it was in the late 1990s, which means that despite fluctuations up and down, there has been virtually no warming trend since the end of the last century.

REMEMBER GLOBAL COOLING?

None of this has diminished the certainty of Ocasio-Cortez and other activists. In fact, they are best understood as part of an apocalyptic tradition that includes environmentalists, religious fundamentalists, cult leaders, population-control fanatics and other types of zealots. In the 1980s I read Hal Lindsey's fundamentalist tract, *The Late Great Planet Earth*. Lindsey was positive—positive!—that a world war was imminent and the Second Coming of Christ was at hand.

It didn't happen. And during the 1970s, much more respectable figures—on the left—drew on predictive "models" to insist, with an equally straight face, that the earth was running out of food, that minerals and other natural resources were being irreplaceably depleted, that growing populations would soon cover every inch of the planet's living space, that the ozone layer was dissolving and that the world was facing the prospect of "nuclear winter."

Perhaps the most famous prophet of the apocalypse was biologist Paul Ehrlich of Stanford, author of *The Population Bomb*, who warned that "sometime in the next 15 years," the earth would run out of food and mineral resources and then "the end will come." That was in 1970. Over the years, Ehrlich made one extreme prediction after another. By the end of the twentieth century, he insisted, "the United Kingdom will be simply a small group of impoverished islands, inhabited by some 70 million hungry people. . . . If I were a gambler, I would take even money that England will not exist in the year 2000." Ehrlich wrote that in 1974.[25]

Ehrlich was so sure of himself that in 1980 he bet economist Julian Simon $10,000 that over the subsequent decade the prices of raw materials—Ehrlich chose copper, chromium, nickel, tin and tungsten—would skyrocket, reflecting their increasing depletion and scarcity. Simon said the prices of those elements would all decline. Ten years passed, and Simon won the bet. Ehrlich paid up, but never admitted his mistake.[26] The progressive media, which was Ehrlich's cheerleader all along, publicized the bet but barely covered the outcome. Still, those in the know could see that another apocalyptic prediction bit the dust.

The left also insisted during the 1970s that we were in an environmental crisis because the earth was cooling. Yes, cooling! Global cooling—not global warming—was the imminent threat. Lowell Ponte's book *The Cooling* is typical of the literature of the time. The book is endorsed by leading climate scientists at Stanford University and the University of Wisconsin at Madison. One of them, Reid Bryson of Wisconsin, says that while scientists disagreed on the issue, a majority of them believed the long-term trend is toward global cooling. This is important because it contradicts claims by activists today that cooling was a minority position among scientists in the 1970s.[27]

Ponte cites a National Academy of Sciences report showing that temperatures in the Northern Hemisphere, where most of the world's population lives, have been in steady decline since the 1940s, leading the NAS to conclude that there is a "finite possibility that a serious worldwide cooling could befall the earth within the next 100 years." In 1975, John Gribbin wrote an influential article, "Cause and Effects of Global

Cooling," summing up the research in the leading scientific journal *Nature*.[28] Gribbin and the NAS even fretted about the possibility that we were heading into another Ice Age, similar to periods when the earth was largely uninhabitable by humans.

Ponte proposed a series of far-out solutions: one of them was to dam up the Bering Strait, essentially closing the sea between Siberia and Alaska, an almost unimaginably costly venture. To justify it, Ponte employed the familiar alarmism: "Global cooling presents humankind with the most important social, political and adaptive challenge we have had to deal with for ten thousand years. . . . The cooling has already killed hundreds of thousands of people in poor nations. It has already made food and fuel more precious. If it continues and no strong measures are taken to deal with it, the cooling will cause worldwide famine, world chaos, and probably world war, and this could all come by the year 2000."[29]

In case you are wondering, none of this happened. Happily, no one followed up on his idea to build the Bridge to Nowhere. Unhappily, the same nonsensical rhetoric—no less apocalyptic, no less sure of itself, no less unreliable than its predecessor, uninhibited by getting it wrong every single time in the past—is now back with a vengeance. This is the genealogy of the Green New Deal. First, it was cooling, now it is warming. Opposite messages, delivered by the same type of idiot. In some cases, delivered by the very same idiots themselves.

By now you are probably getting the idea that the whole Green New Deal is a scam, a massive exercise in globaloney, a transparent excuse to replace capitalism with socialism. The rhetoric of the activists certainly supports this. "The climate crisis," Natasha Fernández-Silber writes in *Jacobin*, "is quite simply a crisis of capitalism. . . . We must either replace capitalism with a more sustainable economic system—or face barbarism and extinction."[30] Extinction or socialism: you get to choose!

THE PROBLEM WITH WALLS—THEY WORK!

Now we turn to a second issue that animates identity socialism, namely, illegal immigration. Even Marcuse didn't guess this one, although I'm confident he would have jumped aboard if he were alive today. He would recognize that this issue is now a critical part of the left's project to assemble a coalition of alienated minority groups to create a pro-socialist majority. An open advocacy of illegal immigration represents a big change for the Democrats. Obama and Hillary were both ambivalent about illegals, whom they considered a problem. Today's Democrats, by contrast, consider them an opportunity.

Labor unions like the AFL-CIO once opposed illegal immigration. The reason was obvious, and it derived from simple economics. If you import large numbers of illegals who are willing to work for less money, the laws of supply and demand will guarantee that they will drive down the wages of native-born workers. Socialists have traditionally opposed illegal immigration because it hurts the working class they profess to care most about.

Today's working class has been buffeted over the past generation by a perfect storm of globalization and outsourcing, which sends jobs abroad; technology, which uses automation and software to do things that previously required labor; and legal immigration, which swells the ranks of the working population. One might think that unions devoted to protecting worker salaries, and a Democratic Party that once stood for the workingman, would do whatever they could to suppress illegal immigration, which can only make a bad situation for workers into a worse one.

But no. Marx, I think, would have been befuddled. What kind of a left, he would think, wants to import foreign workers to hurt the bargaining power of native workers? If anything, this will divide the working class. It will set foreigners against natives, it will cause native workers to blame the foreigners—instead of the capitalist class—for its miseries and it will postpone, if not block, the prospects of a socialist revolution. This is standard socialist doctrine.

So there must be a reason why today's left gives such primacy to this issue.

The reason cannot be that Democrats are courting the illegal vote. Sure, there may be some cases of fraudulent voting by illegals—I know that several such cases came to light recently in Texas—but by and large illegals cannot vote.

Nor can the reason be that "walls don't work." Sure, progressive journals like *Foreign Policy* publish elaborate explanations of why walls don't work.[31] Supposedly, they don't work because desperate people find a way to get through. Yet if walls really didn't work, Democrats wouldn't mind Trump's wall so much. Their determination to prevent the wall is in direct proportion to their fear that it actually would work.

I got into this debate recently with a group of left-wing activists at Stanford University, where I spoke last year. The students gave me the usual humbug about how walls don't work. They looked very surprised when I told them Stanford has a wall. Where, they asked, is the wall? Certainly anyone from Palo Alto can easily stroll onto the Stanford campus.

Stanford's wall, I said, is of a different kind. It's a wall, I said, higher than any wall Trump could build. The wall, I explained, is in the admissions office; it regulates who is let into Stanford. So efficient is that wall, I noted, that never in the history of a university had anyone scaled it. There is no record of any student, ever, sneaking into Stanford, taking courses for four years and graduating. Walls work! The activists stared at me with gaping eyes.

Let's look at what the Democrats are pushing for. They want to shut down what Ocasio-Cortez and Ilhan Omar term "concentration camps," a reference to the admittedly overwhelmed facilities where illegals who show up at the border demanding asylum are temporarily housed. ICE officers themselves, according to Rashida Tlaib, know they are operating a "broken system."[32] Omar, Tlaib and others on the socialist left want to abolish ICE, the immigration enforcement authority. All the leading Democrats are publicly committed to free healthcare for illegals.

None of this makes any sense. If ICE is a "broken system," then it's obviously not a concentration camp. Concentration camps were not "broken systems." On the contrary, they were ruthless and efficient factories of forced labor and, in some cases, mass murder. No one at an ICE facility is forced to work. So for Ocasio-Cortez and Omar to equate ICE facilities with concentration camps is false and wicked.

Now consider free healthcare for illegals. This violates the basic idea of a social compact, which is a mutual bond among citizens who pledge that they are in this together. It violates the premise of the welfare state, in which citizens of a nation through the political process agree to pool some of their resources and insure themselves against certain risks. "Rights" are within that social compact. No group of people owes entitlements, whether subsidized healthcare or anything else, to anyone who is not a legitimate member of their community.

But let's put all of this to the side. If Democrats are so keen on these "reforms," why don't they pursue them through the normal political channels? Why don't the Democrats campaign to change the immigration laws? Go ahead and pass laws that allow open borders. Go ahead and limit or eliminate enforcement. Go ahead and mandate health coverage for illegals and all of Mexico, if you want to go that far. If it's "democratic socialism" they are trying to impose, then do it through the democratic process. Yet interestingly the Democratic left seems to have no interest in this.

Rather, they are in open defiance of existing laws. They portray enforcement of those laws, in a difficult atmosphere where they are flagrantly violated, as hateful, racist and Nazi-like betrayals of basic human decency. While exposing the holding facilities as overcrowded and understaffed, they work with activists in Central American countries to further overwhelm those facilities, apparently seeking the chaos that makes effective administration of the immigration laws more difficult so that more illegals get through.

ASIAN INDIAN IN A SOMBRERO

In a recent book, *This Land Is Our Land,* the progressive writer Suketu Mehta attempts to justify the left's approach to illegals. Subtitled *An Immigrant's Manifesto,* Mehta begins with some fake heroism. "We're here," he declares, "we're not going back, we're raising our kids here. It's our country now." But since Mehta is an immigrant whose parents came legally from India, no one is trying to send him back. Of course it's his country, as much as it is every other American's country. How dumb can this guy be?

He's not dumb. Mehta is playing a clever game, conflating legals and illegals. This has become standard fare among left-wing politicians and also the media left. "We are all immigrants," ranted New York governor Andrew Cuomo in response to Trump's deportation threats. "More Immigrants Face Deportation Under New Rules," headlined *The New York Times*.[33] According to this narrative, my wife Debbie, an immigrant from Venezuela, and I, an immigrant from India, should be living in fear. Trump wants to send us packing! But this is a lie, and Cuomo and the editors of *The New York Times* know it.

Illegals are not "immigrants." Immigrants are people who have lawfully moved to this country. Illegals are not even "undocumented immigrants," any more than someone who forcefully seizes my house is an "undocumented owner." Illegals are, in a very precise sense, "aliens." Even those whose motives are understandable—the desire to relocate to a better society—are still breaking the law. Trump is determined to enforce the law. It is only by erasing the distinction between legals and illegals that the left can insist, as it blusteringly does, that "Trump is against immigrants."

Although he claims to have visited the migrant caravans, Mehta gives no indication of how they actually operate. How do thousands of supposedly starving people move themselves and their families—including small children—hundreds if not thousands of miles? In reality, as Michelle Malkin and others have shown, they do it through an elaborate network of facilities generated by the American and international left. The left assembles the caravans and then sustains them through their trek to the United States border.

Along the way, the caravans benefit from soup kitchens and first aid centers, overnight shelters with baths and medical care facilities, including therapeutic counseling. The migrants even get free calling cards and phone apps that provide immediate access to lawyers and sympathetic journalists in case of detention or encounters with law enforcement. Mehta decides it would be impolitic to mention that the caravans aren't spontaneous; they are orchestrated and sustained by political groups for political benefit.

At one point Mehta challenges Rodney Scott, a San Diego immigration official, about the need for a border fence. Scott responds, "Pick any amusement park that you want, or any movie, or even Black Friday, the day after Thanksgiving, where people line up for hours or days in advance to get into the event, right? So, in any one of those events, if you're standing in line and a family cuts in front of you, you're gonna be a little bit angry about it. Now you complain, and security walks up and grabs the parents and says, 'You can't do this, but it's not your kids' fault that you cut in line, so we're gonna let the kids go in.' Ahead of your family, ahead of all the people that've been waiting in line. Is that fair?"

No, it's not fair. Mehta knows this. Scott's point is especially devastating because it strikes at the very position Mehta is coming from. In other words, Scott is making the case against illegals not from the viewpoint of aggrieved natives but from the viewpoint of other foreigners seeking to come here. Moreover, these others are from countries like India, faraway places where you can't just jump a fence or swim the Rio Grande. Any Indian waiting for a green card would side with Scott over Mehta on this.

Since Mehta has no comeback here, with a grand "Alrighty, then," he simply moves on. His central claim seems to be that illegals have a "right" to migrate to rich countries like England and the United States. Why? Because, in his view, "Migration today is a form of reparations." In other words, England ruined India through colonial occupation, and so Indians should have a right to relocate to England. America stole half of Mexico, so Mexicans should have a right to move north to parts of America that, at one time, were part of Mexico.

But, to take the issue head-on, did England ruin India through colonial occupation? To put it differently, would India have been better off if the English never came? Would Mehta himself be better off? The British built the railways in India. And the ports. They introduced the English language, in which Mehta writes his books. Without British influence, would India be the technologically advanced country it is today?

One could raise a similar set of objections regarding America's alleged theft of Mexican land. Texas used to be part of Mexico but broke off because of tyrannical laws imposed by a Mexican dictator. Texas then opted to join the United States. The Mexican War arose over a border dispute between Texas and Mexico. Mexico lost the war, and ceded the disputed land in a treaty in which the United States paid money and wrote off Mexican debts.

Not only did Hispanic Texans fight on the American side of that war, but the Mexicans who ended up on the American side of the line soon found themselves immeasurably better off than their counterparts in Mexico. I know something about this; my wife grew up in the Rio Grande Valley, and these are her maternal ancestors. They value their history, which strengthens their patriotic identification with America. This is not to say that the Hispanic community in Texas suffered no discrimination, but even the partial deprivation of their rights in America was far preferable to living in Mexico where, as a practical matter, they had no rights at all.

What does Mehta have to say about these questions? The poverty of his argument is that he doesn't even address them. He merely asserts what he has the burden to prove. Yet reviewers seem to have taken no note of this. Mehta himself doesn't see the need to make a case. One gets the feeling that he's playing to an audience he knows very well, or to put it differently, he's a very sly Indian who knows how to assimilate to progressive culture.

"It may make sense for America to let in more skilled Indians and fewer unskilled Latinos," he writes, "but America has hurt Latinos much more than it has hurt Indians. America owes them more, and so it should open its doors more to them."[34] Again, the Latinos who became Americans in 1848 were not hurt; they were helped. I'm not sure if Mehta knows this. One thing he does know are the left's political priorities, and he shows by this statement that he's willing to go to bat for them, even where it makes no sense. That's why this Asian Indian guy puts on a sombrero.

So what's the left's motive here? The short-term motive is simple: use the illegals to portray Trump and the Republicans as racist or anti-Mexican and also anti-immigrant. The point is to alienate Trump and the GOP not from illegals, who can't vote, but from legal immigrants and Mexican Americans, who can. The left also wants to swamp the country with illegals, seeking to make them dependent on the government, so that if they ever get amnesty and can vote, they will vote for the party that sneaked them through and provided them with a steady, if meager, sustenance.

THE TERRORIST NEXT DOOR

Trump and his allies point out that porous borders don't just admit the wretched of the earth who want a better life; they also admit drug smugglers, and gang members, and terrorists. In 2018 Beto O'Rourke insisted that "precisely zero terrorists, terrorist groups or terror plots have ever been connected with the U.S.-Mexico border." PolitiFact—a left-wing site devoted to validating such claims—rejected O'Rourke's assertion. "We rate this claim False."

They had to, because there have been at least a dozen cases of terrorists or terrorist groups apprehended while crossing the southern border or after doing so. One, Mahmoud Youssef Kourani, secured a Mexican guide and entered the United States in the trunk of a car. He moved to Dearborn, Michigan, where he raised money for terrorist groups. He was eventually charged and pleaded guilty.

Ahmed Muhammed Dhakane, a Somali terrorist, furnished bogus documents for terror recruits and showed them how to make false asylum claims at the Mexican border. Dhakane himself was arrested on the border, in Brownsville, Texas, just across from Matamoros, Mexico. He was accompanied by a young Somali girl whom he had instructed to pretend to be his pregnant wife, in the belief that a pregnant wife would improve his chances of U.S. asylum.

Said Jaziri, a Tunisian terrorist, was caught by immigration authorities trying to enter the United States from Mexico at an entry point near San Diego. Jaziri had traveled from Tunisia to Tijuana, where he recruited coyotes to steer him across the U.S. border.[35]

Captured ISIS fighter Abu Henricki, a Canadian citizen with dual Trinidadian citizenship, admitted recently that his mission was to recruit terrorists from Central America and then smuggle them into the United States using false identification and passports. ISIS figured that Central Americans would raise less suspicion than Middle Easterners.[36]

I've given just a few examples, and it may be said that there are just a few more documented cases like this, but let's remember that these are only the cases we know about—the ones who got caught—and let's also recall that it took only a handful of guys to cause all the carnage on 9/11.

Ilhan Omar's 100,000-strong Somali community in Minneapolis is the terrorist recruitment capital of the United States. It is a fertile base for both direct and online recruitment. FBI data show that more men from this community have joined, or sought to join, a foreign terrorist organization over the last dozen years there than in any other jurisdiction in the nation. From this community alone, 45 members left to join either the Somalia-based insurgency al-Shabab or the Iraqi and Syrian wing of ISIS.[37]

Omar herself seems quite protective of these terrorists. In August 2019, Omar called for the protection of a Somali telecom company called Hormuud, invoking its "vital services" and "enormous contribution to the economy." She neglected to mention that the founder, Ahmed Nur Ali Jimale, is known to be one of the chief financiers of al-Shabab. Through Jimale, Hormuud has reportedly provided not only technology and logistical support to al-Shabab but also weapons and ammunition.[38]

Whenever Omar is urged to condemn ISIS or Al-Qaeda, she evades the subject. Her rationale seems to be that Muslims have no special obligation to denounce terrorism conducted in the name of Islam. Thus, she refuses to denounce Islamic terrorism. For Omar the lesson of 9/11 is not to blame it on Muslims. Muslims as a group shouldn't be held responsible just because, in Omar's words, "some people did something." Yet after a mass shooting by a white supremacist, Omar does not hesitate to call out white supremacy and seek to pin the blame on Trump and his supporters.

In 2015, six Somalis were arrested trying to cross into Mexico as part of a plan to join ISIS in Syria. As the case approached trial, Omar, then a state representative, wrote the trial judge requesting "compassion" and lighter sentencing for one of the men who was facing 30 years in prison.

"Such punitive measures not only lack efficacy," Omar wrote, "they inevitably create an environment in which extremism can flourish, aligning with the presupposition of terrorist recruitment. The best de-

terrent to fanaticism is a system of compassion. We must alter our attitude and approach; if we truly want to affect change, we should refocus
our efforts on inclusion and rehabilitation."

I translate this to mean that punishing terrorists causes terrorism, and
the best way to fight terrorism is to seek to include potential terrorists in
our communities and to seek to convince them not to terrorize us. Very
much along these lines, a Minnesota judge in 2010 gave 21-year-old
Abdullahi Yusuf no jail time and a chance at experimental rehabilitation
after he pleaded guilty to attempting to join ISIS. Yusuf was confined
to a halfway house, yet soon found himself back before the judge when
authorities found a box-cutter under his bed. Yusuf denied that the box-
cutter was his, yet the judge ordered him to be imprisoned for the violation. He is now released.[39]

In 2018, Omar was asked about terrorism on Al Jazeera, and she addressed what she called the "quote-unquote legitimate fears" Americans
have. She responded, "I would say our country should be more fearful of white men because they are actually causing most of the deaths
within this country. And so if fear was the driving force to keep America safe—Americans safe within this country—we should be profiling,
monitoring and creating policies to fight the radicalization of white
men."[40]

Here is the standard socialist move, to turn the tables and insist
that whites, not Muslims, pose the greatest terrorist threat; that legals,
not illegals, are the problem; that there's nothing wrong with creating
Somalia-in-America; that Americans, not Somalis, should make the ad-
justment to this; and that even terrorism represents nothing more than
a cry of protest against America's refusal to include and provide for its
foreign newcomers.

Illegal immigration is not merely a mechanism for changing the political, religious and cultural composition of America; it is literally a
mechanism for changing, in ways that Americans have not agreed to
and immigration laws have not authorized, the actual DNA of America. In this way the socialists hope to win the day, not by convincing
a majority of existing Americans but by creating a majority using new
Americans who will overpower and subdue the native population.

RACE AND GENDER HOAXES

Now I take up the third face of identity socialism, namely the race and sex agenda. Again, this is a critical part of an attempt to amass a ruling majority by incorporating a mélange of self-styled victim groups. Strangely, the actual agenda here is pretty thin. The left halfheartedly demands racial reparations, it pushes for paid maternal—and sometimes paternal—leave, it is committed to abortion on demand (even late-term abortion) and it wants biological males to be able to use women's bathrooms and compete in women's athletic events. Most of the legislative action, oddly enough, has been on that last front. Somehow, transgenders are now the front lines of identity socialism.

What does this tell us? It tells us that, once again, socialism cannot be understood purely in economic terms. Marx would not know what to make of biological males with penises choking and pounding women in wrestling matches! If someone had told him this was socialism, he would ask them to seek medical attention. Clearly something new is afoot.

What's going on, I want to suggest, is that race and sex have become more than mechanisms to secure group loyalty for the Democratic left. In addition, they have become tactics of intimidation. The socialist left uses these mechanisms to force people to grovel and submit to its worldview. They want to overturn your moral code and replace it with their moral code. The economist John Maynard Keynes once called this "immoralism," recognizing that it represented a kind of inversion of traditional moral values.[41]

Naturally, the left expects resistance. So the whole race and gender thing is aimed at torpedoing that resistance. The basic idea is to portray whites, males and heterosexuals as evil oppressors, and nonwhites, females and gender benders of all kinds as the most normal, wonderful people in the world. And if you say otherwise, or oppose this view, the left will demonize you as racist, sexist, heterosexist and a "hater." Then they will try to destroy your career and your life.

Of course, the whole thing is based on lies. Let's start with racism, which has become increasingly rare in a society where it is now customary, if not obligatory, to tiptoe around blacks and other people of color, to express deference if not subservience to their demands and to put up with behavior that would be utterly intolerable if anyone else did it. We live in a society of black and brown privilege, yet all that we hear about is "white privilege."

Since racism has become so rare, it now has to be invented. The Jussie Smollett hoax is the most obvious example. My favorite detail from that case was that Smollett—who paid two Nigerian men to fake an attack on him that he subsequently blamed on Trump supporters—was still wearing the noose around his neck when the police arrived at his apartment. I guess this was a case of "method acting," in which the actor stays in his role even when his part has ended.

But what few people know is that racial hoaxes have now become commonplace, especially on the university campus. The gay conservative journalist Andy Ngo has become something of a specialist in tracking down these hoaxes. He has publicized dozens of them. Even this is the tip of the iceberg. Wilfred Reilly in his book *Hate Crime Hoax* counts more than 400 racial hoaxes.

Here's a small sample. In 2016, a Muslim university student received national attention after she claimed a man threatened to set her on fire if she didn't remove her hijab. The university denounced the "hateful attack," which turned out to be a hoax. Students at St. Olaf College in Minnesota boycotted classes in May 2017 in the wake of racist graffiti targeting black students. The event got widespread media coverage until it turned out a black student did it. When a black church in Greenville, Mississippi, was set on fire, *The Washington Post* and other media outlets blamed "the incendiary rhetoric of GOP nominee Donald Trump." Turns out a black congregant set the fire.[42]

Such hoaxes, leftist pundits insist, amount to a small percentage of all hate crimes reported. Still, let's ask why they occur. Why did Smollett do it? It's not enough to say that the hoaxers are trying to call attention to a social problem. Blacks didn't stage lynchings in the late nineteenth and early twentieth centuries, even though they wanted to call attention to the problem. They didn't need to stage lynchings because large numbers of lynchings were going on, and it made more sense to record the evidence rather than to manufacture it.

But for the racial hoaxers of today, like Smollett, the event has to be staged because there is insufficient evidence of the real thing. So the hoaxer is kind of like a cop who feels sure that the suspect did it, but since he doesn't have the evidence, he decides to plant it. The outcome, he's convinced, is just, because he "knows" the suspect is guilty. Of course planting evidence is both corrupt and evil, and one can hardly minimize the practice by saying that cops do it only in a small fraction of cases. Even one case is too many!

Now we turn to feminist and #MeToo hoaxes, which are also fairly common. At Columbia University, Emma Sulkowicz accused her sex partner Paul Nungesser of raping her. A panel of university administrators looked into the matter and cleared him. Sulkowicz then started walking around campus with a mattress on her back to dramatize Columbia's supposed culture of rape.

One might expect that "mattress girl," as she was locally dubbed, might face disciplinary action for making false charges and seeking to destroy a man's reputation. Instead, Columbia embraced her "activism." The School of Arts ultimately allowed her to justify her display as an example of "performance art." She was even able to have it count toward earning her Columbia degree.[43] As with Smollett, we see here how the false charge carries no real consequences, so there is no deterrent to making one.

Now we turn to the various women who accused Trump's Supreme Court nominee, Brett Kavanaugh, of pawing, harassing and raping them. Kavanaugh was even accused of being part of a rape gang that systematically assaulted women en masse at parties. First it was Christine Blasey Ford, who was 100 percent sure that Kavanaugh was the one who attacked her, all those decades ago, but couldn't provide any corroborating evidence. Leland Keyser, the friend she said was present on the occasion—who was fiercely pressured by various Democratic and media activists to corroborate Ford's story—refused to do so, saying she had no recollection whatever of the alleged incident. Later Keyser said she did not believe Ford's story.

Like Keyser, I suspect Ford made the whole thing up, and here's why.

First, her own stated motivation is suspect. According to her lawyer, Debra Katz, she was in part motivated by her desire to protect *Roe v. Wade*. In Katz's words, "When he takes a scalpel to *Roe v. Wade*, we will know who he is, we will know his character."[44] So presumably, if Kavanaugh were a nominee who would uphold *Roe v. Wade*, Ford would have held back on making her public accusation. What kind of victim abstains from reporting a serious crime involving a profound personal violation on the basis of the ideological proclivities of the criminal?

My second reason for thinking Ford is a liar is the pattern of things that she could, and couldn't, remember. Let's say you want to falsely accuse someone. The obvious questions are who, when, where and what happened. Obviously you have to be sure about "who." That's the target. You also have to be sure about "what." That's the assault, which you have to recall with vivid detail to make it believable.

Now what about the "where"? You have to be fuzzy on that because otherwise someone might come forward and say, "I was there." Likewise, the "when" has to be equally cloudy, for the same reason. Ford's story tracks this pattern perfectly: she is vividly clear on the things she needs to peg her target, and yet her story becomes hazy at every point where it might be open to refutation.

The left realized that they needed more women to come forward to get Kavanaugh. One, Julie Swetnick, made a sworn declaration through her lawyer Michael Avenatti that Kavanaugh was part of a rape gang that spiked women's drinks, Bill Cosby style, and then took advantage of them because they were too comatose to say no. Yet when she was asked in a TV interview what she actually saw, she said she merely saw Kavanaugh "around the punch containers," adding, "I don't know what he did. But I saw him by them, yes."[45]

A California woman, Judy Munro-Leighton, who came forward to say that Kavanaugh assaulted her, later admitted to Senate investigators that she made the whole thing up as a "ploy" and a "tactic" to defeat his nomination.[46] Remarkably, the media left created a national hysteria around these accusations, showing no hint of skepticism, actually showing no interest in even finding out whether any of them was true.

And since Kavanaugh has been on the Court, all the women have disappeared, and the media has lost all interest in following up on any of these cases, since they have ceased to be ideologically useful.

For some feminists, all of this is aimed at more than just putting men on notice that they can be accused and ruined at any time. It is also about toppling the heterosexual norm itself. As one writer, Marcie Bianco, recently wrote on the NBC website, "Heterosexuality is just not working." Bianco argued that "men need heterosexuality to maintain their societal dominance over women." But now women are coming to recognize that "they don't need heterosexuality," which is the "bedrock of their global oppression."

The solution: some form of lesbianism! Bianco offers Miley Cyrus as her role model. Most people might consider Cyrus a highly disturbed individual who is unable to maintain a relationship with herself, let alone with anyone else. I cannot help but think that Cyrus is headed for the asylum, or the morgue. Yet Bianco cites Miley Cyrus' split with Liam Hemsworth as more than celebrity gossip. "It's a blow to the patriarchy."[47] Bianco is not kidding about this.

In a way, the notion that women are a sort of proletariat being oppressed by men goes back to the 1970s, when Shulamith Firestone published *The Dialectic of Sex*. Firestone argued that the basic problem for women wasn't just patriarchal culture. It was nature itself, which assigned to women the reproductive function. Therefore, Firestone argued, in the same manner that Marx asked the worker proletariat to seize control of the means of production, women must seize control of the means of reproduction.

This means abortion. The fetus, Firestone argued, is an "uninvited guest." But it also means breaking what she termed the tyranny of the biological family by figuring out ways to have artificial reproduction, which is to say, reproduction outside the womb. This way children would still be born, but mothers wouldn't have to carry them; somehow both sexes would bear equal responsibility for the incubation process. Firestone was unclear about the specifics, but her ideological thrust could not be more clear.[48]

THE MAN WHO MISTOOK HIMSELF FOR A TOAD

One can see the radical gay and transgender movements as picking up on this same thread. Let's think for a minute about what it means to be "transgender." I have the biological equipment to be a boy, but I think I am a girl. So here we have a clash between biology and psychology. The traditional medical approach has always been that nature dictates biology, and when psychology refuses to come to terms with biology, there is an urgent need for therapeutic intervention.

The transgender movement wants to reverse that approach. Psychology trumps biology. Yet can nature be overridden in this way? Let's say that I want to be a toad. More precisely, let's say that I come to believe that I have always been a toad. I become convinced that I am in fact a toad trapped in a human body. Of course I don't have the biological equipment of a toad. But I feel that I am a toad. Therefore, I spend my days acting like a toad, jumping around in ponds and marshes, eating insects and making toad-like sounds.

Does the fact that I believe I'm a toad make me a toad? What happens if I then insist that society treat me like a toad? This means allowing me to audition for toad roles in Disney movies. It means competing in toad races. It means that toad jokes are entirely taboo; if I hear someone call me anything other than a toad, I become furious and accuse that person of being a hater and a neo-Nazi. I threaten to sue for discrimination or file a complaint with the federal government. At this point, I think you'll agree, we have entered never-never land.

There's a difference, you might say, between claiming to be a different gender and claiming to be a different species. Yes, but how is that difference relevant to the point at issue here? If, as leftists routinely say, "gender is a social construct," why isn't species membership also a social construct? Species themselves have evolved out of other species, and moreover, it takes a human and social system of classification to distinguish one species from another.

Recently the progressive online magazine Slate ran an article, "Teaching Young Dogs Old Tricks." This was a profile of a group of older and younger men who "imitate adolescent canine behavior in order to get off." We're talking here about men who put on collars and leashes and run around like dogs, sniffing each other's rear ends and, pardon my French, dog-f*cking each other. Apparently this sort of thing "happens regularly at leather bars across the country."

This particular group includes "two alphas, Turbo and Pup Midnight, who are the leaders . . . then there are two betas, Pup Fawks and Shadow, who are basically vice-alphas . . . one omega pup, Pup Arco, a submissive who services the pack in exchange for protection . . . Bullett who is their 'big and strong' guard pup, and Jumper, Amp and Astro, who don't have specific roles within the pack hierarchy." Slate presents this way of living as normal and healthy, quite a contrast, I'm sure they are convinced, from the oppressive atmosphere of the heterosexual household.[49]

The transgender issue is not a fight just about bathrooms and sporting events. Recently TV personality Mario Lopez said in an interview that he was "kind of blown away" by the whole transgender thing. "If you're three years old and you're saying you feel a certain way or you think you're a boy or a girl or whatever the case may be, I just think it's dangerous as a parent to make this determination then, OK, you're going to be a boy or a girl." Lopez added, "I'm never one to tell anyone how to parent their kids," but "when you're a kid, you don't know anything about sexuality yet. You're just a kid." Lopez concluded that parents should "allow their kids to be kids but at the same time, you gotta be the adult in the situation."

I cannot think of anything more sensible or innocuous, and Lopez took care to make all the appropriate qualifications. Even so, he was viciously attacked in the usual left-wing quarters, including CNN, NBC News and the Daily Beast. Much more troubling, the producers of *Access Hollywood* convened to discuss whether to remove Lopez as host of the program. Lopez seems to have saved his job only by apologizing. "The comments I made were ignorant and insensitive, and I now have a deeper understanding of how hurtful they were. Moving forward I will be more informed and thoughtful."[50]

The real story here is the reeducation of Mario Lopez. Reeducation is of course an old socialist technique, applied here in a new way. To put it in Marcuse's terms, the left had every right to be intolerant of Lopez's intolerance and to beat him into abject submission. And when journalist Andy Ngo recently showed up to cover an Antifa rally in Portland, the activists beat him so badly that he had injuries all over his body and a brain hemorrhage. Ngo's offense was nothing more than publicizing racial hoaxes and recording the violent tactics of Antifa and the left.

So what does the left want from Mario Lopez and Andy Ngo? They want them to embrace their race and gender hoaxes and their Moulin Rouge society. This isn't comprehensive Stalinism—in which, for example, there is an official position on classical music and chess—but rather limited Stalinism, in which there is an official position on every aspect of identity politics. The left's goal here is to stigmatize resistance as discrimination and to ruthlessly punish dissenters so that everyone is suitably warned. Socialism is a scheme for the trampling of human hearts.

Today we are living with an identity socialism that seeks not only an economic upheaval but also a cultural upheaval. Its goal is forced cultural conformity: "Here's our make-believe world that we are going to make you believe is real." They want to bludgeon us into accepting their imagined community in which good is evil and evil is good, in which deviancy of every kind is normal and normal behavior and feelings are rendered pathological, in which aliens are the true Americans and native-born citizens feel like aliens, an upside-down society where walruses can talk and pigs have wings.

4

VENEZUELA, SI; SWEDEN, NO

SOCIALISM AND THE SCANDINAVIAN ILLUSION

Viva Mission Sucre!
Viva Presidente Chavez!
Viva La Revolucion Bolivariana!
Hasta La Victoria Siempre![1]

—BILL AYERS, WORLD EDUCATION FORUM, 2006

The identity socialism we have been exploring so far is in some respects unique. Eager to distance their ship from earlier ones that have crashed into the reefs, American socialists and leftists are trying to chart their own distinctive course. Even so, it's impossible to sail without some sort of a compass, so it's worth asking: What is the guiding model for American socialism? If it's not the socialisms of the past, is there a socialist system today that moves and inspires them? The unanimous response of the American left is, yes there is.

That model, the progressive economist Paul Krugman insists, is not my wife Debbie's native country of Venezuela; it's Scandinavia. "Whenever you see someone invoking Venezuela as a reason not to consider progressive policy ideas," Krugman writes, "you know right away that the person in question is uninformed, dishonest or both." According to Krugman, Venezuela isn't really socialist. He wants us to ignore the insistence of Venezuela's former strongman Hugo Chavez that he was a socialist inspired by Marx and Castro. Or the Venezuelan regime's continuing practice of labeling virtually all consumer products "Hecho en Socialismo," which means "made in socialism."[2]

Krugman concedes that Venezuela is a "mess." But why? "Hugo Chavez got into power because of rage against the nation's elite, but used the power badly. He seized the oil sector, which you only do if you can run it honestly and efficiently; instead he turned it over to corrupt cronies, who degraded its performance. Then, when oil prices fell, his successor tried to cover the income gap by printing money. Hence the crisis."

One might see here the familiar narrative of socialist failure, but Krugman goes in a different direction. "It's a bad story, and not without precedent. Macroeconomic populism has a long history in Latin America, and usually comes to grief." Don't miss the veiled allusion to Trump. Chavez and Maduro were populists, and that's what brought their nation down! Just like the other populist we could name in the White House.

Of course, Krugman knows that Chavez and Maduro's so-called Bolivarian Revolution was carried out in the name of socialism. Chavez too insisted he was creating a new type of socialism, free from the debris of earlier failed versions. He called it "socialism for the twenty-first century." Krugman puts on his most innocent face. Sure, sure, "but what, exactly, does any of this have to do with the policy ideas of Elizabeth Warren, or Kamala Harris, or even a genuine radical like Alexandria Ocasio-Cortez?" I'm not sure if Krugman here is uninformed or dishonest. In any event, in this chapter, I'll supply the answer to his question.

The point of Krugman's rhetorical performance—we have to call it a performance—is to distance the American left from Venezuela and connect it to Scandinavia. What American progressives want, he writes, is for America to "look like Denmark or Norway, not Venezuela." The same point is made by Krugman's allies on the American left. "Europe is not Venezuela," columnist Roger Cohen writes in *The New York Times*. "We're not talking about Maduro in Venezuela," economist Joseph Stiglitz emphasizes in a recent interview.[3]

Historian Michael Kazin, editor of *Dissent*, adds, "What democratic socialists want is closer to what exists in Scandinavia or Iceland." Bhaskar Sunkara in *The Socialist Manifesto* is positively rhapsodic about the Scandinavians. "Sweden in the 1970s was not simply the most livable society in history; it was also the European country where . . . socialists got the furthest along in undermining capital's power."[4] Sunkara wants American socialists to model themselves not just on Sweden but on Sweden in the 1970s, specifically 1974–76. That was the two-year period when the socialists really got things right!

Even Scandinavia today, the socialist blogger Matt Bruenig writes, provides an inspiring example. Lest readers think he is backing away from hard-core socialism, Bruenig insists that "Norway is far more socialist than Venezuela." While both are oil-rich countries, Bruenig solemnly notes that Norway deposits its oil revenues into a capital fund that it specifically labels "the people's money, owned by everyone, divided equally and for generations to come." Venezuela doesn't split its oil bounties in quite this way, and therefore the Norwegians are the true socialists.[5]

Bernie Sanders and Alexandria Ocasio-Cortez both echo these sentiments. Neither one has said a critical word about Venezuelan socialism. Yet they refuse to embrace it. What they do embrace, however, is what may be termed "Nordic socialism." I call it "Sven Socialism"—socialism developed for people named Sven. Even if you don't know a Sven, you know the type. Sven carries a feminine handbag, rides his bicycle to work, recycles his trash and is into some weird sexual stuff he'd rather not talk about. This is the pursuit of happiness, Scandinavian style.

Nietzsche had a name for Sven: the "last man." Nietzsche had nothing but contempt for this insufferable type, who never disturbs himself with a noble thought, who never risks his life for something greater than himself, whose life is defined by a high self-regard and comfortable self-preservation. Even so, Sven fancies himself a pretty nice guy— "I've never killed anybody, you know, and I really hate neo-Nazis"—and Bernie Sanders, himself a member of the breed, agrees. While Soviet socialism failed, Bernie told an audience in Burlington, Iowa, "I think that countries like Denmark and Sweden do very well."

Ocasio-Cortez said in a *60 Minutes* interview that her policies "most closely resemble what we see in the U.K., in Norway, in Finland, in Sweden." She even specified how the model might apply to America. "Your tax rate, you know, let's say from zero to $75,000, may be 10 percent or 15 percent, et cetera. But once you get to, like, the tippy tops—on your

10 millionth dollar—sometimes you see tax rates as high as 60 or 70 percent."[6] This is AOC's take on Sven Socialism, a complete howler, as we'll see, and indicative of how American leftists aren't just clueless but have no genuine interest in how things actually work in the Scandinavian countries.

THANK GOD FOR SCANDINAVIA

The Scandinavian model is crucial to the American left because Norway, Denmark and Sweden seem like relatively nice places to live. So are Iceland and Finland, if you can endure the frigid winters. Thus, Sven Socialism appears to show that socialism at least works somewhere. This is encouraging for American socialists who must typically confront a dreary landscape of failed socialist regimes, past and present. Cuba isn't looking so good, Zimbabwe is a disaster, North Korea is worse, Venezuela is beyond redemption, so thank God for Scandinavia.

After all, from the left's point of view, if there is at least one working model someplace in the world, it salvages the whole concept of a viable socialism. If socialism works there, maybe it can also work here. A Scandinavian socialism, imported to America, would represent a sort of second landing. The Vikings, after all, were probably the first Europeans to land in America. Leif Erikson seems to have visited American shores around 500 years before Columbus. But he left hardly a trace. Now the Scandinavians have another chance to leave their imprint, this time not through raiding ships but through Americans remaking their society according to a Scandinavian recipe.

Recognizing the significance of the Scandinavian model—which is all the rage on the American left—conservatives have set about debunking it. "Sorry Bernie . . . But Nordic Countries Are Not Socialist," reads the headline of a column by Jeffrey Dorfman in *Forbes*. "The Myth of Scandinavian Socialism," from the free market group FEE, stresses that the socialism of the Scandinavians has been greatly exaggerated. In a recent article in *Reason*, John Stossel zoomed in on a single country, making his point in a telling headline: "Sweden Isn't Socialist."[7]

There is a good deal going for this argument, as I'll show later in this chapter. In some respects, Nordic nations seem more free market than the United States. In 2015, the prime minister of Denmark, Lars Løkke Rasmussen, intervened in the debate to clarify, "I know that some people in the US associate the Nordic model with some sort of socialism. Therefore, I would like to make one thing clear. Denmark is far from a socialist planned economy. Denmark is a market economy."[8] True enough. Yet if you think about it, the conservative rebuttal is inadequate.

After all, the left can easily respond, "Fine, if you don't think the Scandinavian countries are socialist, then you should be fine with America following their example. If Sven Socialism is truly capitalism, let's go ahead and emulate it. Let's have 50–70 percent marginal income tax rates. Let's have a 25 percent VAT or value-added tax on all consumer products. Let's have in America the whole menu of Nordic entitlements: free healthcare, free education, ambitious climate change policies and the rest of it. It's wonderful to have you on board for this Nordic capitalist agenda."

Matt Bruenig italicizes the fallacy of the right-wing rebuttal. "On the one hand," he writes, "they say that the Nordic countries are not actually very socialist." They are capitalist! Yet since conservatives know about the lavish array of Nordic welfare state programs, they insist at the same time that "the countries have terrible outcomes." Putting the two themes together, Bruenig draws the logical conclusion that Nordic capitalism produces terrible outcomes.[9] This is a gotcha that confirms the need for reframing the conservative position.

I'm going to make a different argument. I'm not denying the existence of Nordic socialism. Nor do I deny that this type of socialism works to a point. What I deny is that it can be imported here. We cannot have Scandinavian socialism because we don't have the conditions for it. Our type of society doesn't permit it. Moreover—and this is the telling point—the American left doesn't want it. If we could somehow transplant the Scandinavian model here—if we could all "go Norwegian" as it were—the left would consider the result a nightmare. If I'm right, then there is no Scandinavian model for the United States to look to. The left's entire invocation of Scandinavian socialism is a fraud.

Why do I say this? The key to understanding Scandinavian socialism is that it is "unification socialism," very different from the "division socialism" that is characteristic of the American left. Unification socialism is the socialism of the tribe, and its distinguishing features are tribal homogeneity and tribal solidarity. The whole point is to gather the society into a single unit. The motto of unification socialism is that we are one people; we are in this together. The burdens of survival, and the fruits of prosperity, must be broadly shared by the whole society.

In the old Viking days, of course, Scandinavian solidarity was the product of the demands of survival in an extremely harsh climate. Viking tribes gained their booty in part through seafaring raids on other coastal peoples. They then shared it among themselves. The Vikings obviously had chiefs and ordinary raiders, but the key point is that the distance between the chief and the ordinary raider was much smaller than the distance between the Vikings as a group and everyone else. So there was close identification between the chief and his men, preserving the solidarity of the tribe.

Today the climate is no less harsh—those shivering Nordics could use some global warming—but the booty is more peacefully generated. Yet Nordic culture has preserved that sense of tribal solidarity that enables those countries to distribute their wealth fairly widely in the confident belief that they are helping "our people." Gert Tinggaard Svendsen, a political scientist at Denmark's Aarhus University, says that "the Nordic welfare state works due to trust. You have to trust that people work and pay taxes when they are able to do so. The second condition is that you also have to trust the politicians."[10]

Work when you don't have to? Trust the politicians? One can see right away how distant the Nordic psychology is from the American. But my point is not merely that the Nordic approach violates the tradition of the American founding. It also violates the root assumptions of American socialists. The root assumption here is that America is not a single tribe. Diversity, not unity, is our defining characteristic and strength. The left here separates society into various subgroups: rich and poor, black and white, immigrant and native. The whole structure is based on "us" against "them." Socialism in America means forcing groups defined as "oppressors" to submit and pay up to groups defined as "victims."

Nothing could be more alien to the spirit of Scandinavian socialism.

None of the Nordic countries vilifies their rich. None of them preaches the politics of ethnic division. None of them exalts immigrants over natives, or illegal aliens over citizens. On the contrary, they preach the politics of ethnic unity. They stress the uniformity of Nordic culture. There is no "us" versus "them," there is only "us." The Nordics insist that immigrants adopt Nordic culture for themselves, and become very agitated—indeed lose their enthusiasm for immigration itself—when they don't.

For these reasons, American leftists who have thought about the subject realize they don't want Nordic socialism. They realize it can't work in America, and quite separately from that, it holds no appeal for them.

PEOPLE LIKE US

When I think of what makes Nordic socialism distinctive, I'm reminded of Joel Kotkin's book *Tribes*, in which the author discusses some of the world's most successful groups. He names a handful—the Jews, the Mormons, the Asian Indians—and shows how they have not only survived but also thrived in the face of persecution or hardship. One key to their success, Kotkin argues, is their "strong sense of identity."[11] This identity may be based on ethnic kinship, as in the case of the Asian Indians, but it doesn't have to be. It can also be based on religious identification, as with the Mormons, or cultural identification, as with the Jews.

When tribal unity is strong, it generates trust. This trust can be preserved even in diaspora. In fact, it is the basis of international networks that operate with relatively little legal formality. These people don't need airtight contracts, because they are dealing among their kin, which is to say, within the tribe. Asian Indians in Toronto, Dubai and Jackson Heights can send money home, hundreds or even thousands of miles away, in the confidence that it will sustain the welfare of their kinsmen, even if they cannot closely monitor how the money is disbursed.

In the Middle Ages, the Muslim writer Ibn Khaldun used precisely this concept of tribal solidarity—which he called *asabiyah*—to advance a novel theory of history. Tribes that develop strong *asabiyah*, according to Khaldun, become very good fighters, and they also sustain strong communities. Khaldun gives the example of the Bedouins, who survived demanding desert conditions through *asabiyah*. So strong was their loyalty to each other and to their way of life that "if one of them were to find ways and means of fleeing from these conditions, he would not give them up."

Later the Arab Muslims used the same *asabiyah* to launch their military conquests abroad. Arab *asabiyah* was always tribal, but through Islam it was also fortified by a strong religious identity. No wonder, Khaldun writes, that the Arab Muslims were so fearsome in battle. They were able to defeat much larger numerical armies through superior *asabiyah*. Yet success breeds complacency and, just as important, a dissolution of *asabiyah*. When a tribe loses its *asabiyah*, it atrophies or becomes easy prey for a different tribe with stronger *asabiyah*.[12]

This kind of tribal identification that Kotkin and Khaldun both praise is reminiscent of the socialism—even communism—that operates within the nuclear family. The nuclear family, if we think about it, is based on a fundamental Marxist concept: "From each according to his ability, to each according to his needs." Of course, this is not the end of the story. Families strive, at least healthy ones, to prepare the dependent children to become independent. Unlike some modern forms of socialism, they don't promote a condition of enduring immaturity and dependency. Yet while the children are growing up, the Marxist principle prevails.

The earliest forms of socialism, going back to the early nineteenth century, can be understood as an extension of this family principle. I'm thinking here of the small utopian communities in England, France and Germany, created by the likes of Robert Owen, Henri Saint-Simon and Charles Fourier. These were voluntary communities based on a shared vision. They functioned largely through consensus, which means they sought the elimination of faction. Members of the community willingly shared their possessions because they functioned as one extended family, with no sharp lines among the members.

There is an early Christian precedent for this. Brought together through a tight sense of religious identification—an identification strengthened by terror and persecution—the early Christians functioned as a kind of socialist commune. "No one claimed that any of their possessions was their own," we read in the Book of Acts, "but they shared everything they had" and "there were no needy persons among them." Here we see the roots of Scandinavian socialism; it builds on the unification impulse of the early socialists and manifests as a secular version of the huddled unity that characterized the early Christians.

Marx is the founder of the division socialism that has since characterized most of its forms and continues to define the socialism of the American left. Marx ridiculed the early socialist communities as experiments in impossibility, quixotic "bubble-blowing," "ready made nonsense" and "idealistic humbug." Why? Because although they were billed as model communities, they didn't provide a model for anything. They might offer a surrogate community for a small number of people who didn't fit very well into the larger society. But they offered no way to transform society as a whole.

Marx argued that a powerful economic structure like capitalism doesn't give way without a fight. Powerful people like capitalists don't submit unless they are pressured or overthrown. Consequently, socialism can come only via the class struggle. There has to be a Manichean division in society between capitalists and workers, or between the bad guys and the good guys. The good guys win by overthrowing the bad guys. This can be done through revolution, violently, or through democracy, peacefully. But either way, it's a fight.

We see an echo of this Marxist Manicheanism in FDR, who taunted, reviled and sought to humiliate the capitalist class. In a speech in 1936—the very one advancing his Second Bill of Rights—FDR identified his wealthy Republican opponents as plutocrats, describing them as "the forces of selfishness and of lust for power." Of them he said, "They are unanimous in their hatred of me—and I welcome their hatred." In his first term, FDR declared, he had proved their "match," but in his second, he would prove himself their "master."

Here we see how FDR uses the rhetoric of class warfare, of social division, to expand his electoral majority so as to more effectively reduce the power and wealth of the plutocratic class. He literally wants to kick them out of America. If they don't like his New Deal, he says, they are "aliens to the spirit of American democracy. Let them emigrate and try their lot under some foreign flag in which they have more confidence."[13]

In this way, FDR sought to make wealthy Republicans feel like outsiders in the America of the 1930s. This was the beginning of the leftist scheme to make us feel like strangers in our own country.

Identity socialism continues—indeed intensifies—the politics of social division. For identity socialism there are not merely two opposing categories—the rich and the poor—but several: whites against minorities, men against women, heterosexuals against homosexuals and transsexuals and natives against immigrants. Whites, men, heterosexuals and the native-born are all bad, but nothing is worse than the combination of these four attributes. The identity socialists then mobilize a martial rhetoric to crusade against their great reviled totem: the white male native-born heterosexual.

The symbol of this evil—the totem himself—is of course Donald Trump. Beto O'Rourke calls him a white nationalist. Elizabeth Warren says that "he has given aid and comfort to white supremacists." Biden insists that Trump "has fanned the flames of white supremacy." According to Alexandria Ocasio-Cortez, a "core part" of Trump's coalition was racists together with "all sorts of other people that could be susceptible to racist views."[14] Notice how the indictment has moved from Trump to Trump supporters.

The week of Trump's election, the writer Toni Morrison argued that, "unlike any nation in Europe, the United States holds whiteness as the unifying force." And who are the Americans who respond to the call of whiteness? "They are willing to kill small children attending Sunday school," to "slaughter churchgoers," to "set fire to churches and to start firing in them while the members are at prayer" and to "shoot black children in the street."[15] Is there any basis for unity here, for drawing these people into a beloved community? Of course not. Morrison wants them stigmatized, routed, ruined. This is the point of her incendiary rhetoric.

Beto O'Rourke recently said that "this country is founded on white supremacy and every single institution and structure that we have in our country still reflects the legacy of the slavery and segregation and Jim Crow and suppression."[16] In earlier decades, such extravagant rhetoric was rare, but not in today's Democratic Party. Several of the other leading Democrats could easily have said it, and some have said similar things.

For *The New York Times*, it's not enough to trace America's racial sins to the founders, because that still leaves as innocent the Americans who lived before the founding. At the *Times*, the feeling is "let's go get them too." This is the mission of the so-called 1619 Project, recently announced with great fanfare by the newspaper. The whole point of going back to 1619, more than a century and a half before the founding, is to racialize all of American history, to spread the racial indictment to all Americans.

The spirit of the special issue is captured in Nikole Hannah-Jones' contention that "anti-black racism runs in the very DNA of this country."[17] This contradicts what historians—even progressive historians—have been saying for half a century. In his book *Racism*, the Marxist historian George Fredrickson writes that "racism as an ideology of inherent black inferiority emerged . . . in reaction to the rise of northern abolitionism in the 1830s." Moreover, "Antiblack racism peaked in the period between the end of Reconstruction and the First World War."[18]

Fredrickson's dates are important, because they coincide with the rise and humiliating defeat of the Democratic Party. Antiblack racism runs congruent to those developments. Indeed, prior to 1860, the Democratic Party was the party of the slave plantation, and it trafficked in racism as a justification of slavery. After the Civil War, Democrats promoted racism as a doctrine of biological inferiority. Leading Democrats founded the Ku Klux Klan in the late nineteenth century and then, after Republicans shut it down, revived it in the early twentieth century.

This is the elephant—or perhaps I should say donkey—in the living room. Even Fredrickson says nothing about how Democrats backed slavery and segregation, and how Republicans fought to stop them. Today the left continues with this project of concealment. It doesn't want people—especially young people—to know the role of the Democrats in protecting slavery and advancing racism. Hence the pivot back to 1619! This way "America" gets the blame for what the Democrats did.

What we see here is a systematic effort on the part of the American left to use various categories of oppression—race, gender, class and so on—to divide society into good guys and bad guys. Then their good guys band together to create an electoral majority for the left's operating vehicle, the Democratic Party. Through this majority, they seek to overthrow the power of the bad guys. They do not hesitate—indeed, they consider it right and just—to confiscate the earnings and possessions of the bad guys to support and enrich themselves.

In a sense, this is the old Viking model in a transposed form, only the looters and the looted—the raiders and the raided—are now in the same society. Consequently, they can hardly be expected to be friends. Those who are being raided have a natural enmity toward those who are taking their stuff. FDR understood this, which is why he vilified opponents and made no attempt to persuade or appeal to them. Neither does the left today. The left understands that any solidarity that the raided express for the raiders cannot be natural or voluntary; it must be coerced.

Consequently, division socialism takes on its intolerant aspect. This is the "intolerance toward intolerance" that Marcuse advocated. In this Marcusian spirit, the left today makes strenuous attempts to intimidate and bludgeon those whose possessions are being taken to quietly succumb to the takers. Those who protest are branded as bigots and haters who deserve to be silenced, fired, prosecuted or imprisoned if necessary, but in one way or another driven to the margins of society.

The Scandinavians would be appalled and horrified; imagine a Swede or Norwegian doing this to a fellow Swede or Norwegian! No Scandinavian has ever identified American socialism as resembling Scandinavian socialism, even in embryo. The defining features of American socialism and the American left—identity politics, class and ethnic division, and social intimidation to enforce these categories—are simply absent in the Nordic countries.

WHITE ON WHITE

The aversion is actually a two-way street. I'm not aware of a single American socialist who wants what the Scandinavians have. Not even Bernie Sanders. The reasons for this are not merely temperamental. Rather, they go back to Madison's discussions in *The Federalist* about how large extended republics cannot work on the same model as a small homogeneous society.

Small homogeneous societies such as ancient Athens or Crete essentially seek to eliminate factions, especially economic factions. To put this in socialist terms, their goal is a one-class society. Madison insisted that factions are inevitable in a large extended republic. They reflect competing values and interests, and they cannot be eliminated. So the founding architecture is designed to accommodate this brute fact, in Madison's terms, to steer the course of factional politics toward the common welfare of society.

Deep down, the American left agrees with this. That's why leading figures of the left never go to Scandinavia. It's a striking fact. Earlier I mentioned how leftists have, from the early days of socialism, made regular pilgrimages to socialist countries to observe their wonders, to study their greatness, and to report back to Americans on how we should be heading in their direction. Yet how many such reports have we seen from the Nordic countries? Hardly any! Even Sanders, who has Scandinavian roots and seems to have visited every socialist landmark on the planet, has never been to Scandinavia.

If an American leftist visited, let's say, Norway, he or she would find a country that is 90 percent white, with over 80 percent of its population being ethnic Norwegians of Germanic descent and another 10 percent being whites from other European regions. There are fewer than 100,000 blacks in the country. Around 3 percent of the population is Muslim. If diversity is the American left's mantra for America, there's not a whole lot of that in Norway, or in most of the Scandinavian countries. If Elizabeth Warren or Bernie Sanders did an outdoor Christmas photo op with the Norwegian socialists, it would be an all-white image with very white people, many in white outfits, mostly with white hair, against a white background.

The white ethnic Norwegians form a dominant majority bloc. They set the tone for the whole country. And Norway is not alone in this. When journalist Robert Kaiser returned from a three-week trip to Finland, he reported that this tiny country, with just over 5 million residents, is "ethnically and religiously homogeneous." The Finns, he said, look alike and think alike. "Groupthink seems to be fine with most Finns; conformity is the norm." Politics is based on consensus, and the major political parties are no more than a few inches apart.[19]

In Scandinavian countries, more generally, people consider themselves to be of one group, one class. There are no "oppressors" and "oppressed." There is no "white privilege." There are no figures like Christopher Columbus to vilify; no Scandinavian has been known to burn his country's flag. Since there are no taboos to uphold, political correctness takes on a whole different aspect in Scandinavia. In the American sense, it doesn't really exist. So the whole template of leftist politics that we are familiar with in this country, rooted in identity politics, is pretty much inapplicable to Scandinavia.

Nor would the American left find much to emulate in the way the Nordic countries deal with immigrants. For the most part, the black and brown immigrants to Scandinavian countries are largely indigestible. They are visitors of a sort in Nordic society. This is another hallmark of tribal communities. Their tribal identity is rooted in blood, language and culture, and there is no easy way to incorporate outsiders of a different ethnicity, who speak a different language and practice different religions.

The Muslims in Norway, who came mainly as refugees from Syria and Africa, are themselves a sort of tribe, and they could hardly be more different from the Norwegian tribe. The Norwegians are mostly secular; the Muslims are fanatically religious. The Norwegians are sexually "liberated"; the Muslims are not. Norwegians have no intention of dissolving their own tribe; consequently, they have been shutting the door on immigration and have advanced proposals such as a recent one to relocate new immigrants to a small island off the Norwegian coast.

"We're going to minimize the number of ferry departures as much as possible," said Martin Henriksen, a spokesman for the coalition government in Norway. "We're going to make it as cumbersome and expensive as possible." Danish prime minister Lars Løkke Rasmussen, who once boasted that his country had no border walls, now sounds a different tune. Responding to public opinion in Denmark, Rasmussen has stressed that his government's goal is not to have refugees stay permanently but to eventually return home. In his words, "We should not make refugees immigrants."[20]

Carl Melin, policy director at the Swedish research institute Futurion, says that Swedes built the welfare state for themselves, not for outsiders. He remarks that his country has been cutting back on immigration because of the realization that "people are quite open to showing solidarity for people who are like themselves. They don't show solidarity for people who are different." The same note is sounded by Urban Pettersson, a council member in the town of Filipstad, in the lake country of Sweden. "It's interesting to meet someone from another country for maybe half an hour," he says. But living with them and supporting them is something else. "People don't want to pay taxes" Pettersson adds, "to support refugees who don't work."

These problems are not unique to the Nordic countries; to some degree, they afflict all of Europe. In this country, it is possible for a Nigerian, a Korean or an Asian Indian to "become American." But it has proved far more difficult for a Turk to become a German, for a Pakistani to become an Englishman, for a Syrian to become a Swede. This is widely understood throughout Europe, and the Swedish language itself confirms it. The modern Swedish term for "immigrant" does not mean a foreign-born person but rather a non-Nordic person in Sweden.

Part of the problem for the nonwhite immigrants goes beyond race and ethnicity. Scandinavian countries may provide greater security but they also provide lesser social mobility, compared with the United States. Their leaders admit this. Recently Ida Auken, a member of the Danish parliament, wrote in *The Washington Post* that Denmark "scores low when it comes to creating social mobility that may elevate people from the bottom to the top of society. If your parents have no or little education, chances are high you will end up at the same level yourself, even in Denmark." This is broadly true of all socialist societies, and broadly untrue of all capitalist or entrepreneurial societies.[21]

The point is that the American model has proven far more hospitable to nonwhite immigrants than the Nordic model, and leftists in this country realize that. American socialists who look like Rashida Tlaib, Ilhan Omar and Alexandria Ocasio-Cortez would never dream of moving to Scandinavia, because they would be permanent aliens there, even if they secured local citizenship. No American socialist wants America's racial landscape to resemble that of Denmark, Norway, Sweden or Finland. In Scandinavia, "diversity" is perceived as a weakness, not a strength.

DESTINATION CARACAS

If Scandinavian socialism is not the model, then what is? We can answer this question by seeing where American socialists have been going on pilgrimage in the past couple of decades. The short answer is: Venezuela. Venezuela has long been a multiracial society, as America now is. Venezuela has precisely the kind of division socialism that the American left admires and practices. Not surprisingly, a whole troop of American leftists have gone to Venezuela to witness "socialism in the twenty-first century." Many have urged that we import some of it here.

Oddly enough, this is how I met my wife, Debbie. Some years ago, she stumbled across a series of videos made by Bill Ayers. Yes, that Bill Ayers! The former domestic terrorist and cofounder of the Weather Underground had made several trips to Venezuela. Debbie knew I had debated Bill Ayers on television, and she wanted me to help publicize what Ayers was conniving with the Venezuelan socialists.

The tapes represented conversations between Ayers and senior education officials under Hugo Chavez. Ayers could not have been more excited about the socialist indoctrination in Venezuelan schools. He wanted to find a way to do that in America. In a 2006 speech at the World Education Forum in Caracas, with Hugo Chavez himself in attendance, Ayers spoke about how "education is the motor force of revolution" and how "Venezuela is a beacon to the world" because it was "poised to offer the world a new model of education—a humanizing and revolutionary model whose twin missions are enlightenment and liberation."[22]

That same year, the African American scholar Cornel West toured Venezuela as part of a left-wing delegation that included the actors Harry Belafonte and Danny Glover. All three were enraptured by Venezuelan socialism. Belafonte told the Venezuelan dictator, "Chavez, I was retired from politics. Now I'm engaged again." West said, "I love that Hugo Chavez has made poverty a major priority. I wish America would make poverty a priority." Glover gushed later, "We all embraced Hugo Chavez as a social champion of democracy, material development and spiritual well-being."

Joseph Stiglitz, the left-wing economist, visited Venezuela in 2007 and praised the country's "very impressive" growth rate. He praised Hugo Chavez for his "equitable" distribution of oil revenues and said that he "appears to have had success in bringing health and education to the people in the poor neighborhoods of Caracas." The socialist pundit Noam Chomsky found his way to Venezuela in 2009 and appeared with Chavez at a public rally. He reported, "What's so exciting about at last visiting Venezuela is that I can see how a better world is being created."

Jimmy Carter first met Hugo Chavez during his first presidential campaign in 1998. Carter was back in Venezuela in 2012 to declare, amid widespread allegations of voter fraud, that the country's election system was the "best in the world." Carter said of Chavez, "We came to know a man who expressed a vision to bring profound changes to his country to benefit especially those people who had felt neglected and marginalized. . . . We have never doubted Hugo Chavez's commitment to improving the lives of millions of his fellow countrymen."

The Hollywood left was enamored with Chavez. Michael Moore, who met Chavez at the 2009 Venice Film Festival, tweeted on the occasion of Chavez's death in 2013, "Hugo Chavez declared the oil belonged 2 the ppl. He used the oil $ 2 eliminate 75% of extreme poverty, provide free health & education 4 all." Movie director Oliver Stone was also a Chavez enthusiast and made a 2009 documentary, *South of the Border,* celebrating the achievements of Venezuelan socialism. Sean Penn visited Venezuela so often that Chavez once joked that he should be named U.S. ambassador in Caracas. Penn said at Chavez's funeral that thanks to his leadership "Venezuela and its revolution will endure."

Supermodel Naomi Campbell went to Venezuela to interview Chavez and reported that she was "amazed by what I have seen here in only 24 hours." The interview, published in the British edition of *GQ,* is an exercise in hero worship: "The first time I met Chavez, I was a little nervous walking into the palace, but he put me at ease"; "He really admires women and told me that when he completes his term in office, he would like a woman to succeed him"; "He also loves to sing. I believe if he wasn't the president he'd be a very successful Latin singer."[23]

The point of all this is not to test the veracity of these observations— they are pure rubbish, more revealing of the speaker than the subject—

but to show how the left has long considered Venezuela as its actual dream and inspiration. There is no comparable literature of leftist political pilgrimage to Norway or Sweden. There are no comparable paeans to the Finnish prime minister, no Naomi Campbell to say, "I believe if he wasn't the president he'd be a very successful ice fisherman." Venezuela, not Scandinavia, is the left's model, and it is Venezuela that supplies the road map for where we seem to be headed if we choose the socialist path.

WHY ANDREW YANG FEELS SO GENEROUS

Now let's take up the "free stuff" the socialist left is promising Americans—Medicare for All, free college, elimination of most or all existing college debt, Universal Basic Income, a mandated $15-per-hour minimum wage, a generous package of unemployment benefits, childcare subsidies, mandated paid leave and all the rest. Here there is virtually no limit to the craziness. Since most of the leading Democrats want a $15-per-hour minimum wage, Rashida Tlaib ups the socialist ante by proposing $20 per hour. Somewhere I just know there is an even bigger crackpot ready to propose a $100-per-hour minimum wage.

Why not? After all, he's not paying for it. Even the government doesn't have to pay. The government merely mandates that employers pay. If they can't, there is always the option of them going out of business. For socialists, business shutdowns are not a mark of political failure; they are a mark of success, because they involve a diminution of the capitalist system. We can detect the same attitude behind Bill de Blasio's proposal for compulsory paid vacations in the five boroughs because "New Yorkers need a break."[24] If you can't afford it, close down your shop and go to work someplace else, where you can force that guy to pay for your vacation as long as he stays in business.

On the surface, this nonstop, sky's-the-limit welfare state expansion resembles the Scandinavian model, since the Scandinavians offer some (though not all) of this. The Scandinavians justify it in terms of "social insurance," and ostensibly this is what the American left also seeks. Here I will show, however, that the resemblance is merely superficial. Upon examination, we can easily see that the two models are completely different.

The Scandinavian model is based on genuine social insurance. Sweden even has a government-run Social Insurance Agency (Försäkringskassan). Look on the website, and you will see little talk of "entitlements" and even less of "free stuff." Think about what insurance means. Citizens pool their money into a pot, so that if any of them falls into distress, the common pool can be used to ameliorate that distress. This is how the Scandinavians designed their welfare state: everyone is expected to act responsibly, and everyone, including the poor and the middle class, is taxed heavily.

The underlying image of the welfare state is not one of a "safety net" but rather one of the "nest," in which all the birds work diligently to sustain a common habitat. The Finnish use the term *talkoot*, which means "doing work together," or more generally, "we're all in the same boat." The operating principle of Scandinavian socialism is that we're all in this together, so the burden must be shared across the society and everyone has to pay.

By contrast, the American left and the Democratic Party operate on the principle that "free stuff" is truly free. The proposals of free healthcare, free education and free monthly checks all come with the tantalizing promise that someone else is going to pay. Not one Democratic candidate will stand up at a rally, point his finger toward the audience, and say, "The government is going to provide, and you are the ones who are going to pay for it." This would bring an awkward, menacing silence. The reason for the cheering is the audience's excitement over its realization that their bills and benefits will be footed by some other guy.

This isn't social insurance; it's theft socialism. In this country, the socialists want to stick the bill on Wall Street, or the rich, or the vilified "1 percent." The strategy is to target an affluent minority that will be shoved up against the wall and forced to pay for the education, healthcare and monthly expenses of Democratic voters. In this way, the Democrats seek to create a majority coalition of dependent voters who can put, and keep, the left in power.

Let's watch these scams at work. I'll begin with the Universal Basic Income scam, a hot topic in the media and also apparently in the progressive precincts of Silicon Valley, and most closely associated with the former Democratic presidential candidate Andrew Yang. Pete Buttigieg says that Universal Basic Income is an idea "worth taking seriously."

Kamala Harris has also tiptoed in this direction with a "livable incomes" proposal that would provide cash grants to working families earning up to $100,000.

Innumerable leftist writers tout the promise of Universal Basic Income.[25] The general idea here is for the government to give everyone money, regardless of income, regardless of need. Harris' proposal is in this sense anomalous; most basic income proposals have no wage or work limitations. The typical scheme calls for the government to provide all American adults with a fixed monthly sum, typically in the range of $500–$1,000 a month, to cover their basic needs.

In theory, Universal Basic Income is intended to replace existing government handouts. In this respect, it's appealing because of its simplicity and because it gives people a choice in how to solve their own problems. Instead of saying, "Here are some food stamps that can only be spent in this way" and "Here is a housing subsidy that must be applied in that way," the government says, "Here's some cash. Now go take care of yourself." The conservative economist Milton Friedman proposed his own version of this—which he called a "negative income tax"—a generation ago.

Yang's program involves a government giveaway of $1,000 a month to every adult. Now to send 150 million Americans a monthly check for $1,000 would obviously cost a great deal of money. I'll do the math for you: it works out to $150 billion a month, or just under $1.8 trillion a year. That's half the entire federal budget. As *Wired* magazine notes, the only way the nation could bankroll this sort of program would be to get rid of many if not most existing social programs.[26] But there's the rub. No Democrat wants to do that. Not even Yang.

Many poor people get existing subsidies that far exceed $1,000 a month. Consider a poor person of retirement age with health problems. Obviously $1,000 a month would scarcely provide a "safety net." His basic needs are much greater. So existing federal programs target the needy and don't seek to provide "basic income" to the entire adult population. Yet if you keep existing programs and add Universal Basic Income, you've basically come up with a formula to bankrupt the federal government.

No Scandinavian country has Universal Basic Income. In a much-heralded experiment, Finland briefly tried one in 2016. A Finnish welfare agency proposed paying every adult Finn between 550 and 700 euros a month. The Finnish government decided to try the idea on 2,000 people, but to limit it to those receiving unemployment benefits.

So it was no longer a "Universal Basic Income plan" but rather an "unemployment benefits" plan. The government then decided that its goal was not to guarantee a standard of living, but rather to get people who weren't working to find jobs. It declared that the "primary goal" of the experiment was "related to promoting employment." Once the Finns realized that the plan didn't do that, they got rid of it in early 2018, less than two years later.[27]

Yang regularly promises on the campaign trail that he will "give every American adult $1,000 a month until the day you die." He has Washington, D.C., resident David Han, who counts himself a member of the "Yang Gang," convinced. "No other candidate is going to cut that check. Andrew Yang will cut that check for all of us."[28] But of course Yang isn't cutting any checks out of his bankbooks. In fact, he's not giving away anything. As a high-tech fellow, he's reasonably well-off, but he can't afford to give $1,000 a month to people in his neighborhood, let alone all American working-age citizens.

What is Yang saying? What he's saying to me, if I read between the lines, is that he has designed a program for the federal government to give all eligible Americans, including me, $1,000 a month. So far, so good! I'm not going to be hard to convince that I'm "entitled" to it. To fund this program, he intends to tax an affluent segment of the population, which is to say, people like me.

The plot thickens! And now I get it. Basically I'm going to end up paying $5,000 or more per month for Yang's program, and then he'll turn around and return $1,000 a month to me. Obviously he could have saved himself the trouble by simply taxing me an additional $4,000 a month.

So why doesn't he do that? Because he wants to make it look like he's giving me a benefit, when he's actually ripping me off. If he said to me, "Dinesh, why don't you go around to four of your neighbors every month and hand them $1,000 apiece?" I would hardly believe what I was hearing. Then the following dialog would likely ensue:

> Me: In exchange for what?
> Yang: In exchange for nothing.
> Me: What! Just to prove I'm a nice guy?
> Yang: No, to prove that *I'm* a nice guy! Then you can all send me a
> thank-you note for arranging the transaction.

Sounds insane. Yet this is the precise clinical description of what he is saying. Yang hopes, however, that by processing the transaction through the state he can camouflage its true nature and claim dishonest credit for "giving" citizens what amounts to their own money. Instead of proposing the familiar type of transfer program, Yang seeks to create the illusion that everyone is benefiting and no one is being ripped off. After all, Yang is the one who is "giving" us all free income to which we are presumably "entitled," regardless of whether we work or need it. In short, a transparent scam.

DO FINNISH DOCTORS WORK FOR FREE?

Now I turn to the free college scam. Many leading Democrats are on board—Cory Booker, Kirsten Gillibrand, Kamala Harris—but the two obvious standouts are Bernie Sanders and Elizabeth Warren, both of whom have proposed schemes not merely for tuition-free college but also for canceling all existing student loan debt.[29] Sanders and Warren make earlier college subsidy schemes, of the kind advanced in 2016 by Hillary Clinton, seem downright ungenerous and frugal. Sanders and Warren are competing for who can be more generous with other people's money; in short, they are competing for Democratic primary votes.

While Warren would cancel up to $50,000 of debt for students who make less than $100,000 a year, and give "substantial debt cancelation" to households earning between $100,000 and $250,000, Sanders would make everyone eligible for debt cancelation. Even Warren Buffett wouldn't have to pay off his grandchildren's college loans, presuming of course that they have any.

There is a philosophy here of undeniable popular appeal: Who says that loans are genuine obligations? Sure, you made all those agreements, but you don't have to keep them. Bailouts, baby! The banks got them; now it's our turn. Fiscal responsibility is for suckers. The federal government doesn't exhibit it, so why should we? Once again, the American socialist message comes through loud and clear: let some other fellow foot the bill.

Recently I saw a medical student lament on TV that his higher education debt was causing him great anxiety. Joe Babinski told *60 Minutes* that he could focus so much better on his medical study, and presumably be a much better doctor, if he didn't have to worry about working while in school or paying off his loans. No wonder he planned to vote for a Democrat like Warren or Sanders. They would stick his graduate school loans on someone else. And this way the fellow could feel so much better that his education costs were essentially free.[30]

Throughout, interviewer Lesley Stahl nodded with appreciative idiocy. The one question Stahl didn't think to ask was, "What about when you have completed your education and become a doctor? Do you plan to work for free?" I think I know the answer to that one. The guy had absolutely no intention of doing this. Hadn't even occurred to him! The whole point for him was to work as a doctor and enjoy the accompanying lifestyle. "Give me a free education, so that I can get my training and earn half a million bucks a year for the rest of my life." Sure, education isn't really free, but let the other guy pay!

We find exactly the same approach when we turn to Democratic healthcare solutions. Here the left proposes a range of answers, from Biden's full-throated defense of Obamacare to a number of leading Democrats who favor Medicare for All. Sanders and Warren are explicit that the government would run the entire healthcare system. No private plans! This is too much even for Whoopi Goldberg, whose leftism typically borders on the robotic. "You have to allow people to make these decisions for themselves," she erupted on *The View*. "So I want them to back off."[31]

The radicalism of the scheme can hardly be understated. Over 100 million Americans would be booted off their private insurance. "Can you imagine," John Delaney asked during one of the Democratic primary debates, "if we tried to start Social Security now but said private pensions are illegal? That's the equivalent of what Senator Sanders and Senator Warren are proposing with healthcare."[32] Delaney's riposte exposes how far left the Democrats have moved; FDR-style socialism now seems quaintly conservative.

So what's the case for Medicare for All? Bernie Sanders tweeted out on March 6, 2019, that "in the United States it costs, on average, $12,000 to have a baby. In Finland it costs $60." Clearly Bernie's intention was for America to take a page out of the Finnish book. He added, "We've got to end the disgrace of our profit-driven health care system and pass Medicare for All."[33]

Now one can read this to mean that the actual cost of child delivery in Finland is actually $60. How do the Finns manage to do what America does at 0.5 percent of the cost? This would imply that Finnish doctors work for little or nothing, Finnish hospitals run for free, and postnatal care is performed on a volunteer basis. None of this is true. Sanders doesn't mean that having a child costs $60 in Finland but that the thousands of dollars it actually costs to have a child is not paid by the couple itself but rather by other Finns, through various tax measures and the mechanism of the welfare state.

Admittedly, Finnish healthcare costs less than American healthcare. This is no surprise, since it's inferior in quality and offers a smaller array of services. Children, for example, are not typically delivered by doctors but by self-taught midwives. There is a simpler, more basic, regimen of tests. Problems are not anticipated or screened for; the general attitude is that if they arise, we'll deal with them then.

The relatively poor quality of Finnish—and more generally Scandinavian—healthcare is illustrated by the fact that although the government covers the vast portion of the tab, a significant portion of the population still buys private insurance. Private insurance has been growing in Norway and Denmark. In Sweden for example, more than half a million Swedes have private insurance. None of this would be necessary if the Scandinavian government plans provided satisfactory care.[34]

What the Scandinavian—and more broadly the European, and we can also throw in the Canadian and Australian—healthcare schemes provide is unsatisfactory care: limited coverage, waiting periods, limited or no choice when it comes to doctors. That's what drives affluent citizens in those countries to find alternative, private healthcare solutions. Bernie implies that under his program, private care would not exist, so if he gets his way this option may be unavailable to Americans.

The real difference between the Finnish plan and the Sanders plan, however, is not the overall cost or even the scope of the coverage but rather the one paying. Who pays for the Democrats' Medicare for All schemes? Here the unanimous answer is, the rich! Someone else! Other people must pay. Now we have only to imagine this transaction occurring in the private sphere to see how unreasonable this is. Imagine Sanders walking around his neighborhood, informing his neighbors, "I'm going to have a kid in nine months. I'm here to collect the $500 that is your share toward the delivery process for my kid."

The neighbors are likely to respond, "Why should we pay for your kid? Why is it our responsibility?" Sanders responds, "Under democratic socialism, healthcare is a social responsibility. We all have to pay our fair share." The neighbors say, "So what's your fair share? You had the fun of making the kid. Why don't you pay for delivering the little guy?" Sanders becomes indignant. "Who says I'm shirking my responsibility? Once I've collected $500 apiece from everyone in this neighborhood, I'm going to chip in $60 myself." This is the illogic of Sanders-style socialism. The product of his loins becomes a bill on someone else's dinner table.

EVERYONE MUST PAY

By contrast, in Finland and in Scandinavian countries more generally, the unanimous answer is that everyone must pay. This process starts with the patient. Most Scandinavian countries have significant healthcare deductibles and copayments. This contrasts with Bernie Sanders, who emphasizes that his plan would involve no deductibles and no copayments. The point here is not the amount but the difference of philosophy. The Scandinavians insist that patients are partly responsible for covering their healthcare costs; Sanders insists that they are not.

And here's the biggest difference of all. While taxes cover the majority of healthcare costs, the Finns, like all Scandinavian countries, do not target the rich or the 1 percent. They target the entire society. The whole society is responsible for providing not just healthcare but also education and paid leave and all the other services that form part of the social insurance package. This means high taxes across the board. In some respects, the Scandinavians impose higher proportionate taxation on the middle and lower classes than they do on the rich.

Comparisons between America and the Scandinavian countries typically focus on the top marginal tax rate. In America, it's around 46 percent when you combine federal and state income taxes. This compares with Norway at 39 percent, Sweden at 56 percent and Denmark at 60 percent. Norway's top marginal income tax rate is actually lower than that of the United States. Sweden and Denmark's rates are substantially higher.

But as the Tax Foundation points out in an illuminating study, the top marginal rate in America kicks in at $400,000. That's more than 8 times the average income, so comparatively few U.S. taxpayers pay at that rate. In Scandinavia, however, nearly half the society is taxed at the top rate. In Denmark, the 60 percent rate kicks in at 1.2 times the average income, which is to say, at $60,000. Norway and Sweden apply their top marginal tax rate to all income roughly 1.5 times their average income. Similar rules apply in Finland. The Scandinavian norm is to impose high rates of taxation not just on the rich but on the middle class as well.

Moreover, the Scandinavian countries also impose a value-added tax—the so-called VAT—on virtually all consumer items sold. Sweden, Norway and Denmark all have a VAT rate of 25 percent. These countries collect around 10 percent of their gross domestic product through VAT levies. This compares with much lower sales taxes in America, which are levied at the state and not the national level. Even New York and California, which have the highest sales taxes in the country, tax consumer goods at around 10 percent; other states have much lower rates. Only 2 percent of America's gross domestic product comes through this form of taxation.[35]

Economists recognize that taxes on consumer items are typically regressive. This means that they proportionately fall more heavily on the poor and middle class, because the poor and middle class spend a higher ratio of their income on consumer goods. The net effect is that Scandinavians tax all working citizens at a rate of around 50 percent, but when you figure in the VAT, the poor and middle classes pay the same, or higher, rates than the rich. This of course is not the case in this country. Here the top brackets—the top 1 percent, the top 10 percent—are responsible for the vast majority of the revenue collected from income taxes in America.

So are the Scandinavian countries capitalist or socialist? We can resolve the contradiction by saying that they are capitalist in wealth creation and socialist in wealth distribution. "The Nordic countries," writes Jeffrey Dorfman, "are smart enough not to kill the goose that lays the golden egg."[36] And the Finnish journalist Anu Partanen, in a book recommending the Nordic model for America, points to the success of Swedish and Danish companies like Ikea, H&M, Spotify, Volvo, Ericsson and Maersk to emphasize that "the Nordic model goes to extraordinary lengths to support entrepreneurs."

Partanen adds, "Government in the Nordic countries tends to be like a referee who makes sure that the field is level and the rules are followed, but who then steps out of the way and lets the competitors determine who gets the highest score. If the referee were to . . . take points away from the winner and give them to the losers . . . of course no one would want to play."[37] Yet this is exactly what Bernie Sanders, Elizabeth Warren and many of the leading Democrats seek to do in this country.

Unlike the American left, the Scandinavian countries don't demonize either corporations or the rich. In fact, they have low corporate tax rates, comparable to the United States: 20 percent in Finland, 22 percent in Denmark and Sweden, 23 percent in Norway. No Nordic country imposes financial transaction taxes of the kind that Bernie Sanders has proposed here. Scandinavian countries also have fewer regulations. Corporations can easily hire and fire people. Virtually no Nordic country has a minimum wage law. Most have no inheritance tax.

Sweden veered sharply in the socialist direction in the 1970s, vastly expanding its welfare state. The most dramatic evidence of this was its introduction, at the suggestion of economist Rudolf Meidner, of "employer funds," in which private ownership of firms and companies would gradually be transferred to workers through labor unions. The American socialist Matt Bruenig still gets chills when he thinks about this. He insists that American socialism needs, in some form, to revive the Meidner Plan.[38]

But the Swedes themselves killed the Meidner Plan. As socialist policies dragged the Swedish economy into a slowdown, the Swedish Social Democrats were ousted from power and replaced by a new government that ignored the Meidner Plan. When the Social Democrats returned to power in early 1983 they revived it, but in such a diluted form that Meidner himself said, "None of the original tasks has been achieved and the whole scheme must now be considered a rather symbolic gesture."[39] You know your idea is a dud when your own side suffocates it.

Scandinavian countries have been lurching away from socialism in the past two decades in an attempt to revive their sluggish economies. The attempt has worked. Norway and Sweden both privatized state-owned enterprises. They increased legal protection of property rights. Sweden reduced taxes and unemployment benefits and streamlined welfare programs. In the past, most Nordic countries tried wealth taxes like the ones Elizabeth Warren now proposes; all but Norway abandoned them. Sweden offers parents a voucher program to choose their children's school, and private and even for-profit schools are eligible.

So the irony is that while the American left wants to move toward Scandinavian socialism, the Scandinavians have been moving away from it. The Nordics have learned from their experience with socialism; American leftists seem determined to pick up the Nordic model from the 1970s, ignore the lessons of subsequent experience and make all the same mistakes. Many on the left here will find it surprising that Denmark, Sweden and the Netherlands now rank higher than the United States on the Heritage Foundation's "Index of Economic Freedom." This is what Sven Socialism means now.

The greatest admirers of Nordic socialism are now in America, not in the Nordic countries. In fact, some Nordic socialists are looking wistfully to the possibility of an American model that they can emulate. Writing in *Jacobin*, two Scandinavian scholars say that when it comes to digesting refugees and immigrants, in other words to creating a model for "a comprehensive welfare state in a multiethnic country," the Scandinavians hope to learn from America, since their own model is proving to be a disaster.[40] The Nordics simply have no idea what to do in a nest of sparrows when a flock of crows shows up.

To sum up, the Scandinavian model is social insurance for "people like us," while the American left subscribes to what may be termed "theft socialism" for the benefit of various favored constituencies, including illegals. In Scandinavian countries, Peter and Paul both contribute to the commonweal in the understanding that they are both expected to be responsible, and the government is not stealing from one to provide for the other but rather providing social insurance to both. The Scandinavian political parties compete for the votes of both Peter and Paul.

American socialism, by contrast, is not based on genuine social insurance, since the majority of citizens are not expected to fund the programs the Democratic left is promising. This is not a common pool but a "1 percent" pool. The socialism proposed in this country is based on promising free stuff and getting someone else to pay, thus fostering social irresponsibility and dependency on the left for political gain. The American left's motto comes from the English Fabian socialist George Bernard Shaw: "Any government that robs Peter to pay Paul can always count on Paul's support."

HUGO CHAVEZ'S GANGSTER SOCIALISM

Finally, I want to show how the left's model for socialism in this country is not Scandinavia but Venezuela. Yes, Venezuela. My wife's native country, which is now in ruins, with runaway inflation, a useless currency, no food in stores, shortages of medicine and water, regular electricity blackouts, the highest crime rates in the world, a starving population, an exodus of the productive class and now some 4 million Venezuelans fleeing the country—this is the socialism the left is attempting to import here.

Of course they won't admit it. They keep repeating the mantra that their goal in America isn't dictatorial socialism of the traditional stripe; it's democratic socialism. But Venezuela has, or at least had, democratic socialism. Hugo Chavez was democratically elected in 1998. There have been subsequent elections, sustaining first Chavez and then, after his death, his handpicked successor Nicolás Maduro, although virtually every ballot since 2000 has been contaminated with charges of election-rigging and voter fraud, both phenomena not entirely unknown in this country.

Even so, the left's denials seem at first glance to have some credibility, because Venezuela is a Third World country. Why would the American left seek to emulate Third World socialism? The answer, of course, is that Venezuela was not always a Third World country. In the 1960s, it was the richest country in Latin America and the fourth-richest country in the world, with a per capita income many times higher than its neighbors Brazil and Colombia and not far behind that of the United States. Venezuela, after all, has one of the largest oil reserves on the planet. Now that wealth is largely gone.

Debbie's aunt, who once lived a comfortable, middle-class life, has been reduced to near-starvation. We have figured out a way to send her money to get by; her pension, once sufficient to cover her food and medical expenses, has been rendered useless because of inflation. Debbie's cousin, with an engineering degree, now travels the remote countryside with a generator that he has rigged to his van. He sleeps in his vehicle, cooks outdoors and lives somewhat like a caveman. Socialism made Venezuela into a Third World country.

But at the same time—and this is part of the appeal—it created a wealthy ruling class of Chavistas who run the country like their own private domain. They rewrite the constitution. They have their own private army. They are a governing elite exempt from the misery and desperation of ordinary citizens. They have uninhibited access to what remains of Venezuela's oil wealth. In fact, their lifestyles are the envy of American leftists. Why be a millionaire and own three homes like Bernie Sanders when you can be a billionaire, like the Chavez family, and have mansions around the world? In Venezuela you don't need a Clinton Foundation to trade favors for cash; the country itself is your private foundation.

Let's examine the ingredients of Venezuelan socialism and see if they sound familiar. First, identity politics. Venezuela is a multiethnic country. In this respect it resembles America, not Scandinavia. When Debbie grew up in Caracas and Maracaibo, she encountered blacks, browns and whites; Italians, Asian Indians, Iranians, Jews and of course indigenous populations descended from the native peoples who originally inhabited the continent.

Politics in Venezuela was generally based on two factors: economics and religion. There were two main parties, Acción Democrática and Copei. The former was the secular party; the latter nominally the Christian party. The former leaned to the left; the latter to the right. But there were meeting points in the middle. There was corruption, of the usual sort, and it infected both parties. The country's economy was to a large degree dependent on the price of oil, making it vulnerable to fluctuation and instability.

Hugo Chavez was elected as a third-party candidate who eventually got the backing of Acción Democrática. He didn't campaign as a socialist—in fact, he denied that he was a socialist. Remarkably, Chavez founded the Socialist Party in Venezuela only in 2007, eight years after he became president. Initially he sounded more like Barack Obama; he portrayed himself as a thoughtful centrist who sought "hope and change." Yes, this was his actual slogan.

But Chavez also introduced an explosive new element into Venezuelan politics: the politics of race and ethnicity. Chavez highlighted the fact that he was a *pardo*, a term used in the colonial era to designate someone of mixed racial heritage. He also liked to call himself "the Indian from Barinas," explaining, "My Indian roots are from my father's side. He is mixed Indian and black." Chavez noted that his grandmother was a Pume Indian.[41] Chavez's term for whites was *mantuanos*, which tellingly covers not only whites but also colored people with European pretensions. He also called them *miameros*, a reference to their alleged penchant for shopping in Miami.

Knowing that nearly 70 percent of Venezuela is mestizo or mixed-race, with 20 percent white and 10 percent black, Chavez sought to mobilize the native Indian, black and mestizo populations against the whites. The Yale legal scholar Amy Chua is one of the few to remark on this "ethnic dimension" of Venezuelan politics. Chavez used the anticolonial model: whites of European descent are the foreign oppressors, and blacks and browns are the victims. Columbus, once honored as a great explorer, became the poster boy of white imperialism.

Chavez turned Venezuela into a racially polarized society to an extent that it never was before. The socialists introduced a new cultural policy termed Misión Cultura aimed at vilifying whites and elevating previously marginalized groups to hallowed status. Chavez even pressured the referees in Venezuelan beauty pageants not to award prizes to so many light-skinned Venezuelans and to give preference to those who looked more like him. As Chua notes, Chavez ordered that two oil tankers named after former white Miss Venezuelas—the *Maritza Sayalero* and the *Pilín León*—be renamed *Negra Hipólita* and *Negra Matea* after two black women who supposedly raised Simón Bolívar.[42]

Chavez created a new Chavista class heavily populated with blacks and browns, although sprinkled with whites who are happy to serve as "race traitors" in order to enjoy the benefit of being part of a ruling elite. In Venezuela, as in America, identity politics serves to topple old social and cultural hierarchies and to foster a multicultural left that then controls and dominates the society.

Then came the attack on entrepreneurs and the rich. Chavez demonized the productive class—notably the Europeans, Americans and Venezuelans who collaborated in the oil industry—and invoked their alleged greed and selfishness to justify a government takeover not only of the oil industry but nearly all industries. The socialists stacked the banks with directors drawn from Chavez's allies and cronies. The regime set wages and prices for basic goods, restricting the ability of entrepreneurs to make a profit, driving many of them out of the country and then ruining their businesses, so productivity ground to a halt.

The Chavistas took over the oil industry, which had been officially nationalized in the 1970s, but which still operated with a measure of autonomy, along with considerable foreign expertise. The foreign expertise was necessary because Venezuela's greatest oil deposits are in the Orinoco heavy oil belt, and this type of oil is more difficult to extract, requiring a special process of liquefaction before it is ready for sale. Venezuela's oil executives invited British and American companies to collaborate with the state-owned oil company Petróleos de Venezuela (PDVSA) in getting out the oil and sharing the profits.

During the 1990s, international firms like ExxonMobil, Chevron, BP and ConocoPhillips were actively involved in unlocking Venezuela's heavy oil deposits. These companies had invested billions of dollars in technology and infrastructure as part of a joint venture with PDVSA. Denouncing PDVSA and its foreign partners as a "state within a state," Chavez rewrote the terms of their contracts, sharply hiking the royalties the foreign firms would have to pay the government. Chavez insisted that the government needed the lion's share of the oil profits to fund its socialist programs.

"He was ignorant about everything to do with oil, everything to do with geology, engineering, the economics of oil," said Pedro Burelli, a former PDVSA board member who quit when Chavez took over. "His was an encyclopedic ignorance."[43] The foreign companies attempted to negotiate with Chavez, but to no avail. A few, such as Chevron and BP, submitted to the heavy-handed edicts of the socialist government. Others, including ExxonMobil and Conoco, moved their operations out of Venezuela.

Chavez then proceeded to get rid of the professional class of Venezuelans that ran PDVSA. He fired PDVSA's president, the respected Guaicaipuro Lameda, and 18,000 other employees, most of them managers and skilled technicians, replacing them all with political allies loyal to the socialist government. For Chavistas who found themselves with grand titles, occupying corner offices, it must have felt like winning the lottery! These apparatchiks, through that familiar socialist combination of corruption and ineptitude, ran the oil industry into the ground. At one point they insisted that PDVSA should produce and distribute milk; later they ordered it to supervise the importation of cooking oil and rice.

Some of these incompetents, who learned more from socialist pamphlets than they learned from petroleum engineering, mouthed off about "climate change" and how Venezuela needed to make a transition from fossil fuel to hydroelectric power. In this respect, they sounded a bit like their oil-rich Norwegian counterparts. The Norwegians, however, are smart enough to blabber about climate change while doing nothing to let it interfere with the nation's oil industry. The Chavistas, however, actually sought to replace fossil fuels with hydroelectric power. This, together with a mismanaged grid, is the root of today's regular blackouts.

But the real problem was that the new PDVSA crew was running an oil-drilling operation they had no idea how to run. Kind of like Elizabeth Warren running a bank, or Bernie Sanders leading a platoon. "Hurry up, fellas, you're not doing your fair share." Suddenly the wells weren't pumping the way they used to, and the refineries weren't operating as smoothly as they used to, and so the goose that laid the golden eggs in Venezuela became weak and sterile.

Imagine an oil-rich country having to import oil! It's embarrassing. Actually, the United States was in that position for a long time. Only now with its discoveries of huge deposits of oil and natural gas has America achieved energy independence. Venezuela, alas, has moved from energy largesse to energy dependence. Imagine having gas lines in a country that has one of the largest gas reserves in the world. Well, Venezuelans don't have to imagine those lines; they are standing in them every day.

Then began the socialist confiscation of land and property in Venezuela. Debbie's grandparents had a ranch; the Chavistas took it. They allowed Debbie's family to live on the ranch, but the family no longer owned it. The government reserved the right to dictate who lived there, and on what terms. Today in Venezuela, if you leave the country and return, you are quite likely to find someone else—someone designated by the socialist regime—living in your house, or what used to be your house. Chavez himself liked to parade through neighborhoods, seizing property simply through finger-pointing. "We want that place. And that one. And that one." These confiscations were triumphantly featured on Chavez's reality TV show *Aló Presidente* (Hello President).[44]

To oppose the socialist government is futile. Why? Because of the third feature of Venezuelan socialism, which is the rigging of the system to make it beholden to the socialist regime. Chavez and his cronies rewrote the Venezuelan constitution, dismantling provisions for separation of powers and essentially stripping the document of its protection of economic and civil liberties. They "packed" the Venezuelan Supreme Court, increasing its size from 20 to 32, in order to ensure that it was dominated by Chavistas. Today there is no judicial independence, and the Venezuelan high court is a rubber stamp for the socialist regime.

Sure, there is an elected National Assembly—now largely made up of dissenters who oppose the socialist government—but it is largely powerless, because all legislation must go through another body, the Constituent National Assembly, which is controlled by the Chavistas. As I go through all this, I realize that I am describing a wet dream for the American left. They have been working since the days of FDR— and how hard they tried in the Clinton and Obama eras—to stack the odds in this way. They haven't yet succeeded, but it's easy to see how the Venezuelan blueprint points the direction in which they would love to go.

DESARMA LA VIOLENCIA

A fourth feature of Venezuelan socialism is gun confiscation. Here too we see how Venezuela resembles America, and how both countries are different from Scandinavia. There is no gun debate in Scandinavia, because the citizens were never armed. In Venezuela, however, citizens once possessed guns as a matter of right. The socialists began a systematic propaganda campaign to demonize guns and gun owners. This campaign was termed "Desarma la Violencia" (Disarm the Violence).

In one government-sponsored commercial, we see a young man getting ready to go out on the town. A fashionable fellow, he zips up his leather jacket and packs his gun. Then the image fades, we hear a loud explosion and once again we see a zipper moving slowly, but now we see that it's a zippered body bag, and it contains the same young man's dead body. His gun got him killed! The message is: Guns are dangerous. Turn in your guns.

The Venezuelan socialists organized a "buy-back" program, very much along the lines of what Democrats like Beto O'Rourke are proposing here. Of course the term itself is Orwellian nonsense. How can you buy back something that you never owned in the first place? How can you buy something when you are using the money of the very people that you are taking the guns from? There, as here, the whole thing is a fraud. But as the Venezuelan case shows, it is fraud with a political purpose.

The political purpose is to disarm the citizens, so that they are vulnerable to the depredations of the socialist regime. We now turn to the fifth feature of Venezuelan socialism, which is the unleashing of armed militias—the so-called *colectivos*—against dissidents and protesters. If you blame the government for shortages or blackouts, the government will send a motorcycle gang of armed thugs to beat you and members of your family. In 2005 the *colectivos* took control of a region of Caracas and unleashed an orgy of terror on tens of thousands of citizens protesting against the socialist regime.

These thugs are Venezuela's answer to Antifa. They are not part of the government. They are civilian thugs who work in cahoots with the socialist regime. Some of them are criminals who have been armed and released on the condition that they serve the regime and target its opponents. No surprise, Bill Ayers—one of the founders of Antifa—praises the *colectivos* as a necessary militarized force to defeat the enemies of Venezuelan socialism. "Venezuela must be defended," Ayers writes, in part because it "is today's proving ground for socialist alternatives."[45]

A common sight in Caracas today is a group of *colectivos* grabbing a fellow who has gotten into a dispute while standing in a long line for gas or groceries and bludgeoning him into submission to send a message about who is in charge and what kind of conformity is expected even from a suffering population. And how convenient for the government and for the *colectivos* that the population has been disarmed in thoughtful preparation for this government-led onslaught.

Conformity. That's the sixth theme of Venezuelan socialism. The whole education system has been designed not for debate but for conformity. This isn't an allegation I am making; it's the law. The socialist government has mandated that all education in the country be conducted according to what it terms "Bolivarian socialism." Never mind that Simón Bolívar, who liberated much of Latin America from the Spanish, wasn't a socialist. He was for the most part a classical liberal who admired George Washington and the American founders.[46]

The Chavistas have made him into a socialist. If the textbooks say he was a socialist, then, from the students' point of view, he must have been a socialist. There is no one to say any different. And Venezuelan socialism has an anti-American thrust that vilifies everything that America stands for. No wonder Ayers and the Hollywood left are so enthusiastic. That's why they rave about socialist "literacy programs"—they are 100 percent political propaganda.

And that of course is the direction in which the American left has been moving education in this country. Propaganda on climate change, on identity politics, on gender and race and inequality, now dominates elementary and secondary education, and the debate that once occurred on American campuses is now a rarity; Antifa blockades and the shouting down of speakers has now become the norm. I can testify to it; I have seen it. And Debbie, who travels with me, can hardly believe it. It is all so chillingly familiar to her. We haven't reached the Venezuelan destination, but we're clearly headed down that road.

Finally—and this is the seventh familiar theme of Venezuelan socialism—there is getting rich off politics. Once again, that does not occur in Scandinavia. There is not a single politician in Norway, Sweden or Denmark who has gone from zero to $10 million—or $200 million—while largely employed in the public sector. But in Venezuela, as in America, it is quite possible for "public servants" to become very rich. In fact, it is hard to name any prominent figure on the Venezuelan left, as on the American left, who hasn't profited handsomely from their politics. Apparently they all came to do good and stayed to do very well.

While the Venezuelan people starve, the Chavistas post photographs on Facebook of their European vacations, their lavish parties, their designer outfits, the bouquets of fresh flowers that adorn their homes. One of them is Debbie's childhood friend, married to a man who is now one of Maduro's generals. Another is the wife of Vice President Tareck El Aissami. It's as if these people live in a different country. And these are the bottom apples in the Chavista barrel; the top ones live at the scale of the richest people in the world, enjoying private airplanes, domestic staff, Hollywood soirees, and Michelin-starred restaurants.

The current ruler, Maduro, a former bus driver, was recently spotted puffing on a cigar at a private banquet in Istanbul hosted by celebrity chef Salt Bae. His two stepsons Yoswal Gavidia Flores and Walter Gavidia Flores managed to spend $45,000 on a lavish spree at the Ritz Hotel in Paris. The U.S. government confiscated millions of dollars from Maduro's second in command, Diosdado Cabello, probably a small fraction of his private fortune. His daughter Daniela lives a celebrity lifestyle and is regularly photographed by paparazzi in Madrid and the Cote d'Azure; her boyfriend is Latin pop singer Omar Acedo.[47]

In Barinas, the late Hugo Chavez's family owns 17 country estates, totaling more than 100,000 acres. *Forbes* named Chavez, during his lifetime, as one of the 400 richest men in the world. He reportedly had looted $2 billion from the Venezuelan people. His daughter, María Gabriela, apparently models her lifestyle on Paris Hilton. She has a special affection for toy dogs. She is also the wealthiest individual in Venezuela. A Miami newspaper, *Diario las Américas*, estimates her net worth as $4 billion, most of it stashed away in foreign bank accounts.[48]

Who said socialist countries don't have their own top 1 percent? Only in this case the 1 percent is made up of the socialists themselves. For Venezuelans, it makes their suffering all the more unendurable. It's one thing to be in pain; it's another to watch the people proclaiming to be your champion stamping their boots in your face to keep you down while they live high on the hog. These people seem like heartless monsters, and of course they are. Just like the heartless monsters in this country who sound like them and, deep down, long to be like them.

When we consider the major themes of Venezuelan socialism, we can see right away that every one of them parallels the themes of the American left. American leftists are wannabe Maduros pretending to take their cues from Sven. If we continue to move in the direction that the left is taking us, we are going to end up not where the Scandinavians are but where the Venezuelans are. Pack your bags, and make sure you label them correctly. It's not "Stockholm, here we come" but "Caracas, here we come." It won't be pretty.

5

JUST DESERTS

THE MORAL BASIS OF ENTREPRENEURIAL CAPITALISM

To feel much for others and little for ourselves, to restrain our selfish, and to indulge our benevolent affections, constitutes the perfection of human nature.[1]

—ADAM SMITH, *THE THEORY OF MORAL SENTIMENTS*

The best thing going for socialism in America is the moral anxiety over capitalism. This by itself is a puzzle. Capitalism has proven enormously successful in relieving suffering, raising people out of poverty and multiplying the technological marvels of everyday life. Even Bernie Sanders admits that China has "made more progress in addressing extreme poverty than any country in the history of civilization."[2]

Bernie is silent about the reason for this, but he's not that dumb. He knows! China, one of the poorest countries in the world, has become one of the richest by casting aside socialism and embracing capitalism. Chinese capitalism may be state-run capitalism, capitalism contained within an authoritarian political structure, but it is capitalism all the same.

In America, as in much of the world, we have witnessed a technological revolution, a second communications revolution that matches in scope the one that accompanied the Industrial Revolution. The first communications revolution gave us the railroads, the car and the airplane; the second one has given us the computer, the internet and the iPhone. Of course, these transformations bring a whole new range of products in their wake. Do you watch Hulu? Read on a Kindle? Find your way with GPS? Shop on Amazon? Listen to Spotify? Get to the airport with Lyft or Uber? Book with Airbnb? Use Instagram? If so, you are a beneficiary of twenty-first-century technological capitalism.

Yet—and to some this will seem incredible—the anxiety over technological capitalism is perhaps stronger in America now than at any time since the Great Depression. We are accustomed to seeing hostility to free markets from groups that do not seem to benefit from it. A flourishing capitalist economy, for example, doesn't do much for a single mom who spends her time raising her children and is not otherwise employed. I can understand the rage of a sociologist or political scientist who, despite making $100,000 a year, despises a capitalist economy that confers vastly greater rewards on a fat Rotarian with gold chains on his chest who sells pest control or term-life insurance. Envy is not a justification, but it often provides a good explanation.

But today we see whole groups in society that seem to revile capitalism even though they are its greatest beneficiaries. On my campus tours, I frequently encounter students who are living off the proceeds of the small businesses operated by their parents, yet, in evident disregard of this, they unhesitatingly call themselves socialists. In some cases, the most pungent critics of capitalism are themselves capitalist success stories.

At one time such strange behavior was confined to Jews. The late Irving Kristol, my former colleague at the American Enterprise Institute, used to say, "Jews are the only group that earns like Episcopalians and votes like Puerto Ricans." Kristol, who was himself Jewish, pondered this seeming political "irrationality" on the part of Jewish Democrats. But now Jews are no longer an anomaly; many rich people earn like Episcopalians and vote like Puerto Ricans.

In 2016, I took note of the fact that Highland Park, the most affluent section of Dallas, was thick with Beto signs. Signs for Cruz were scarce. Hillary raised far more money from big donors than Trump did. Overall, Trump raised $850 million, Hillary $1.4 billion, and Trump got more of his total from small donors than Hillary did. If you peruse the list of America's wealthiest men and women, you'll see that a sizable majority of them now are Democrats, even though the Democratic agenda would seem inimical to their economic interests.

In fact, several of capitalism's biggest names have gotten themselves elected to high office—as Democrats! Billionaire Jay Pritzker, heir to the Hyatt hotel fortune, is the Democratic governor of Illinois. Ned Lamont, the Democratic governor of Connecticut, is a scion of the Morgan banking family, with a net worth exceeding $100 million.[3] What's going on here? How do we make sense of Buffett, Soros, Zuckerberg and the whole crop of Silicon Valley leftists who agitate for higher taxes and work closely with the Democratic Party?

Here, I make sense of it. Here I intend to confront head-on the strongest moral arguments against capitalism. These are the arguments from inequality, from selfishness and greed and from "fair share" or just deserts. I intend to show that these arguments are typically rebutted by arguments that stress the efficiency or expediency of free markets. Even the best advocates of capitalism, from Adam Smith to Friedrich Hayek to Ayn Rand, emphasize its efficiency, how well markets "work." And they have proven successful, but only to a point.

Capitalism has won the economic debate, but it has never won the moral debate. The critics of capitalism are currently winning because their moral indictment goes largely unanswered. No wonder that billionaire hedge fund manager Ray Dalio says that "capitalism basically is not working for the majority of people." The left has convinced him to feel bad that it works only for him! Seattle entrepreneur Nick Hanauer warns his fellow one-percenters that they had better embrace the leveling socialist schemes proposed by leading Democrats or else "the pitchforks are coming for us plutocrats . . . and then there's no time to get to the airport and jump on our Gulfstream Vs and fly to New Zealand."[4]

We know that capitalism has a problem when the capitalists themselves are surrendering to the other side. What is needed, therefore, is a moral case for a market economy, an argument that goes beyond "why capitalism works" to "why capitalism promotes individual virtue and social justice." This chapter not only makes an original case for the morality of capitalism, but it also shows how the moral claim of democratic socialism—that it reflects popular consent or the will of the people—is vindicated not by socialism but by capitalism itself.

THREE STRIKES AGAINST CAPITALISM

For a full-throated expression of the anticapitalist sentiment, we could hardly do better than Alexandria Ocasio-Cortez. Speaking at the South by Southwest conference in Austin, Ocasio-Cortez pronounced capitalism "irredeemable." She explained, "The most important thing is the concentration of capital, and it means that we seek and prioritize profit and the accumulation of money above all else and we seek it at any human and environmental cost. That is what that means. To me, that ideology is not sustainable and cannot be redeemed."[5]

Yes, well. Moving beyond the bartender community into the precincts of journalism and academia, I find three arguments that seek to expose what the progressive economist Joseph Stiglitz calls "fundamental flaws in the capitalist system." Together these arguments make the case for fixing—or even eliminating—capitalism in the name of social justice.

First, the argument from inequality. This argument doesn't merely focus on the existence of inequality but also on the degree of it. While America has seen unprecedented prosperity in the last few decades, Stiglitz writes, "all of the wealth accumulation in this country has gone to the top."[6]

The storyline goes like this. In the three decades following World War II, the American economy grew rapidly, and of course some prospered far more than others—but even so, the rewards of prosperity were fairly widely distributed. This period is sometimes referred to as the "great compression," as it represents a key interval in which the nation's distribution of wealth and income became more equal. A top executive, for example, might earn 50 times the salary of the average worker, but he—and it was typically a he—didn't earn 500 times that sum.

Since the 1970s, however, inequalities have grown much starker, and they are even greater when it comes to wealth than income. Recently Ilhan Omar tweeted, "Walmart CEO's salary last year: $23,618,233. A

Walmart worker's median pay last year: $21,952." Then she commented, "The issue isn't that these employees aren't working hard enough. It's that our system doesn't value workers. And it's a moral outrage."[7]

Omar is right that many heads of companies do earn 500–1,000 times what their employees make, and wealth gaps are so large that the top 1 percent of Americans now own as much wealth as the bottom 90 percent. It is not enough to attribute these huge chasms to "capitalism," since America was capitalist between the 1940s and 1970s. Clearly something within capitalism has changed, which inspires the socialist chant, "If we can't have socialism, then in terms of income and wealth distribution, let's at least go back to the 1970s."

A second anxiety about capitalism is focused on an issue that we may term "fair share" or "just deserts." "The twenty-first century economy," writes Nathan Robinson in *Why You Should be a Socialist*, seems "more feudalistic than meritocratic." In short, people aren't getting their fair share! I am using the term "fair share" in much the same manner that Obama did, but I use it to point to something a little different. Obama used the term in the context of how much people pay in taxes; I am using it in the context of how much people earn in the first place. Does capitalism return to Americans in proportion to the share that they have contributed to the economy? Does it give them their "just deserts"?

This issue of fair share and just deserts is encapsulated in Obama's claim, going back to 2012, that "if you've got a business—you didn't build that. . . . If you were successful, somebody along the line gave you some help. Somebody else made that happen." As Elizabeth Warren explained at the time, "You moved your goods to market on the roads the rest of us paid for; you hired workers the rest of us paid to educate; you were safe in your factory because of police forces and fire forces that the rest of us paid for."[8]

This argument is flawed on its face. The "rest of us" didn't pay for the roads and the schools and the police protection; the entrepreneurs paid also. So why should entrepreneurs incur some special or additional obligation to reimburse society for things to which they have already contributed their fair share? Should entrepreneurs be penalized because they made better use of their education, or because they used the roads to transport their goods while the rest of us used them for less productive purposes? This makes no sense.

But the question being raised by Obama and Warren—are the rewards of a capitalist society proportionate to what people actually contribute?—remains valid. In a recent interview, Alexandria Ocasio-Cortez said, "No one ever makes a billion dollars. You take a billion dollars." Here's the argument from personal incredulity once again. Sitting in her congressional office, twiddling her thumbs, Ocasio-Cortez can't imagine what anyone can possibly do to earn a billion dollars. She presumes, in her words, that billionaires make their money "off the backs" of "single mothers," "black and brown people" and "undocumented people."[9]

Recently Bernie Sanders put it in a different form. He tweeted out, "If we are a nation that can pay baseball players hundreds of millions of dollars, don't tell me we can't afford to pay teachers the salaries they deserve."[10] There is some typical Sanders obfuscation here. "We" don't pay baseball players hundreds of millions; the owners of the teams do. The taxpayer doesn't bankroll baseball salaries the way he bankrolls teacher salaries.

But even so, Sanders' core point persists. What is it that baseball players do that justifies such a large compensation difference? Teachers require the appropriate degrees and training to qualify for the profession. They work reasonably hard, even granting the three-month break they get in the summer. Moreover, teaching serves a vital social function; what could be more important to a nation than educating its young? Many of us—this is certainly true of me—had our lives transformed by one or a handful of teachers.

Baseball seems, by comparison, a trivial pursuit, which is why we call it a game. Baseball players practice, to be sure, but most of their talent seems to be based on natural gifts. Did Babe Ruth really work that much harder than all the other hitters? Baseball is entertaining, but it is hardly socially indispensable; America could survive just fine without it. What possible compass could warrant pay differentials so obscenely large between them and teachers? The outcome seems like a classic illustration of social injustice.

Capitalism, the social theorist Michael Walzer argued several years ago, is inherently unjust because it does not recognize the "intrinsic value" of work or the "individual qualities" of the worker. Walzer gives a telling example. "Imagine a novelist who writes what he hopes will be a best seller. . . . His novel appears, let's say, during a depression when no one has money for books, and very few copies are sold; his reward is small. . . . Years later, in better times, the book is reissued and does well. Has its author become more deserving? There is too much luck involved here; talk of desert makes little sense."[11]

Walzer's point about just deserts is deepened by the philosopher John Rawls, who in his classic work *A Theory of Justice* argued that all our good qualities—our intelligence, our creativity, even our proclivity for hard work—are basically assets that have been provided to us as a consequence of luck. If we think about it, we don't really deserve them. Consider Steve Jobs. How did he become Steve Jobs? His genes came from his parents. We may presume that his habits of application and concentration, along with his marketing prowess and other skills, came largely from his environment, which is to say, from those who influenced him over the years.

And the same may be said of all successful people. Either they were born with their aptitude and gifts—Rawls invokes what he terms a "natural lottery"—or they acquired those things from their environment, what Rawls terms "happy family and social circumstances." Therefore, Rawls argues, the ingredients of their success are the product not of what they somehow deserve but merely of good fortune or luck. And luck, Rawls concludes, is "arbitrary from a moral point of view."

We are not, Rawls argues, entitled to the benefits of luck. This does not mean that the state should attempt to take away people's productive capacity. Rawls is not calling for the society described in Kurt Vonnegut's short story "Harrison Bergeron," where intelligent people have scramblers attached to their brains and good dancers have impediments fastened to their bodies, all for the purpose of neutralizing their undeserved intellectual and artistic capacities.

Rather, Rawls contends that we should seek "a conception of justice that nullifies the accidents of natural endowment and the contingencies of social circumstances." The basic idea is now a core element of progressive doctrine, namely that, through state intervention, the fruits of all good fortune must be shared with society, specifically with the least advantaged. In Rawls' view, this is not quite socialism, but some of his progressive admirers regard it as pretty close.[12]

A third and final argument against capitalism is that it is based on the worst qualities in human nature, namely, greed and selfishness. Capitalism is summed up in the infamous speech delivered by Gordon Gekko in the movie *Wall Street*: "Greed is good." Now we may expect that a socialist society, or any other kind of society, would also have greed and selfishness, but the progressive indictment of capitalism holds that these low qualities are incidental to other systems and intrinsic to capitalism. As a recent article in *Teen Vogue* instructs its young readers, capitalism doesn't merely exhibit greed and selfishness; it fosters greed and selfishness.[13]

Entrepreneurs are successful, according to Rutger Bregman, writing in *The Guardian*, in proportion to how greedy and selfish they are. It has little to do with what they produce. Bregman gives us a familiar rant. "No, wealth isn't created at the top. It is merely devoured there." Bankers, he writes, are a "giant tapeworm gorging on a sick body." They specialize in "sucking others dry." In Bregman's view, oil drilling, pharmaceutical and tech company executives are also greedy selfish leeches. How else, Bregman asks, could they end up with such massive boatloads of other people's money?[14]

The rich are "more likely to be despicable characters," Charles Mathewes and Evan Sandsmark write in *The Washington Post*, and what's more, their vast sums of money "poison not only those who possess them but even those who are merely around them." That's because, as Tylor Standley writes in the progressive Christian magazine *Sojourners*, "capitalism is the single most powerful tool for habit formation in Western society," and "the selfishness of our exemplars trickles down to the rest of us."[15] Capitalism is responsible for the moral depredation of American society.

A SINGLE ARGUMENT

Three separate arguments against capitalism, all made in the name of social justice, and yet if you think about it, they are all part of a single argument. This argument revolves around a simple question: Who gets what? Or to put it in moral terms, who's entitled to what? The arguments about equality and greed, which seem like separate arguments, are all reducible to the single argument about fair share and just deserts. That's the heart of the issue, and the whole case against capitalism turns on that. Let's see why this is so.

"Is justice equality?" Aristotle writes, and then he gives this enigmatic answer: "Yes, it is, but not for all people, only for those who are equal."[16] What does Aristotle mean by this? He means that justice is not a matter of giving someone an equal or unequal share but rather of giving everyone what they are actually due. If someone deserves more, it is just to give him more; if someone deserves less, it is just to give him less. The question of inequality is subordinate to the question of just deserts.

We can see Aristotle's point by imagining a mother who has two children, a six-year-old and an infant. She spends most of her parenting time on the infant. The six-year-old is indignant; he protests he's not getting equal time. The mother, however, recognizes that while she loves both children equally, her infant child needs more time. She's not neglecting her older child by treating him "unequally." On the contrary, in giving more time to one child and less to the other, the mother is acting justly by giving each one its due.

Similarly, the greed and selfishness critique doesn't stand on its own; it involves implicit judgments about fair share and just deserts. Here I'm going to borrow an example from the left-wing economist Amartya Sen. Sen envisions three individuals—Anne, Bob and Carla—fighting over a flute. Carla made the flute. Anne is the best flute player of the three. Bob claims never to have had a flute of his own. So who owns the flute? We are tempted to give the obvious answer—Carla—but Sen does not agree.

In typical progressive fashion, Sen insists that given the multiple claimants to the flute, "there is a difficult decision that you have to make." An egalitarian analysis, he claims, would give the flute to Bob, the poor lugubrious boy who never owned a flute. A utilitarian calculation might assign it to Anne, since she might derive the greatest pleasure from its use. A libertarian may favor Carla, whose labor produced the flute. Sen concludes that there is a social choice to be made here. To whom, he pompously asks, should we give the flute?[17]

The giveaway term here is "we." This is the precise point at which we catch Sen in the act. Sen has made the hidden assumption that ownership of the flute has silently transferred from the person who made the flute to some societal "we" that now determines who gets the flute. Yet where does the issue of redistribution even arise here? A flute didn't magically appear out of nowhere. No one "distributed" the flute to Carla, and therefore there is no question of "redistributing" the flute. The flute always belonged to Carla, who created it. It's obviously Carla's flute. Absent Carla, there wouldn't be a flute.

Now imagine someone—Sen, or a teacher, or a judge—seizing the flute and giving it to Anne or Bob. Carla would naturally be outraged. And rightly so! It's her flute. Is Carla "selfish" for wanting to keep what she made? Is she "greedy" for seeking to hold on to what belongs to her? Of course not. She is no more greedy or selfish than the A student who produces A-quality work and then expects to receive—what else?—an A. There is no greed or selfishness in claiming what is legitimately our due.

So we return to the basic question: Who owns stuff in the first place? Who has a moral right to it? This is the justice question that is at the heart of any inquiry about social justice. Rawls rightly makes it central. "Justice," he writes, "is the first virtue of social institutions, as truth is of systems of thought. A theory however elegant and economical must be rejected or revised if it is untrue; likewise, laws and institutions no matter how efficient and well-arranged must be reformed or abolished if they are unjust."[18]

I agree with this, and therefore the central question for me is whether capitalism truly distributes its rewards in proportion with what people actually deserve. If it does, it's just. If it doesn't, it isn't. So let's find out what the great apologists for capitalism have to say on this topic—which, as it turns out, is surprisingly little.

VOTING IN THE MARKETPLACE

Capitalism has been a controversial institution virtually since its origin, and most certainly since Marx and other socialists unleashed their diatribes against it in the early nineteenth century. Given the ceaseless dispute over it, one might expect that, over the years, the defenders of free markets would have sought to fully demonstrate that the allocations of capitalism are right and just. We might expect this, but we would be wrong.

In fact, ever since Adam Smith, the defenders of capitalism have mostly emphasized its efficiency, not its morality. They have sought to show that capitalism "works," not that it gives people their just deserts. Smith acknowledged that capitalism is based on the motive of self-interest. As he famously wrote in *The Wealth of Nations*, "It is not from the benevolence of the butcher, the brewer or the baker that we expect our dinner, but from their own interest. We address ourselves, not to their humanity, but to their self-love, and never talk to them of our own necessities but of their advantages."[19]

Did Smith, then, consider selfishness to be a high virtue and empathy and concern for others to be a useless indulgence? He did not. Consider the quotation that begins this chapter, in which Adam Smith insists that empathy and consideration for others, and restraining one's selfish impulses, constitute human nature at its best. That quotation is from Smith's first book, *The Theory of Moral Sentiments*. One should not consider this work to be one of Smith's side pursuits. He was, by profession, a professor of moral philosophy.

Yet the doctrine of unselfishness expounded in that book would seem to directly contradict the whole system that Smith himself outlines in his subsequent and best-known work, *The Wealth of Nations*. Thus, we have what the German scholars of the nineteenth century called "Das Adam Smith Problem." The Adam Smith "problem" is that we have two apparently contradictory teachings from the same teacher. In his earlier work, Smith ascribes elevated human action to sympathy and unselfishness; in his later one, he ascribes productive human action to self-interest or, to use his term, "self love." Did Smith change his mind? How to reconcile these two positions?

The conventional way to do it is the progressive way, which is to hold that Smith conceded the moral inadequacy of capitalism—its rootedness in selfishness and greed—while insisting, nevertheless, that this greed could be channeled, through the invisible hand of competition, to promote the material welfare of the community. In this understanding, the moral logic of free markets is the law of unintended consequences. While the intention of capitalists is purely selfish, the effects of those actions advance the prosperity of the larger society.

While Smith seems to have vindicated the utility of capitalism, he has not vindicated its morality. *The Theory of Moral Sentiments* seems to hover in stern judgment over *The Wealth of Nations*. By his own moral compass, as outlined in the first book, Smith seems to concede the low motivation of the entrepreneur. The good man looks out for others, while the entrepreneur looks out for himself. And Smith does not even make an effort to show that the allocations of free markets—what Smith terms the "system of natural liberty"—correspond with merit or just deserts.

Perhaps, we might think, there are more recent champions of free markets who have taken up the challenge where Smith left off, to make the case for the unselfish motivations of capitalism, or to show how it leads to just deserts. Not so. Most notorious here is Ayn Rand's book *The Virtue of Selfishness*, which, far from disputing the selfish roots of free markets, celebrates them. Selfishness, Rand insists, is a virtue. There is no way that Adam Smith would agree with this. There is no way that I can either.

Equally striking is a statement made by Friedrich Hayek, whose work cannot be bettered in demonstrating the efficiency of capitalism. Yet when it comes to the morality of capitalism, Hayek sounds a different and, by his own admission, more problematic note. Hayek writes in *The Constitution of Liberty*, "In a free system, it is neither desirable nor practicable that material rewards should be made generally to correspond to what men recognize as merit, and it is an essential characteristic of a free society that an individual's position should not necessarily depend on the views that his fellows hold about the merit he has acquired."[20]

Neither practicable nor desirable! So we have here the remarkable concession—from a leading apologist for capitalism, no less—that capitalist allocations neither are, nor ought to be, based on a recognized standard of merit. Hayek's statement, "strange" and "shocking" as he himself terms it, appears to be a full surrender to the progressive indictment. However efficient a capitalist system may be, if it fails to give people their due, it fails the basic test of justice. In Rawls' words, it must be reformed or abolished.

The alternative, of course, is some form of democratic socialism. And from where does socialism derive its morality? "To me socialism means everybody has a seat at the table and everybody gets a slice of the pie," Michael Moore said recently. "We have to believe that if it's a democracy. Everybody has to participate." Here's the socialist writer Irving Howe from his autobiography *A Margin of Hope*: "We believe that the democracy more or less prevailing in our political life should also be extended deeply into economic life."[21]

We can see from these statements that the moral force of socialism derives from its appeal to democracy. In fact, the statements would carry no weight—they would be downright risible—in any other context. Consider the comedy of saying, in monarchical France or aristocratic Spain, "Everybody has to participate" or "Everybody gets a slice of the pie." The dauphin would turn you over to the court jester. The Spaniards would summon the Inquisition! The logic of mass participation and popular consent are simply opaque in nondemocratic systems of government. Only in a democratic society, like this one, can one talk like this.

I realize, and showed in an earlier chapter, that America is a democracy only in a qualified sense. We have a system that both reflects and places constraints on the will of the majority. Even so, the founders clearly recognized popular consent—the consent of the people—as the moral basis of the free society. Lincoln affirmed the same principle. So democratic socialism today rides on the wagon of majority rule and popular consent. Its moral core is that our economic system, no less than our political system, must reflect the will of the people. That's what is meant by the term "social justice."

Far from disputing this criterion of justice, I embrace it. Thus, the burden of this chapter is to meet the moral critique of capitalism and to show that capitalism satisfies the requirement of justice no less than efficiency. And in addition, I seek to refute the socialists on their own terms by showing that capitalism, far more than socialism, reflects the will of the people and expresses democratic consent. To see this, we must recognize that we are, each of us, not only citizens but also consumers. These are overlapping categories: every citizen is a consumer, and with the exception of illegals, every consumer is also a citizen.

The consumer, like the citizen, is a voter. In this respect, we are all voters in a dual sense. As citizens, we vote once every two or four years; as consumers, we vote many times a day. The citizen votes with a ballot on which he expresses a preference; the vote costs him nothing except the inconvenience of going to the polls, or sending it in. The consumer votes with his dollar bills, which are his hard-earned money, which represent the time and effort he has put in to get those dollar bills.

Only a fraction of citizens is eligible to vote at the ballot box, but every consumer votes in the marketplace—even felons, even children. Illegal aliens cannot lawfully vote for political candidates, but they too vote with their dollar bills. And while citizens participate in a system of representative democracy—their views are filtered through the politicians who represent them—consumers vote in a system of direct democracy. If you prefer an Audi to a Lexus, or Fox to MSNBC, or the Apple iPhone to the Samsung Galaxy, you don't have to elect some other guy to exercise these preferences; you do it directly yourself, by paying for them.

Thus, I will show that a market economy involves a level of popular participation and democratic consent that politics can only envy. We don't need to extend democracy from the political to the economic sphere; we already have it. And the moral grounding of free markets, just like that of our constitutional system, is in the will of the people—in the latter case, a will expressed only on Election Day; in the former case, a will expressed deliberately, emphatically, constantly.

"If we are not competent to rule ourselves, then let us misrule ourselves."[22] Barack Obama Sr., the former president's father, said that in 1959 when he was a student in Hawaii. He was making the case against colonial rule in Kenya. His point is obvious. Let the Kenyan people decide their own fate, even if they decide badly. And so it is with capitalism. Consumers have the right to vote for the products they want and, in this sense, to elevate the entrepreneurs who produce those products. If they make foolish choices, that is regrettable, but it is their right. Capitalism, like democracy, is rooted in popular will and popular consent. Thus capitalism, like democracy, is a form of social justice.

WHO GETS THE SURPLUS?

I'll begin my analysis of the morality of free enterprise by considering an ordinary man's complaint against it. One of my favorite hotels in America is the Trump International Hotel in Washington, D.C. I've stayed there several times, and I've gotten to observe the staff—the concierge, the doormen, the valets—at work. Consider, for a moment, the fellow who parks cars at that hotel and earns, let us say, $100 a day.

Now if I put myself in his place, I would ask myself this question: How many cars do I park each day? Let's say the average is a hundred. And it costs $30 to park a car overnight, a rate comparable to the Ritz Carlton or the Four Seasons or any fine resort hotel. So how much does the Trump Organization make each day on the parking? It makes, on average, $3,000. So that's interesting! The hotel makes three grand and it pays the parking guy just $100.

So, from the point of view of the parking guy, he's being cheated. Why? Because he's the one doing the work. Yet virtually the entire profit goes to the Trump Organization. Why does he get so little? Who gets the remaining $2,900? Our indignant parking guy imagines a member of the Trump family using the money to help pay for a Hawaiian soiree. Notice the parking guy doesn't view himself as a "taker." Rather, he's a "maker." It's the Trumps who are the "takers," depriving their employees of their fair share.

The parking lot guy wants to know, "Where are my just deserts?" And this is a legitimate question. We cannot convince him—and countless others like him—by simply chanting, "Free markets!" "Capitalism!" "America—Love It or Leave it!" We have to show where the other $2,900 went. In other words, we have to show that he is being paid commensurate with what he is producing. If we can, we will have shown that the rewards of the free market system are not only efficient but also fair. If we cannot, some socialist-type redistribution becomes not only plausible but also irresistible.

We can generalize the parking guy's question by putting it in the context of Marx's celebrated criticism of capitalism, one that is taught in schools and universities today, and one that Marx regarded as his most original contribution to economic thought. This is the critique on the basis of "surplus value." It is intended to show that the outward cooperation between entrepreneurs and workers is illusory, that at bottom there is a deep conflict between them, and the result of the conflict is thievery and exploitation. In short, the capitalist is a dirty rotten scoundrel, and he, not to mention the capitalist system that sustains him, deserves to be overthrown.

The strength of Marx's critique is that it does not apply to capitalist "excess": to crisis situations or monopolies or predatory pricing environments like airport concession stores and eateries in sporting stadiums. Rather, Marx attacks capitalism in its normal functioning; this gives his critique a universal character. And nothing vindicates it in the minds of young people so much as the fact that it is rarely confronted and never answered. I have never heard a single Republican—not Trump, nor any congressman or senator—ever discuss, let alone rebut, the Marxist critique.

Marx considers the operations of a normal business, let's say an automobile company or a delivery service like FedEx. Marx recognizes that it costs money to start and operate a business; these represent its total costs. The total costs would include such things as rent, machinery, insurance, travel and so on. Typically, the largest cost is for labor, in the form of salaries and benefits, so Marx factors this in as well. And when you have added these all up, you get the total cost of running the business.

Now, Marx says, one might imagine that a business would price its products in such a way that it would recover all its costs, but in fact, businesses are not content to do that. Rather, they price their products as high as the market will bear. And so, Marx says, businesses generate an income stream that we can call total revenue. Total revenue typically exceeds total cost. And when you subtract total cost from total revenue, you get a crucial number. That number Marx calls "surplus value." We call it "profit."

Now Marx asks a profound question: Who gets that? The profit, Marx argues, belongs entirely to the workers. Why? Because they are the ones who have produced the product. What about the capitalist? Marx insists that the capitalist has produced nothing. The capitalist has—like the name says—contributed the capital. Marx concedes that capital counts for something, but we know what capital counts for: it counts for interest. And paying the going rate of interest on capital is part of the cost of doing business. So a business that does this has already repaid its capitalists. They are not due anything above and beyond that.

Yet although the workers are the ones who are getting the job done, Marx notes that it is the entrepreneur who swoops in and takes all the profits. The workers produce the "surplus value" but the capitalists steal it. Here, for Marx, is the true meaning of exploitation and social injustice. Here are the roots of the class division. And here is the moral argument against capitalist exploitation and in favor of socialist redistribution. Here's where Obama and later Elizabeth Warren got their diatribes about "fair share." It's not about realizing some vague goal of equality; it is simply giving workers their due, using the agency of government to return, one may say, the "stolen goods" that have been taken from them.

The Marxian critique is open to an immediate objection that I regard as telling, though not decisive. Marx insists that the capitalist contributes nothing but the capital, and the workers do all the work to make the business run profitably. Ilhan Omar offered a softer version of this critique in comparing the relative salaries of Walmart's CEO and its median worker. But if this is indeed the case, why don't the workers dispense with the CEOs and start their own companies?

No one is being forced to work at Walmart, so why don't the workers leave and create their own Walmart? Sure, they may lack the initial capital, but they can borrow that at a going rate of interest. This way, there is no one to exploit them and they can share all the profit among themselves. I find it interesting that workers never do this, and even more interesting that Marxists and socialists never even call on them to do it. Deep down, the Marxists seem to realize that they don't do it because they can't.

But why not? Here we get to the heart of Marx's fallacy. Marx was a highly theoretical thinker, and I intend to show that he had no idea of how businesses actually operate or what entrepreneurs actually do. Let's recall that Marx never ran a business. He never even balanced his checkbook. He was a lifelong leech, a Bernie Sanders type, who had most of his expenses paid for by his partner, Friedrich Engels, who inherited his father's textile companies. Incidentally, Engels didn't run his family business either; he had people do that for him. Freed from the need to work, Engels was a man of leisure and a part-time intellectual.

Ironically Marx and Engels were both dependent on the capitalist system they scorned. And one reason American progressives are continually drawn to this duo is that they too have little understanding of what entrepreneurs do. Nor do they really care. They have no aspiration to become entrepreneurs. Rather, they prefer occupations like community activist or professor of romance languages at Bowdoin College. And they aspire to be, like Marx, lifelong leeches, agitating against capitalism even as they subsist off its largesse.

But what is it that Marx and the progressives are ignorant about? I'm going to answer this question by considering two men, an economist and an entrepreneur. The economist is Joseph Schumpeter, who is famous for his theories about the cultural impact of capitalism. Schumpeter wrote a little-known book called *The Entrepreneur* that is one of those rare documents to make the moral case for capitalism and entrepreneurship.

Tellingly, however, Schumpeter doesn't say this. He merely describes what capitalists do. But this is very instructive. Schumpeter shows that the one thing Marx says that capitalists do, they in fact do not do. Schumpeter does show that capitalists do at least four important things that Marx either ignored or had no idea about, calling his whole critique into question. Entrepreneurs earn what they make because of the vital functions that they—and they alone—perform.

The entrepreneur I'll focus on is a familiar person, who happens to be president of the United States. But we're not looking at him in that capacity; instead, we'll look at him in the capacity in which he functioned for most of his career. Donald Trump is a businessman and a builder; he is the quintessential American capitalist. He actually did the things that Schumpeter talks about, and it's fun to see how he did them. Together these two will help me provide my full and complete refutation of the Marxist critique and a persuasive answer to that sullen parking attendant at the Trump Hotel in D.C.

THE SECRET OF TRUMP'S SUCCESS

The starting point of Donald Trump's career, he writes in his best-known book, *The Art of the Deal*, was his realization that "I didn't want to be in the business my father was in." A strange thing to say, since his father was in real estate. But Fred Trump made his money through rent-controlled and rent-stabilized housing units in Queens and Brooklyn. A cautious, self-effacing man, he liked to say that collecting rent was the ideal way to make money. Donald Trump—who was not his father's son in this respect—disagreed.

Trump wanted to cross the bridge and do business in Manhattan, and collecting small rents could not have been further from his mind. "I was looking to make a statement," he says. "I was out to build something monumental—something worth a big effort. . . . What attracted me was the challenge of building a spectacular development on almost one hundred acres by the river on the West Side of Manhattan, or creating a huge new hotel next to Grand Central Station at Park Avenue and Forty Second Street."[23]

What does Schumpeter have to say about this? One defining feature of an entrepreneur, he writes, is "the dream and the desire to found a private kingdom." In fact, the secret dream of the entrepreneur is to found a "dynasty," to project the dream beyond his own life. It is, Schumpeter admits, "the nearest approach to medieval lordship possible to modern man."

The motivation of the entrepreneur, according to Schumpeter, is not primarily monetary success. Rather, it is "the will to conquer, the impulse to fight, to prove oneself superior to others, to succeed for the sake, not of the fruits of success, but of success itself." Schumpeter likens it to sport. "The financial result is a secondary consideration, or at all events, mainly valued as an index of success and a symptom of victory." It is entirely subordinate to "the joy of creating, of getting things done, or simply of exercising one's energy and ingenuity."[24]

Early in his career, Trump set his sights on the Commodore Hotel—built in 1919 and named after "Commodore" Cornelius Vanderbilt. Yet in the depressed real estate market of the mid-1970s, this historic property had become a sorry sight. "The hotel and the surrounding neighborhood were unbelievably run down," Trump says. "Half the buildings were already in foreclosure." The brick façade was filthy, the lobby dingy, and derelicts reclined in the hallways. Management didn't mind; no one wanted to stay at the Commodore, despite paltry room rates.

"But as I approached the hotel," Trump writes, "something completely different caught my eye. It was about nine in the morning and there were thousands of well-dressed Connecticut and Westchester commuters flooding onto the streets from Grand Central Terminal and the subway stations below." Here we have a critical scene. A progressive academic might interpret it one way, such as to note the ironic contrast between the upbeat commuters and the depressed Commodore. Once the hotel was historic, but now history had passed it by.

Trump's interpretation was more prosaic: there's a business opportunity here! "What I saw was a superb location." Affluent prospects were passing through it every day. "The problem was the hotel, not the neighborhood. If I could transform the Commodore, I was sure it could be a hit. Convenience alone would assure that."[25]

So Trump has an idea for a business: to buy the Commodore. It's a crazy idea for a brash kid who just came across the bridge from Queens. But it's a big new idea, and that's what counts to get things started. So here's the first thing entrepreneurs do: they come up with a big new idea for a venture. They don't necessarily invent something new—in fact, invention takes an entirely different skill and sensibility—rather, they envision a new product, a new landscape, a new way of doing things or a new way of living.

This new idea—this new combination the entrepreneur sees—is

invisible to others. "Most people," Schumpeter writes, "do not see the new combinations. They do not exist for them. Most people tend to their usual daily business," and that effort alone "exhausts their energies and suppresses all appetite for further exploration."[26] They have neither the creativity nor the disposition to envision something new. In fact, they view the entrepreneur as reckless, "out there," even as a bit of a crackpot.

It's one thing to have the vision for a new business, Schumpeter writes, but entirely something else to figure out how to do it. Here we have the second element of entrepreneurship, which involves organizing the business. In Trump's case, he didn't have the money to buy the Commodore. Nor was his daddy much help. "I went to my father and told him I had a chance to make a deal for this huge midtown hotel. . . . He refused to believe I was serious." Trump had to figure out how to buy the Commodore, and how to run it, even though he lacked the funds to purchase it or to renovate it, and he had no experience in operating an upscale Manhattan hotel.

First, Trump negotiated a bargain price for the hotel with its owners, who were eager to unload it but who had to be convinced that Trump could afford to buy it. Trump convinced them to sign a paper listing the terms. Then Trump went to banks and told them the owners of the Commodore had consented to sell to him, so if the banks loaned him the asking price, plus the money to upgrade the hotel, he could put up the Commodore itself as collateral. It was, as Trump himself admits, a "juggling act."[27] But the banks went for it and the sellers came through, so Trump got the Commodore.

Schumpeter calls the entrepreneur a *Mann der Tat*, a German phrase that translates to a "man of action."[28] What he means is that, quite apart from conceiving the idea for a business and figuring out how to organize it, you must take action notwithstanding the risk involved. So here we have a third distinguishing feature of the entrepreneur; unlike his employees, who receive a guaranteed paycheck, as per their contracts, the entrepreneur takes virtually all the risk. The entrepreneur gets paid only after the profit is calculated—that is to say, after everyone else is paid—and if the venture fails, he does not get paid at all.

Trump knew the risk: if the Commodore failed, he would not only make no money, he was basically out of the real estate business in Manhattan. It would then be back to Queens and collecting rents. Yet how could Trump be sure that the Commodore would be successful? He couldn't. Trump confesses he hates risk. "People think I'm a gambler. I've never gambled in my life. It's been said I believe in the power of positive thinking. In fact, I believe in the power of negative thinking. I always go into the deal anticipating the worst."[29]

With the Commodore, as with most business ventures, there are known risks that one can compute, but there are also unknown risks. A known risk is one you can insure against. An example of a known risk is tossing a coin: you know in advance that there is a 50 percent chance to get "heads" or "tails." Unknown risks are risks you cannot insure against because you cannot compute the probabilities.

Imagine starting a new business in luxury goods that is highly dependent on the state of the economy over the next several years. What is the chance that the economy will remain strong? Or drop into recession? This is like tossing a dice with an unknown number of sides; there is no way to know. Economists call this second type of risk Knightian uncertainty, after the economist Frank Knight who studied the concept. Knight pointed out that unknown risks are the hallmark of a capitalist economy.

Entrepreneurs must go ahead in the face of risks that cannot be known, let alone mitigated. Sometimes they must do so with very limited information, indeed with little more to go on than personal intuition. This, Schumpeter writes, involves the entrepreneur overcoming the greatest resistance his venture will ever encounter, not resistance from the outside but resistance from within the mind of the entrepreneur himself.

Yet at some point, Schumpeter says, the entrepreneur has got to quell this resistance, to stop calculating and agonizing, and make the leap. It is a leap into the unknown, because the new thing the entrepreneur wants to make does not exist yet; it is only the "figment of his imagination." He is carving out a new road, and Schumpeter notes that this is an entirely different matter than walking along a road that someone else has already carved out.[30]

A GENIUS FOR SPECTACLE

Trump wasn't making a new road, but he was determined to make a new hotel. He unveiled his plan to remake the Commodore. He intended "to cover the . . . brick façade with an entirely new curtain wall of highly reflective glass." Trump's plan drew fire from city planners, architectural critics and media pundits. This was friendly fire; Trump was not a Republican, so he didn't get the unrelentingly savage opposition he gets now. The critics groused that Trump was violating the architectural norm of the area, breaking away from the classical look of Grand Central Station and the ornamented brick-and-limestone buildings along the block.

Trump had a different idea. The point of the reflective glass, he felt, was to make the hotel a kind of mirror of the grand landscape of New York City itself. "By choosing this highly reflective glass, I've created four walls of mirrors. Now when you go across Forty Second Street or go over the Park Avenue ramp . . . you see the reflection of Grand Central Terminal, the Chrysler Building, and all the other landmarks, which otherwise you might not have noticed at all."[31]

What we see here is Trump's genius for spectacle, which gives us the fourth characteristic feature of entrepreneurs: the branding and marketing of the business. Trump has shown this marketing flair throughout his career. When he built Trump Tower, he pitched it as the most desirable place to live in New York. "We were selling fantasy," he admits. His business team informed him that a competing property—Museum Tower—had lowered its prices. "We're in trouble," they told Trump.

Here's how Trump reacted: "I thought for a minute, and I realized that actually the opposite was true: Museum Tower had done itself damage. The sort of wealthy people we were competing for don't look for bargains in apartments. They may want bargains in everything else, but when it comes to a house, they want the best, not the best buy. By pricing its apartments lower than ours, Museum Tower had just announced that it was not as good as Trump Tower." Trump summarized his marketing strategy for Trump Tower as "play hard to get."[32]

I once saw a media panel on television chuckling over the fact that Trump claimed to have a $10 billion valuation for his businesses.

Trump's actual net worth was much less—perhaps in the $4 billion range—but the rest he attributed to the value of the Trump name. The pundits could barely contain their amusement and derision over Trump's apparently inflated self-evaluation. What a ridiculous egomaniac! "Why doesn't he admit he's worth just $4 billion?" Yes, I'm thinking, and how does that compare with your net worth?

Moreover, business consortiums all over the world put up hotels in resort and urban locations and pay the Trump Organization to brand these hotels as part of the signature "Trump Hotel Collection." Even before he became president, Trump created one of the country's most recognizable brands. And today he has the biggest brand in the world; I'm not even sure one can place a monetary value on it.

Finally, Trump solved the problem of how to operate the Commodore. He partnered with the Hyatt hotel chain to do it. At first, Trump's people advised him against splitting the profits 50-50 with Hyatt. Hyatt wanted to rename the Commodore the Grand Hyatt, and Trump agreed. His reason was that, in Hyatt, he had found a partner that was not only experienced in running hotels but was also willing to share the financial risk by reimbursing Trump a significant portion of the funds expended to acquire and upgrade the old Commodore.

And it paid off for him. The Commodore reopened as the Grand Hyatt, it was successful, and Trump and Hyatt split the profits. Eventually a dispute arose between the two parties, which they settled in a conventional business way: in 1996 Hyatt gained complete ownership by buying out Trump's half-share in the hotel for $142 million.

Today, decades later, Trump has the experience, and he doesn't have to go to Hyatt; he operates his own hotels, resorts and casinos across America—indeed, in foreign locations also. And he employs thousands of people, including, of course, the parking guy at his D.C. location. "The entrepreneurs," Schumpeter writes, "are the workers' best customers." This is a very clever way to look at it: the worker is a salesman who markets his labor to his employer, who is, in that sense, his customer. "A continuous improvement of the workers' situation stems from them."[33]

Contrary to Marx, the entrepreneur undertakes projects that the worker has no comprehension of and would not undertake himself, but that nevertheless result in paid employment commensurate with the value the worker provides to the employer. Imagine the workers at the old Commodore figuring out how to transform the hotel, and then making it happen, and then marketing it, and taking all the risk, and finally, when the venture is successful, splitting the cash among themselves. They could scarcely get started! That's why they didn't. It took Trump to do it. That's why Trump is the boss and they are the workers.

I've given only a tiny window into Trump's entrepreneurial world, and we can see from it the inadequacy of the Marxist critique. Marx implies that capitalists only supply the capital, yet typically this is the one thing that capitalists do not supply. Most entrepreneurs get their capital from banks—as Trump did—or venture capital firms. What entrepreneurs do supply—the idea for the business, the organization of it, the marketing, the assumption of risk—are all critical elements completely ignored by Marx. He simply had no conception of what capitalists do. This ignorance renders the Marxist critique of who gets what under capitalism completely useless.

Although Trump may be a walking refutation of Marxist nostrums, Trump's story is by no means one of unalloyed entrepreneurial success. In Trump's book *The Art of the Comeback*, he describes seeing a homeless man holding a begging cup on the street. This was in the early 1990s, and two of Trump's big properties—the Trump Taj Mahal and the Trump Plaza Hotel—had just gone bankrupt. Trump owed $900 million. Pointing to the homeless man, Trump remarked, "He's a beggar, but he's worth $900 million more than me."[34]

Reviewing this passage in the book, Dylan Matthews, a writer for the website Vox, reacts with revulsion to Trump's casual, almost whimsical, attitude here. "You'd think this kind of story would result in some kind of self-reflecting," Matthews writes. But in Trump's case, "Nah." Trump seems "uninterested in his failures."[35] In progressive academic and journalistic precincts, self-reflection is what you do when things take a downward turn. Failure is an occasion for some high-toned navelgazing, asking whether your busts and bankruptcies are a real measure of your worth as a person.

To such minds, Trump's willingness to assume gargantuan debt and then forge unreflectively ahead seems downright surreal. The man must be demented! Total lack of introspection! Yet Trump weathered the storm and went on to massively successful new ventures, including some, like hosting NBC's reality TV show *The Apprentice*, that were quite remote from his familiar territory of real estate. He won some and he lost some, but he won more than he lost, and he's got a vastly bigger brand, and the vastly bigger bank account, than all his critics put together.

I'd like to conclude this section by addressing the parking guy at Trump's hotel. If he wants to know why he isn't being paid more, the answer is that his work is not worth more. It's not worth $30 to park a car. If the guy parked my car, I'd pay him a dollar. The reason people pay $30 to park overnight is that they are at a resort. The overall ambience and amenities of the resort, and not merely the simple task of parking a car, is the "value" that people seek when they park their cars overnight. Deep down, I suspect the valet knows this.

Someone—in this case Trump—had the idea for that resort. He organized it. He marketed it and established a coveted brand. His brand attracted the clientele. He took all the risk. The parking guy did none of this. So Trump, not the parking guy, deserves the lion's share of the profit. Both of them—the boss and the menial laborer—are getting their just deserts. If the parking guy wants more, he should work to be the parking supervisor. Or go back to school and study hotel management. Perhaps, one day, he will run his own business and, once he has paid all his employees and managers, justly keep the balance for himself as profit.

WHO GAVE THE ORDERS

I now want to turn to a different kind of entrepreneur, whom I'm going to call the "supply-side entrepreneur." We can understand the supply-side entrepreneur in contradistinction to the traditional entrepreneur. The Austrian economist Ludwig von Mises had traditional entrepreneurs in mind when he told the story of Beatrix Potter. Potter and her husband, Sidney Webb, were Fabian socialists who despised Beatrix's father, Richard Potter, a wealthy businessman.

In Potter's memoirs, she described working as her father's secretary. "In the business of my father everybody had to obey the orders issued by my father, the boss. He alone had to give orders, but to him nobody gave any orders." Von Mises shrewdly observes, "This is a very shortsighted view. Orders were given to her father by the consumers, by the buyers. Unfortunately, she could not see these orders . . . because she was interested only in the orders given within her father's office or his factory."[36]

That's what traditional entrepreneurs do. They respond to consumer demand, to "orders" issued by the consumer. But there is another type of entrepreneur who creates products in response to no existing consumer demand. Think of the iPhone. Did consumers write to Steve Jobs, demanding a phone that connected them to the internet? That did email? That took pictures? No. In the case of that product, the supply preceded the demand. Jobs, in a sense, built the phone in recognition of what people wanted even before they knew they wanted it.

Putting himself in the place of his potential customers, Jobs realized that they didn't like the existing keyboard and stylus that dominated the BlackBerry, Motorola and Palm smartphones of the day. Why not have everything work off a touchscreen, using nature's own stylus—the finger—to navigate the device? Wouldn't it be great to move effortlessly from phone calls to music to web surfing? And, no less important, a device with no instruction manual—you just look at it, and you can see how to use it![37]

The supply-side entrepreneur is an economic revolutionary. He or she thrives in a revolutionary environment, which is to say, during a technological revolution. During normal periods, entrepreneurs and CEOs respond to consumer demand. Their task is fairly routine administration. Think of the CEO of General Motors or Ford during the 1960s, the "golden age" of relative equality that progressives rhapsodize about today.

What did those guys actually do? They were, for the most part, routine administrators; they merely ran their companies, and truth be told, some of them ran their companies into the ground, because they did not anticipate the oil shock and the economic downturn of the 1970s. If they received mediocre compensation for what they did, that's because they were mediocre at what they did. They produced modest consumer welfare, and they were modestly rewarded for it.

Contrast their performance with that of the supply-side entrepreneurs in revolutionary periods, such as the one we're living in today. These are a select group of entrepreneurs working alongside traditional entrepreneurs, but distinguished from them in that they pursue radical innovations. These innovations produce unprecedented consumer welfare. But they also widen inequality, because they channel huge profits to the supply-side entrepreneur.

So this is the real reason why inequalities today are wider than they were in the postwar period. That's why we see the huge agglomerations of wealth in places like New York City, Silicon Valley and Seattle. Seattle alone is home to Microsoft, Amazon and Starbucks. Progressives who say we are living through a new Gilded Age miss the point. The Gilded Age, at the turn of the nineteenth century and the dawn of the twentieth, gave us the telephone, the car and the airplane. Now we have the cell phone, GPS, ecommerce and huge advances in artificial intelligence and medicine.

Can anyone who has lived through this great transformation of the past couple of decades not see the massive improvements they have produced? Is there a progressive or socialist alive today who would give them up? Are there young people who can even imagine what life was like before them? It is the enthusiasm of customers in America, and worldwide, that has produced the inequality that progressives bewail today. The moral justification of those profits is that they represent the wishes—and welfare—of delighted consumers. This is democracy in action, whether the left admits it or not.

Of course, there were supply-side entrepreneurs in the postwar era. One of them was Ray Kroc, who created McDonald's. I can't eat at McDonald's anymore—the food no longer appeals to me—but when I first came to America, it was far and away my favorite place to eat. And even today, despite all the hoopla about the horrors of fast food, McDonald's is an American institution and, with stores in thousands of cities in 100 countries, it is one of the world's most recognizable brands. But why is it called McDonald's? Why not Kroc's?

The reason is that the McDonald brothers, Dick and Mac McDonald, started McDonald's as a single restaurant on Route 66 in San Bernardino, California. Kroc, who at that time sold soft drink dispensers, visited the restaurant to check out their milkshake mixers. He saw a curvaceous young woman eating one of the McDonald's burgers in the parking lot. "It was not her sex appeal," he later said, "but the obvious relish with which she devoured the hamburger that made my pulse begin to hammer with excitement."

Kroc met with the McDonald brothers and told them that he admired the simplicity, efficiency and affordability of their meals. He proposed they go into partnership with him to take McDonald's nationwide. Kroc even spelled out his supply-side insight. America in the postwar era was becoming more mobile. That meant Americans would be spending a lot of time in their cars. Kroc's idea was that people might come to appreciate "fast food" that was predictable, affordable and, as I could testify from my student days, downright delectable.

Yet the McDonald brothers were not interested. They took Kroc to see their brand-new Cadillacs and nice homes on the hill, and they were content with their prosperous lifestyle; they had no intention of working any harder or taking huge risks that might jeopardize the good thing they had going locally. So Kroc took it national. The McDonald brothers of course retained a share, and eventually Kroc took out loans so that he could buy them out. Each of them got a very nice million-dollar check, a great deal of money in those days, and the equivalent of nearly $10 million today.

Later, of course, the McDonald brothers resented the mammoth success of McDonald's. This success, of course, was only obvious in hindsight. It was Kroc, not they, who spotted the opportunity to expand into something big. They had a chance to bet on that success, but opted against taking the gamble. Determined to "show" Kroc, the McDonald brothers started a new burger franchise under a new name. But it was a failure.[38] The duo is no longer around, but if they were, I wouldn't be surprised to see them on MSNBC these days complaining about Kroc's "selfishness" and "greed."

THE GUILTY PARTY

We identify the communications revolution today with Apple products—
the iPhone, the iPod and the iMac—but a predecessor of Apple's iPod
was the Sony Walkman, which took America by storm in the 1980s. It
changed the way people experienced music. I couldn't dream of owning
a Walkman in those days, but I remember meeting Sony CEO Akio Morita at a *Forbes* conference in the 1990s. How, I asked him, did he (and
Sony) come up with the idea for the Walkman, a brand that had become,
at that time, as big as McDonald's and Coca-Cola? Did consumers ask
him to make a little radio that could be attached to their heads?

Morita laughed. Of course not, he said. He told me that he would
go to the beach with his children, and the kids and their friends would
listen to loud music from boom boxes from morning to evening. Teen-
agers are a cultural plague we must all endure, you might say. But not
Morita. He began to think in a supply-side mode. He asked himself,
"Why do I have to listen to this ghastly music?" And further, "Why do
they have to carry those cumbersome boom boxes?"

Morita asked his engineers to figure out a way to build a small radio
and cassette player that would sound like a high-quality car stereo and
yet could be attached to a person's head. Morita didn't want a recording
function; just a music player with an ear connection. That way people
could take their music with them, they could listen to it without an-
noying others and they could ride bikes and do other things with their
hands while listening to music.

The Sony team was dubious. The marketing department, in particular, was aghast. Morita was basically calling for a tiny car stereo with
earphones, but earphones were considered anathema at the time because
they were used mainly by deaf people.[39] Morita, however, insisted, and
the rest is entrepreneurial history. His supply-side venture seized the
public imagination, and the Sony Walkman, launched in 1979, almost
instantly became a regular accompaniment for teenage and even adult
consumers.

Finally, I'd like to talk about what made Amazon an ecommerce
behemoth, and Jeff Bezos—the son of a sixteen-year-old mom and a

deadbeat dad—the richest man in the world. It's tempting to think that it was Amazon's decision to go from selling just books and DVDs to selling, well, just about everything. But Amazon's big jump didn't come from that. In fact, Bezos got that idea from one of his customer surveys. He asked his book buyers what else they'd like to get on Amazon. One of them responded that he was looking for an obscure gadget that he couldn't find locally. Then it hit Bezos that Amazon could sell literally everything, as long as they could figure out how to ship it.

The shipping! This was Amazon's greatest challenge. It took time to get products to consumers, and for some products—furniture, tools, wine, foodstuffs—the transportation was problematic on several counts. How to send perishable items? The biggest obstacle was cost. If Amazon shipped in two days, or overnight, the cost was prohibitive. Try sending a couch by UPS or FedEx overnight, and the price of shipping might be higher than that of the couch itself!

Bezos proposed Amazon Prime. For an upfront payment of $79, customers would get two-day delivery on their orders. In one shot, Amazon changed the rules of online shopping. No more long waits to get your stuff; Amazon could now compete with the immediacy of brick-and-mortar storefronts. Bezos' original goal was great customer service for his existing customers. As he told his team, "I want to build a moat around our best customers."

But the team at Amazon protested that there was no way to make this work. Amazon at the time had most of its inventory in the Midwest; how could the company afford to ship an unlimited number of items to consumers across the country in two days? Marc Onetto, who headed Amazon's operations, told Bezos that air freight cost ten times as much as land or sea delivery, and this alone rendered the whole idea inoperable. Bezos' response to Onetto was, "You aren't thinking correctly."

Bezos' point was that Onetto was considering the situation as it existed then and not the altered situation if Amazon Prime attracted a sufficiently large base of paying customers. In that case, Bezos figured that the upfront $79 payment multiplied, say, a million times over would give Amazon the capital to create dozens, eventually hundreds, of regional distribution facilities. Amazon's products would no longer need to go out from central warehouses via UPS or FedEx overnight. Rather, they could be stored at fulfillment centers in every part of the country and then be driven to customers at a cost that made the whole venture practicable.[40] And this is precisely what happens now.

How did these supply-side entrepreneurs and their core teams get so rich? If you listen to the progressives and the socialists, you'll hear a lot about "appropriation" and how these guys enjoy a disproportionate share of "the nation's wealth." But it's not the "nation's" wealth; it's their wealth. They got it by producing things that have enriched people's lives so much that they were thrilled to pay for them, and probably would have been willing to pay a lot more. So the entrepreneurs didn't appropriate anything; they earned what they have acquired through their entrepreneurial ventures. Contrary to Obama and Warren, they really did build that!

And how did they do it? We have spoken earlier of the critical elements of entrepreneurship, but I left one of them out. That element is a most surprising one, because it runs counter to all the anticapitalist propaganda. It is unselfishness, empathy, the ability to identify with the feelings and wants of others. More than any other profession—with the possible exception of the clergy—entrepreneurs, and especially supply-side entrepreneurs, restrain their own selfish impulses and put themselves in the place of their customers. They focus obsessively on the customers' wants and needs, and on how best to fulfill them. In some cases, as we have just seen, through some sort of empathetic leap, they anticipate consumer desires even before consumers themselves have them.

Recall, from the quotation at the beginning of this chapter, that these qualities of self-restraint and empathy constitute, in the words of Adam Smith, "the perfection of human nature." Thus, we can see a way to resolve the Adam Smith "problem." Smith's own emphasis in *The Wealth of Nations* on self-interest as a description of entrepreneurial motivation must now be qualified to acknowledge the operational empathy that is critical to entrepreneurial success. The entrepreneurs' profits are nothing more than a measure of the degree to which they have effectively satisfied the wants and needs of others.

Inequality, in sum, is here by democratic mandate. Who can still contend that this inequality is unjust? Entrepreneurs are not responsible for it; we are. We conferred these gargantuan rewards on them not irrationally or unwittingly but purposefully, through millions of transactions aimed at making our lives faster, easier, more fulfilling. We are fortunate, not cursed, to be living through an entrepreneurial revolution. If we weren't, we might still be driving around with old maps and making expensive long-distance calls on wall-connected rotary phones.

At some point, of course, this revolution will stabilize, and the inequality that came in its wake will flatten out. We don't need policies to make this happen; it will happen by itself. High tech and ecommerce superprofits will shrink back to normal profits. In the meantime, a certain measure of inequality is the direct and inevitable product of this second communications revolution, so let's enjoy the benefits and stop whining about a just outcome that we ourselves have, through our actions as consumers, ordained and sustained.

TRYING OUR LUCK

I want to further probe the issue of just deserts by considering the role that luck plays in human success. We can consider a successful person lucky in two separate senses. First, his luck could simply be a matter of good timing. Here—to pick up Michael Walzer's example from earlier in this chapter—we might consider a book that enjoys an explosive success largely due to the timing of its release.

In the 1990s, David Maraniss published his biography of the legendary coach Vince Lombardi called *When Pride Still Mattered*. This book was published during Bill Clinton's presidency, at the height of the Monica Lewinsky scandal. It became an immediate bestseller. It helped many Americans cope with their disgust about their leaders and to recover from the past a sense of dignity and honor. Arguably, had it been published at another time, it would have enjoyed only a modest success.

What if McDonald's, instead of being launched a few decades ago by Ray Kroc, was launched instead today by someone else? It seems quite likely that in this era of mass obesity, and with all the public consciousness about the health risks of fast food, a newly created McDonald's would be a disaster. Or consider today's software programmers, with their highly coveted and well-compensated math skills—what if those guys were born a century ago? What could they do with those math skills, aside from winning bar bets and impressing their friends by multiplying large numbers in their heads?

So, to put the question broadly, where is the justice or "merit" in being in the right place at the right time? Philosopher Robert Nozick considers this question through a thought experiment involving a society of individuals, each of whom has a certain amount of money. The initial distribution, Nozick says, doesn't matter; pick your favorite distribution and call it D-1. Let's say it is a socialist society with complete economic equality!

Now let's say that someone in that society is a really good basketball player, like Wilt Chamberlain, or writes gripping horror stories, like Stephen King. Not surprisingly, we see a whole bunch of people fork over some of their money to buy tickets to see Chamberlain play or to purchase one of King's books. This produces a new economic distribution that we can call D-2. Admittedly the new distribution D-2 is less equal than its predecessor D-1. Even so, Nozick writes, if D-1 is a just distribution, then why isn't D-2 also just?

Nozick concludes that it is. "A distribution is just," he writes, "if it arises from another just distribution by legitimate means."[41] No one who participated in these transactions has a right to complain, even if their shares are changed, because they freely chose to participate in them with an eye to their own benefit. Third parties have no right to complain because their shares are not changed. Everyone started out with their fair share, and notwithstanding the inequality, everyone ended up with their fair share.

Nozick argues that a free society that permits such exchanges will necessarily produce inequality, and any socialist attempt to equalize outcomes will require constant state intervention to undo the effects of voluntary human action. In this way, socialism is inherently inimical to freedom. It undermines freedom not merely due to tyrannical "excess," à la Stalin or Mao or Hugo Chavez. It undermines freedom because it refuses to let people exercise free choice in the way they deploy the fruits of their labor.

Even so, where is the "merit" in what Chamberlain and King produce? Where is the justice in the rewards they rake in? Their merit, Nozick argues, is not some external standard dictated by a third party but rather the value that has been created for the consumer. In commerce, as in politics, value is in the eye of the beholder. Buyers no more have to justify their choices to outside parties than voters do. Both groups confer rewards based on their own standards of value, regardless of whether those standards can withstand external scrutiny.

Presumably, those who bought tickets to see Chamberlain or a book by King derived more satisfaction from the entertainment than from the money they parted with to make their purchases. Now if Chamberlain lived in a society that didn't care about basketball, his skills would be useless, not because he didn't objectively possess them but because consumers subjectively didn't value them. Thus, if we define merit not objectively but subjectively—to refer to what consumers value and are willing to pay for—then capitalism is obviously a meritocratic system par excellence.

It should be noted that Chamberlain took a great deal of risk in becoming a professional basketball player. Not only do youngsters, even tall and talented youngsters, aspiring to the NBA have a low chance of making it, but even if they do, their careers might last only a few years, shortened either by injury or the brief window their talent allows them to be among the best at their brand of intensely physical sport. Chamberlain, one may say, entered a lottery with an infinitesimal chance of winning and a high probability of enjoying only a short tenure on the winning stage. We can assume that Chamberlain was aware of these risks when he set aside other options and took his chances on becoming an NBA star.

Now, these risks could be mitigated if the participants in these ventures chose to do so. We can envision a group of talented aspiring athletes—or authors, or actors—coming together to create an insurance pool. Taking into account the risks of their profession, they create a "cooperative" whose members agree in advance to share income receipts roughly equally. Perhaps the deal is that the one who makes it big time—i.e., "hits the jackpot"—gets to keep half of his earnings, but must split the balance with the rest of the pool. This would reduce the risk for everyone.

Yet no one does this. In fact, the very absence of such risk-sharing pools, in sports or publishing or Hollywood, clearly shows that those who venture into these professions are ready to assume the hazards that go with them. I know I am. We would rather assume individually the risk of failure, and in the event that we are successful, the success would be ours; it does not belong to others who "also ran." So good timing or not, winning is Chamberlain's, and King's, and my just prerogative.

THE OVARIAN LOTTERY

Having, I believe, established the justice of luck in the sense of good timing, I now turn to luck in a broader or Rawlsian sense. John Rawls contends that the talents of people like Wilt Chamberlain and Stephen King are, by themselves "neither just nor unjust." Rawls argues that "these are simply natural facts. What is just and unjust is the way that institutions deal with those facts."[42] In other words, it is society that creates just or unjust distributions based on what it does with the earnings of individuals like Chamberlain and King.

The investment tycoon Warren Buffett, a disciple of Rawls, is on board with this. It is his acknowledged basis for backing the Democrats and continuing to urge higher taxes on the top income brackets. The Obama administration trotted Buffett out like a poster boy. "Here's our tycoon who confesses that he pays more taxes than his executive secretary." Buffett says successful people like Chamberlain, King and, well, himself, have won the "ovarian lottery."[43] They got lucky in their selection of genes, and parents, and where they were raised.

Buffett is echoing the key Rawlsian point that none of these people deserve credit for talents that they were either born with or were conferred by their surrounding environment. Since luck cannot be earned, Rawls and his disciples contend that the benefits of luck should in justice be widely shared. While Rawls did not favor the state intervening to prevent Chamberlain or King from doing their thing, he did favor the state taking over and reallocating the fruits of their labor in a manner aimed at reducing inequality and "sharing the wealth."

I'm not concerned with Rawls' own formula for doing this. No one is discussing that formula today, and I intend to respect that general indifference. There is no point disputing about solutions before we have correctly identified problems. What then is the "problem" with luck, as Rawls would have it? Is it really true that all the good things we produce, that anyone produces, are the result of luck or natural lottery? Is it really true that we deserve no reward—or even credit—for them?

If so, it follows that all the bad things that people do, including all the crimes and horrors they commit, are also the result of luck or natural lottery. To pursue Rawls' logic, either Ted Bundy was born a serial killer or he became one as a result of his environment. Either Hitler was born evil or his environment made him that way. Why then do such people deserve punishment? Why do they even deserve criticism?

Rawls' theory applies to the entire system of rewards and sentences, or even of praise and blame, not merely in the market but in every sphere of human action, from performance in school to the criminal justice system. It declares all of it, without exception, to be null and void. Does Rawls seriously propose that we "go there"? He does not. Nowhere does Rawls even acknowledge, let alone consider, these far-reaching implications of what he is proposing.

Moreover, Rawls assumes that the outcome of a natural lottery is both unjust and undemocratic; I intend to challenge this by arguing that lotteries are inherently just and democratic, for the simple reason that they give everyone an equal chance to succeed. Consider the guy who wins $10 million in a lottery. Let's say that 20 million people entered and each bought a single ticket. In this case, each of them had an identical chance to win. Obviously, someone had to win, and it happened to be this guy, but it could just as easily have been one of the other players. Each ticket, and therefore each player, had equal opportunity. What could be fairer than that? Rawls assumes that the lottery winner has some sort of obligation to share. But why? Can anyone reasonably demand this of lottery winners? Can the other players justly gang up on him and seize his winnings? This would be outrageous.

The economist Milton Friedman illuminates this topic further with an example I draw from his book *Capitalism and Freedom*. "Suppose you and three friends are walking along the street and you happen to spy and retrieve a $20 bill on the pavement." Friedman concedes it would be generous if you decided to share the money equally, or to use it to buy a round of drinks for everyone. (This was in 1974, when $20 could in fact buy drinks for four people.)

Then Friedman cuts to the chase. "But suppose you do not. Would the other three be justified in joining forces and compelling you to share the $20 equally with them?"[44] This is a crushing example, because it reflects the tyrannical logic of democratic socialism. Friedman's point is that it would be wrong for the others to use their majority power to confiscate your newfound $20. He concludes that even if your "lucky winnings" were in some respect considered unjust, it would be more unjust to force you to give them up to produce another distribution favored by someone else.

Entrepreneurs have a name for luck: they call it risk. As I noted earlier, they enter the field recognizing that there are all kinds of uncertainties and unknowns. And they do seek, as far as possible, to minimize risk. Machiavelli understood this as an attempt to control the swift current of fortune. But even he, ambitious as he was, believed that only half of it could be controlled. The rest is inscrutable, unforeseeable, "up to chance." There is no alternative but to submit to it. This is what it means to take risk; it is to test your luck.

In life, as in business, our luck may be whimsical, capricious, even random in her dispensations. Even so, we have a right to try our luck, and then to enjoy its rewards or suffer its slings and arrows. Contrary to the Rawlsian mumbo jumbo, no one has the right to our rewards who did not assume the risks we did. This is the human predicament—nature's bargain—and it is as fair and just as anything we are likely to experience this side of Paradise.

ENDLESS PURSUIT

I'd like to close out this chapter making the moral case for capitalism by addressing two remaining questions. The first is whether we have reached in America a situation in which robots and other forms of technology can do all the work, leaving nothing left for entrepreneurs and workers to do. I think we can see, reflecting on what we have observed of how entrepreneurs operate, that this is not a realistic fear. Entrepreneurs never run out of ideas, for the simple reason that humans never run out of wants. The fulfillment of old wants gives rise to new wants. The Book of Ecclesiastes had this figured out ages ago: "The eye never has enough of seeing, nor the ear its fill with hearing." Nor, one might add, does the heart have enough of desiring.

Just as farming gave way to manufacturing and manufacturing to services, services will eventually give way to something else. What? What's the next invention just over the horizon? I wish I knew, because then I would have invented it! Senator Rand Paul recently tweeted, "Instead of sending men to Mars we should send oxygen producing organic life modified to grow under the harsh conditions on Mars. Creating livable atmosphere should be our first goal."[45] Yes, it's a little nuts—precisely the kind of crazy thinking that helps stimulate revolutionary advances in the human condition.

Bottom line: we will always need entrepreneurs and workers because human beings never run out of things to dream, and make, and do. Even as we approach our destination, defined as the sum total of our aspirations, that destination keeps receding, which is to say our aspirations keep growing. For some, this may be a reason to despair of the human condition. But we can all be consoled that idleness and boredom are not in our future. The pursuit of happiness that Jefferson spoke about is an endless pursuit. We had better learn to enjoy ourselves along the way.

The second question I wish to explore is whether highly successful entrepreneurs need so much money. Think about it: we can only eat three meals a day, wear one set of clothes at a time and so on. Even the most lavish, indulgent lifestyle costs only so much. Why, then, should we leave tycoons with so much surplus when that money can be put to relatively good use by the state to provide food, education and healthcare to others?

This is an argument based on practicality, not morality. I hear it quite often. In fact, when I presented the idea for this book to the head of the publishing house, this was her immediate reaction: "I just don't get it why some people need so much money." And of course, in truth, they don't. But it is a fallacy to suppose that because they have no plausible use for it themselves—at least none that we can conceive—they should therefore be willing to relinquish it or the state should have the right to confiscate it.

What, let us ask, would we ourselves do if we somehow came into a gargantuan sum of money? One option is to spend it. This is the obvious initial temptation, but as noted above, there is a limit to how much we can spend. A second option is to invest it. That means putting the money into a bank or into the stock market. In the case of entrepreneurs, it might mean reinvesting it in their own business. However the money is invested, it will most likely help create jobs, satisfy consumer wants and stimulate the economy.

A third option is to give it away. The richest of American tycoons have almost inevitably given away large parts of their wealth. This was true of the Rockefellers and Carnegies a century ago, and it is no less true today. Rockefeller built schools and hospitals and supported Christian missionaries around the world. He backed antipoverty and relief efforts in America and abroad. He funded life-changing medical research through the Rockefeller University and the Rockefeller Foundation. Andrew Carnegie was also a prodigious philanthropist who endowed the Carnegie Foundation and built more than 2,500 public libraries across the United States as well as in his native Scotland.

Ray Kroc was a generous benefactor during his lifetime, and after he died, his widow Joan Kroc continued his philanthropy, erasing a good chunk of the family fortune by giving $1.5 billion to the Salvation Army. Bill Pulte, scion of a big industrial concern, prefers to give away money directly to veterans and families that have experienced tragedy. Bill Gates has already siphoned off a large fraction of his wealth for the Bill and Melinda Gates Foundation. Among innumerable projects, the Gates Foundation buys mosquito nets for poor families in Asia and Africa and sponsors research into altering the genetic code of mosquitos to render key species infertile or unable to carry the malaria parasite.[46]

Now it is possible to argue about whether these tycoons, past and present, are giving away their money in the wisest way. Sure, the Gates Foundation is trying to fight malaria with those mosquito nets, but there have been reports of people in coastal villages taking them down and using them as fishing nets.[47] To which my response is: big deal! Let them use the nets as they see fit. I've seen some skepticism on Twitter about Pulte, because he announces his giveaways and then demands a minimum number of retweets as a condition for making the gift. Some cynics speculate that Pulte's philanthropy is a shrewd marketing campaign to build his social media following.

I don't know. But I do know that people who have made their own money are likely to spend it more carefully and discerningly than a group of politicians and bureaucrats. We all have a natural tendency to be more responsible with our own possessions than with those that belong to someone else. Ask yourself: How often have you taken a rental car to the car wash? I never do. And why not? Because it's not my car! For this reason, I think entrepreneurs are more likely to promote social welfare through their own efforts than by turning over their assets to the federal government.

THE BUSINESS OF POLITICS

Does it follow, then, that progressives and socialists are entirely wrong when they say that there are rich people in the top 1 percent who are greedy selfish leeches, who don't deserve their money and who have gotten it by contributing little or nothing to society? Actually, no! Such people do exist, and they can be found among the ranks of the progressives and socialists themselves. Let's consider a few notorious examples.

Michael Moore accumulated a $50 million fortune by making documentaries bashing capitalism. Moore—who wears a trademark baseball cap to communicate that he's a regular, working-class guy—nevertheless got "outed" in his divorce in which it came to public light that he and his wife owned nine properties in Michigan and New York, including a 10,000-square-foot lakefront home in Traverse City and a Manhattan condo so large that it was once three separate apartments.[48]

Bernie Sanders' public career as a socialist, most notably his presidential runs, have catapulted him from the middle class to "one of those rich people against whom he has so unrelentingly railed," as Politico put it in a recent profile, "The Secret of Bernie's Millions." Bernie cashed in on his wife's severance package after she ran Burlington College into the ground. He also did well with real estate appreciation and with the proceeds of a bestselling book, which he boasts "sold all over the world, and we made money." Bernie and his wife now own three homes, including a lakefront summer pad.[49]

Another basher of free markets, Elizabeth Warren, accumulated a net worth estimated by *Forbes* to be $12 million through a long career of bashing free markets and passing herself off as a Native American. The latter fraud—Warren is in fact 1/1,024 Native American, which is to say, she is not Native American—made her eligible for affirmative action hiring and promotion at elite universities such as Harvard. She was hired at an inflated salary as Harvard Law's first "woman of color."

Of course, as a woman, Warren was already eligible for affirmative action. But she wanted to be a "two-fer," in other words, to claim the "double oppression" of being not just a woman but also a Native American. This would smooth her path to being hired at top academic institutions. Whatever one thinks about affirmative action, no one can justify a white woman masquerading as a Native American to capitalize on benefits reserved for historically disadvantaged minorities. Warren now owns two homes, a $3 million Victorian in Cambridge and a posh condo in Washington, D.C.[50]

What's striking here is the shamelessness of Moore, Sanders and Warren.

We all know about the Clintons, who went from zero to $200 million since Bill Clinton left the White House. The Clintons made money every which way: by renting out American foreign policy, by selling pardons, by siphoning off earthquake aid intended for poor Haitians. I have written about this previously, so I won't go into it here. But in profiting handsomely from their office and connections, the Clintons are not alone; rather, they are part of a Democratic trend.

The Obamas are now worth 30 times more than when they entered the White House in 2008, giving them a net worth in excess of $40 million. Much of this came from lucrative book deals, from speeches delivered by both Obamas at $200,000 a pop and from a sweetheart deal with Netflix that is reportedly worth $50 million. For the Obamas, no money-making scheme is too petty; Michelle rakes in the bucks by charging even nonprofit groups $225,000 to speak and sells 25 different items of merchandise—mugs, shirts and candles—on the speaking circuit.

The Obamas do not seem abashed to enjoy their newfound largesse. They now own a $2.5 million home in Chicago's Hyde Park and a mansion in Washington, D.C., worth $8 million. The D.C. property, in the exclusive Kalorama neighborhood, has 8,200 square feet, including nine bedrooms, a two-tiered flagstone terrace with a courtyard and parking space for 8–10 cars. The Obamas' most recent acquisition is the $12 million beachfront property on Martha's Vineyard. Addicted to luxury vacations, Obama has been spotted relaxing on Hollywood mogul David Geffen's yacht and kitesurfing on Necker Island with Britain's flamboyant billionaire Richard Branson.[51]

While Joe Biden has throughout his career referred to himself as Middle Class Joe, a recent report in Politico titled "Biden Inc." tells a different story. Biden has raked in millions in recent years, enabling him to live in a 12,000-square-foot home in McLean, Virginia, with 5 bedrooms, 10 bathrooms, marble fireplaces, a gym and sauna and parking for 20 cars. The Bidens also own a beach house in Rehoboth Beach, Delaware, to complement their 7,000-square-foot lakeside home in Wilmington, Delaware.

For the Bidens, it's not just about Joe; it's a family racket that includes his son Hunter and his two brothers, James and Frank. All of them have become millionaires by trading on Biden's political name and connections. "In the early 2000s," Politico reports, "Hunter had opened a lobbying practice that landed clients with interests that overlapped with Joe's committee assignments and legislative priorities."

In 2006, Biden's brother James and son Hunter took over a hedge fund, Paradigm Global Advisors. After firing the president and assembling the rest of the team, James Biden laid out his vision for the fund's future. "Don't worry about investors," he said, "We've got investors lined up in a line of 747s filled with cash. We've got people all around the world who want to invest in Joe Biden." The hedge fund, according to Politico, "would soon attract attention for its associations with several criminal frauds."

In November 2010, James Biden was named head of a New Jersey construction firm, HillStone International. Even though Biden had no experience in construction and HillStone had little experience in home-building, the firm landed $1.5 billion in contracts to build homes in Iraq. "At the time," Politico notes, "Joe Biden was leading the adminis-tration's Iraq policy."

Biden's other brother, Frank, has used his proximity to power to negotiate profitable deals in Costa Rica and Jamaica. One year after Joe Biden helped push through a $6.5 million taxpayer-backed loan to build solar power facilities in Costa Rica, that country's government in 2016 signed a letter of intent with Frank Biden's company Sun Fund Americas to operate those facilities. The previous year, right around the time USAID announced a $10 million renewable energy project in Ja-maica, Frank Biden's Sun Fund Americas had signed a power purchase agreement to build a 20 megawatt solar facility in that country.

In December 2013, Hunter Biden accompanied his father aboard Air Force Two on an official visit to China. In Beijing, the vice presi-dent met with Hunter's Chinese partners who had just formed a new investment partnership, Rosemont Seneca Partners. Two weeks later, the Chinese authorized a joint venture—now worth more than $2 billion—between Rosemont Seneca Partners, the China Development Bank and China's social security fund to invest in China's fast-growing economy, including state-owned IPOs normally closed to foreign investors.[52]

In 2014, as Joe Biden commandeered the Obama administration's response to Russia's annexation of the Crimean peninsula in southern Ukraine, Hunter Biden was appointed to the board of Ukrainian nat-ural gas company Burisma Holdings. Despite his utter lack of energy expertise—pretty much all he had to offer was his access to his father—Hunter Biden was paid in excess of $50,000 a month.[53] Somewhat com-ically, the Democratic House sought to impeach President Trump for raising the subject of the Biden family's crooked dealings on a phone call with the Ukrainian head of state. The attempt was swiftly and appropriately thwarted by a Republican majority in the Senate.

The Obamas, the Clintons and the Bidens are now living the billionaire lifestyle. Warren isn't there yet, but that's only because she hasn't yet made it to the highest echelons of government, where there is more access to sell. These people are all political entrepreneurs for whom politics is a business. I wonder if they joke in private: "What's wrong with socialism? It's good business!" They are in the mode of Hugo Chavez and other Third World kleptocrats who speak the language of social justice even as they rake in gargantuan piles of cash.

How long are Americans going to be suckered by this sleazy crew? Leave aside the hypocrisy of these pompous frauds talking about "public service" even as they cash in on their titles, leverage their offices and deliver political favors for personal recompense. What social value have Democrats like Warren, Obama, Clinton or Biden created in exchange for the wealth they have obtained? Virtually none. Essentially, they have used their political name and office to enrich themselves.

They—not entrepreneurs—are the greedy, selfish bastards. They are the ones playing the system and skirting the law. This is the progressive, socialist parasitic class, feeding off the wealth of society while reviling the free market system that produced that wealth. If anyone deserves to be horsewhipped, it's these progressive and socialist Democrats. As for entrepreneurs, we need more of them. If the socialists are helping to destroy the country, entrepreneurs are helping to make America great again.

6

THE ART OF WAR

BATTLE PLAN TO DEFEAT THE SOCIALISTS

The fiery trial through which we pass will light us, in honor or
dishonor, down to the latest generation.[1]

—ABRAHAM LINCOLN, ANNUAL MESSAGE TO
CONGRESS, 1862

When after multiple ballots the Republican Convention nominated Abraham Lincoln as its presidential candidate for the 1860
election, a Committee of the Convention—senior Republicans,
mainly from the East Coast—were sent to give Lincoln the official notice. Many were Seward men; they had preferred William H. Seward for
the nomination. But Seward had somehow disqualified himself on the
basis of a controversial speech, so the baton went to Lincoln.

Some of those Republican leaders had never met Lincoln before.
They were genuinely heartbroken about the divisions in the Republican
Party. Lincoln received them in his house. He served nothing but water.
After he sat down with them and talked to them, they came away satis-
fied. One of them said, reflecting the sentiments of the group, "Well, we
might have chosen a handsomer article, but I doubt whether a better."

Lincoln was the man for the occasion. He was the right man for an
incomparably difficult task, one that was, in his own words, greater
than the one faced by Washington. Yet oddly enough, the Republicans chose Lincoln for the strangest reason. One might even call it

the providential blunder. Seward, by giving his "Irrepressible Conflict" speech, had seemed to invite civil war. He was deemed to be too radical, too uncompromising.

Lincoln seemed a more moderate—which is to say electable— candidate. Yet once the conflict escalated, Lincoln, who could have de-fused it by giving in (as many of his fellow Republicans urged), refused to give in. Some Republicans pressed him to abandon the Republican platform that rejected any extension of slavery and accept the Crittenden Compromise, which would have extended the Mason-Dixon Line all the way to the Pacific and permanently legalized slavery south of the line.

Lincoln refused. "I will suffer death," he said, "before I will consent . . . to any concession or compromise which looks like buying the privilege of taking possession of the government to which we have a constitu-tional right."[2] Thus, Lincoln refused the only compromise that could have prevented the Civil War. And when the war came, he toughened up even more. He did not stop until the bitter end. As Lord Char-nwood notes in his marvelous Lincoln biography, "The Convention rejected a man who would certainly have compromised, and chose one who would give all that moderation demanded and die before he yielded one further inch."[3]

It was with this historical example in my mind that I recently stood with my family in the Oval Office, chatting in nervous excitement and awaiting our meeting with President Trump. I had spoken twice with Trump on the phone—once while he was running, a second time when he called me about my pardon—but I had never met him. I had my own ideas about Trump, but I was eager to see him up close, just like the Seward Republicans were eager to see Lincoln, to take the full measure of the man, to see if he was up to the hard and unfinished task that lay before him.

Suddenly the door burst open and Trump entered the Oval Office, beaming. He immediately recognized my daughter, Danielle. "Hey," he told her. "I just retweeted you." "I know," she said, with a thrill in her voice. "A few weeks ago you retweeted me four times." He laughed. "I saw your beautiful face," he said, "and you have such a great way of ex-pressing yourself." My stepson, Justin, said to Trump, "I just graduated, and now I have a job in an architectural firm, thanks to your strong economy." Trump grinned and patted him on the shoulder.

We sat down on the two sofas across from Trump's desk. Trump sat in his chair and beckoned me to an unoccupied one. "You move over here, Dinesh. Come sit next to me. We're going to have you sit in the dictator's chair. I call it the dictator's chair." Right away, we launched into the topic of contemporary politics. "It's crazy out there," Trump said. "The other side is relentless. Crazy. Totally dishonest. No regard for the truth."

My wife, Debbie, talked about Venezuela. She also thanked him for my presidential pardon, which wiped out my felony conviction on the campaign finance violation. "It was the right thing to do," Trump said. "You didn't even ask for it, but I did it, because your case was bullshit. And look! Now they are trying to do the same thing to me that they did to you." Trump paused. "But I fight back. I have the means to fight back. Like you fought back. We have to. These people are just disgusting."

I said we were no longer in the Reagan years, and the relative civility and decency of those years was now a thing of the past. Debbie said, "Mr. President, I see how you are attacked all over the place, nonstop, without any kind of restraint or respect for the office. Frankly, I don't know how you do it." At this point, the two of us expected Trump to say, "Ha, ha, ha. Whoop-de-do. It's fun for me because I couldn't care less what they say."

But Trump didn't say that. "Well," he said, learning forward, "to tell you the truth, it gets to me after a while. I'm out there trying to get the job done, and no matter what I do, these people are after me. Look at this Baghdadi situation." Trump had just directed one of the most successful antiterrorist operations, resulting in the death of the world's number-one terrorist, Abu Bakr al-Baghdadi, as well as his second in command. In scale, it resembled the Bin Laden operation carried out under Obama.

Yet while Obama's action was greeted with hosannas and cheers—the media went into full genuflection mode—Trump's action received an entirely different response. "They act like it was nothing. It was a one-day story. And even then," Trump said, with a tone of disbelief, "all they wanted to talk about was the dog. For them it was all about a meme."

Our talk turned to impeachment. "It's such a sick joke," Trump said. "There was nothing wrong with that call. But I have to tell you, I am really lucky to have the transcript. If I didn't have a transcript, I'll be honest with you, I'd be in big trouble. Why? Because all these people, these Never Trumpers and all these dishonest people, they would come forward and make up all this stuff, and say I said things I never said, and there would be no way for me to prove what I actually said."

I looked over at my wife, Debbie, and I noticed that she was close to tears. We thought Trump didn't care one whit about what people said about him. But now we saw a side of him that was hurt, uncomprehending, vulnerable. Without quite intending it, Trump had showed us his human face.

Even so, Trump remained the warrior. He had no intention of retreating from the field. At one point he said, "So many people on our side are weak." I agreed. "It gives the bad guys a sense of immunity," I said. "We have to do to them what they are doing to us, otherwise they will never stop." He said, "Republicans are just not mean." He paused and added, "Well, I am." We all laughed. "But I have to be. Look at what I'm up against. And so I fight back, at my rallies, and on Twitter."

I told Trump, "One of the most common things I hear from Republicans is, we agree with him on a lot of things, but please—please!—take away his Twitter." He raised an eyebrow. I added, "I think it's crazy. I'm thinking to myself: Take away his Twitter? And do what—give it to you? What would you do with it?"

Trump said, "I reach 140 million people on all my social media platforms. These people don't realize it's the best way—it's my only way—to reach the American people."

"Without," I said, "the filter of the media."

He said, "Exactly."

We talked about many other things—45 minutes of just him and us in the Oval Office—from India to Venezuela to who should succeed him. What struck all of us about the meeting was how congenial he was, and how candid. He wasn't self-absorbed, as he is typically portrayed in the media. He looked us in the eye. Later, my daughter would say that he was so "real," which I took to mean authentically American, authentically himself. "People tell me that they love his policies but not his personality," she said. "But I love his personality. It inspires me to stand strong in my beliefs, even when I am treated badly because of them."

I told Trump that I had just one piece of advice to give him, and it concerned what he should do after the presidency. "You should start a news network. Not another Fox News. Another CBS or NBC. A network that reaches 50 million, not 5 million, people." He looked at me, contemplating, I suppose, what his life would be if he got out of the real estate business and went into the news business. "You are one of the few people," I told him, "who could pull this off."

Then the White House photographer took photographs. Before it was over, the president invited us to the White House lawn to watch him take off in his helicopter to a rally in Kentucky. There we stood, with the wind beating against us, watching this intrepid fighter for the restoration of his country's greatness, with a task ahead of him greater than that which faced Reagan, lift off into the air and disappear gradually into the clouds.

CHECKING THEM OUT

It is important for us as citizens to closely examine our leaders, but it is also important, when the situation warrants, for our leaders to closely examine us. On February 11, 1861, Abraham Lincoln gave a brief farewell address to a group of friends and supporters in Springfield, Illinois, and began a train journey to Washington, D.C., to assume the presidency. He didn't take the direct route, however, but traveled meanderingly through various cities and towns, covering nearly 2,000 miles and making nearly 80 stops along the way to engage with crowds of admiring locals who had come to see the new president-elect.

The conventional view of historians is that Lincoln, a relative newcomer to national prominence, "apparently felt an obligation to present himself before the people who had elected him."[4] My view, however, is that Lincoln wasn't doing this for the people to check him out; rather, he was checking *them* out. They had voted for him, but were they really with him? Lincoln sought to discover for himself whether Americans—specifically Republicans—had the strength and stamina to endure the coming storm. What were they prepared to do, and to suffer, to save the country?

Today we are not in a civil war, and I don't think that we are headed for a civil war in the conventional, nineteenth-century sense. We are, however, in a cold civil war. It's a cold war, but not like the one Reagan fought, because it is domestic rather than international. And it's a civil war because now, as in 1860, there is a deep dividing line that runs through the country, not a regional line but rather an ideological one. It separates Americans from each other in a manner unprecedented in my lifetime and cuts deeper than any other schism since Lincoln's time. Therefore Lincoln's question—how prepared are we for the severities of our time?—remains pertinent for us.

This chapter focuses on the tactics of the socialist left. One of the tactics we have already discussed: the left routinely practices the politics of division, not only rich versus poor but also white versus black, male versus female, heterosexual versus homosexual, legal versus illegal. This politics of perpetual turmoil, of pitting Americans against each other, is a tactic aimed at assembling a democratic majority of aggrieved so-called victims. While it takes new forms today, the division formula itself goes back to Marx and is intrinsic to socialism. Therefore, I have dealt with it separately.

But beyond this division, why do the socialists need tactics? For the simple reason that their ideas are a flop. The socialists can't even win their "natural" constituencies: even now, many women, gays and minorities are skeptical of their racket. Moreover, if the socialists debated their ideas in an open forum with their critics, they would be crushed. I myself have trouble finding progressive academics and pundits who are willing to take me on.

So, unable to assemble a majority and win over critics and dissenters through honest persuasion, the left seeks to achieve its goals through naked propaganda, shameless deception, various forms of intimidation, outright coercion and the politics of personal destruction. They are in "wartime" mode; this is not the Democratic Party of JFK and Jimmy Carter. In fact, starting in the Clinton years and continuing through the Obama presidency to the present, the Democratic left has become gangsterized.

How do they get away with it? They do so because they have created a massively powerful array of forces. This is not a straight fight between right and left, between Republicans and Democrats. The Democrats have three institutions that are closely allied with them: academia, Hollywood and the media. By Hollywood, I mean not just the movie industry but also Broadway, the music industry, virtually all the comedians. These three institutions, representing education, information and entertainment, have the largest megaphones in the culture. They work largely as unpaid propagandists for socialism and the Democratic left.

Orwell had their number. And I can imagine his dour smile were he to discover that under the Clintons and Obama, the left has also recruited a shadowy new group into its orbit. This is the group conventionally described as the "Deep State." These are the police agencies of government—the IRS, the Department of Justice, the FBI, the CIA—that are supposed to be neutral enforcement agencies but have been working in close concert with the Democratic left to overturn the Trump presidency and go after prominent Trump supporters, usually, if I may use the term, on some trumped-up charge.

In *1984*, Orwell spoke of Big Brother as composed of two elements: the "outer party," which in this case would refer to the Democrats and their allies in Hollywood and the media, and an "inner party," which would here describe the spook world inhabited by Deep State figures like Robert Mueller, James Comey and James Clapper.[5] The Democrats name their enemies, the Deep State goes after them, the media is quietly alerted to do its public strafing, Hollywood is recruited into the propaganda machine—and this is the real collusion, the only collusion that poses a clear and present danger to our republican system of government.

These are not people who have "fallen" for the lie; they are part of the lie, they create the lie. And to what end? Their ultimate objective is far more insidious than just taking away our money; it is to turn us into worms, to establish tyrannical control over our ordinary lives. That is the point of the left's relentless determination, to trample on our hearts and force us to invert our moral instincts. That's why they want us to succumb to them in whatever they say, even if it's the opposite of what they said yesterday. They want us to concede that they are right in all things, even if they say that up is down and two plus two equals five. In this respect, the socialists are all the same: they represent the boot stamping on our faces!

It is essential that we understand this threat, and understand that it means we are living in a new reality. This is not Reagan's America anymore, nor is it the "kinder, gentler" America to which George H. W. Bush aspired. What this means is that the conservative and Republican strategies derived from that period are now largely obsolete, even though, scarily enough, there are many Republicans and conservatives who are still pursuing these strategies—seeking to stop Antifa, for instance, with a well-crafted op-ed on the need for civility.

None of these antediluvian approaches works anymore. American politics is no longer a debating society. We have been utterly incompetent in our Supreme Court nominating strategy, but if by some miracle we gain actual domination of the Court and manage to overturn *Roe v. Wade*, the left would unleash a massive convulsion that would make Trump Derangement Syndrome look mild by comparison. And my point is that we are not ready for it. Even Reagan would be a fish out of water in the roiled political milieu of today.

Lincoln, however, would not, because the waters for him were even more roiled than they are now. And we are in the position that Lincoln was in when he took that train journey to Washington, D.C. Lincoln knew by that time that the Democrats of the 1850s were not the Democrats of the past. Even that old crook Andrew Jackson would have been startled to see the gangsterization of the Democrats that occurred under the leadership of a new breed of thugs: James Buchanan, Franklin Pierce, Stephen Douglas and John C. Calhoun.

Think of the craziness that Lincoln confronted then, and it will seem eerily familiar, even across the chasm of time. Determined to break up the country because of their outrage that Lincoln won a free and fair election, Democrats shrieked that Lincoln—not they!—posed a mortal danger to the democratic form of government.

In prior years, Democratic street gangs, the nineteenth-century precursor to Antifa, sought to disrupt the public appearances of abolitionists like Frederick Douglass and to beat up the speaker. On one occasion, Democratic congressman Preston Brooks invaded Republican senator Charles Sumner's office and beat him with a cane to within an inch of his life. When the assault was announced in Congress, there was raucous applause from Democrats both in the South and in the North.

Lincoln was a moderate man who found himself in an immoderate environment. And that's where we are also. We are the party of the nice guys, the party of the straightlaced people, facing opponents who recognize this about us and ruthlessly exploit it. To vary the analogy a bit, we are the innocents going westward in covered wagons, only to discover that there are outlaws who seek to seize our land and violate our wives and daughters; suddenly we realize that our normal, decent ways of resolving conflict ("Call my lawyer") don't work anymore. Only fools—by which I mean Never Trumpers and other dwellers in la-la land—don't see this.

Lincoln saw it in 1860, and he became a different man. He became a wartime commander in chief, and he adopted policies no less savage than those of the Confederacy. And the Republicans won the war by becoming sterner, harder people than they were previously. We must learn from these examples from our Republican forebears and become, as they did, the dread and ruin of the opposition. So how do we do this, and how do we remain good people even in a very bad situation? Stiffen your spine, my friends, and read on.

STORMY, STORMY!

We cannot understand the tactics of the socialist left without penetrating its most powerful institution, the media, and that institution's staple product, fake news. The media is critical because it is the channel through which the American people get virtually all of their political information. Even Trump's Twitter account, which avoids the distorting filter of the media, must pass through the channel of a digital media platform. Of the left's three big megaphones—academia, Hollywood and the media—the media is unquestionably the most important. Without the media, no one in America—not even critics of the media—has any comprehensive idea of what's going on.

This simple truth gives the media its terrifying power. It answers the question my wife, Debbie, once put to me. "Why is it," she asked, "that even when our side is in control, we are never in charge?" In other words, Republicans currently control the Senate, and the presidency, and—even if by a narrow majority—the Supreme Court. So how has the Democratic left set the agenda for most of Trump's first term? Why are they on the attack, and why do we feel up against the wall? Why are so many of our leaders—Paul Ryan, Jeff Sessions and the rest—so ineffective?

It's not because they are RINOs—Republicans in name only—or because they are in thrall to the other side. They don't secretly want Hillary or Nancy Pelosi or Chuck Schumer to win. Rather, they are intimidated by the power of the media. Unlike Trump, they have no idea how to fight it. They recognize that the power of the media is the power to humiliate. They know that if the media puts them in its sights and opens unceasing fire on them for weeks, their reputation will be in ruins. Even their own side will run away from them! This explains how ordinarily sturdy people on the conservative side become invertebrates.

Now I recognize, of course, that media is a plural term. We are talking about many powerful outlets, from the print media (*The New York Times*, *The Washington Post*) to the networks (notably ABC, NBC and CBS, but also the cable networks, MSNBC and CNN), to public information channels (PBS and NPR), to entertainment channels (HBO, Showtime, Netflix), to digital media platforms (Twitter, Facebook and Instagram). How is it possible for such a disparate group of institutions to work in such close concert to generate, as they typically do, a single ideological narrative?

The answer is not conspiracy. These people don't all get on a conference call every morning and settle on the story of the day. They don't compare notes on how to spin the narrative. They are not clever enough, and well organized enough, to do this. Rather, they operate like birds in flying formation—each one on its own strength—by instinctively picking up cues from the others and maintaining a consistency of flight pattern. The question, however, is how that flight pattern is determined. What makes news into news, as far as these people are concerned?

We think of fake news as the distortion of a given news event, spinning the interpretation to support the left and the Democratic Party. Case in point: even if the Bidens were collecting huge payoffs from Ukraine by promising access to Joe Biden's influence, the media spin is that none of it matters, nothing has been definitively "proven" and the real issue—the only issue—is whether Trump sought to pressure the Ukrainian government to investigate the Biden family corruption. It's almost funny to watch CNN panels where every analyst offers an identical interpretation, as if there were just one way to see the issue.

Now imagine that it were Donald Trump Jr. who received those payments from the Ukrainian company, and it was Joe Biden who demanded that Ukraine investigate the corruption. In this case, the media narrative would take the exact opposite tack, focusing laser-like on the nature of the Trump family dealings with Ukraine and praising Biden for attempting to root out corruption at the highest levels of the U.S. government. The same facts have one meaning in one context and an entirely different meaning when the political roles are reversed.

While the conservative view of fake news as a systematic twisting of news events to fit the leftist narrative is correct as far as it goes, it doesn't go far enough. The real power of fake news is in deciding what news actually is: what to cover and what to overlook. Through this process of news creation, the media in a quite literal sense invents political reality. If they don't cover something, it might as well not have happened, because it has no effect on the political process. I'd like to illustrate the point with a single comparison, and I'll begin with that famous and titillating porn star, Stormy Daniels.

Stormy Daniels has become a household name. She wasn't a household name before, but she has become a household name. Who hasn't heard of Stormy Daniels? There she is on *60 Minutes*, being interviewed by Anderson Cooper. She also has a book out, *Full Disclosure*. Despite Stormy's unsavory background as a porn "actress," her coverage has been unswervingly positive. "Stormy Daniels, Feminist Hero," reads one headline in *The New York Times*.[6]

Lily Burana in the *Huffington Post* views Stormy as the pioneer of changing perceptions about "women who've worked in adult entertainment." Burana is literally thunderstruck by Stormy. "My God, her chutzpah in taking on Donald Trump is commendable." Burana can hardly contain herself; she finds Stormy "volubly sassy and articulate." She is a "curiously sympathetic folk heroine." There is a "pleasing softness to her facial features," and moreover, "she's a working wife and mother, protective of her child."[7]

When Stormy Daniels showed up to a porn store in West Hollywood, she was greeted by the local mayor, John Duran, and an admiring crowd chanting, "Stormy! Stormy!" Duran declared it "Stormy Daniels Day" and presented her with a key to the city.[8] Stormy was never all that famous as a porn star. In saying this, I feel obligated to note right away that I'm not familiar with porn star reputations. I wouldn't know Ron Jeremy if I saw him on the street.

In any event, Stormy found her career jumpstarted by all this attention. Stormy now performs a sort of solo routine on the road, part exhibitionism, part political sassy talk. It's called *Make America Horny Again*. She's cashing in. And people line up to meet her. "It's Stormy." She is now in the category of people like "Madonna" and "Beyoncé," known exclusively by her first name. She has *60 Minutes* and *The New York Times* to thank for that.

What is the value of Stormy Daniels to the left? What made her the darling of the media? We cannot answer this question without recognizing a progressive strategy that works almost every time. The strategy is based on a recognition that conservatives, Republicans and Christians are the straightlaced people. Exploiting virtue, and making virtue an accessory of promoting vice—this is what the Stormy Daniels "play" is all about.

Stormy Daniels, we all know, is kind of a pervert. The left doesn't mind this at all. If you know anything about the rootless, nomadic life of journalists, you'll recognize that many reporters are at least as perverted as Stormy Daniels. Moreover, virtually no one on the left has any objection to Stormy Daniels' perversion. But they know that conservatives do! And Republicans! And Christians!

So now the left's strategy becomes clear. Hurl Stormy Daniels in the face of Trump. Then just sit back and laugh your head off. Because you know what's going to happen. What's going to happen is that Trump's own side will be outraged. They will not put up with this sleaze. They never have. Therefore, the left can count on Trump's own side to knife him over this, and to bury his political carcass.

Now, incredibly, the same strategy that has always worked, that would have worked with any other Republican, didn't work with Trump. Here, in my imaginative rendition, is how it went:

"Hey, Mr. Trump, we got something for you."

"Oh yeah, what have you got?"

"Stormy Daniels!"

"What else you got?"

Trump has this uncanny ability to brush off scandal, to lower the bar and then jump nimbly over it. The left could hardly believe it. So the Stormy tactic didn't work in the end. But how they tried!

THE ESSENCE OF FAKE NEWS

Now of course the left will contend that Stormy Daniels' accusation against Trump—that they once had sex, and that Trump's attorney paid her a settlement sum to keep it quiet—is a legitimate news story. Admittedly, the payment by itself proves very little; lots of famous and wealthy people are extorted on the basis of mere accusations, and it is hardly unknown for them to settle with their accusers, just so that they can avoid a protracted legal battle and the attendant bad publicity. Even so, from the left's point of view, the very fact that Stormy accused the president and received a hush payment makes the story a legitimate one—and a big one!

Meet Larry Sinclair. I did recently in Miami's South Beach, where I interviewed him for the documentary movie that corresponds to this book. Larry—I'll use his first name to maintain the parallel with Stormy—knew the area. He was once homeless in Miami, he told me, and he used to climb the fire escape to get into a room on the top floor of an old hotel that no longer exists where he would sleep and take a shower, and then slip out in the early morning before the maids showed up.

Larry has been a vagabond, an odd-jobs man, a petty criminal with a rap sheet for forgery and writing bad checks and a drug dealer and drug user. In his younger days, he admits, he used to cruise Chicago's neighborhoods looking for guys to pick up to do drugs and have sex with. I tell him I can't even imagine the sort of things he's seen and done. Larry tells me he's a different person now; he has rehabilitated his life, and he now works for a nonprofit group that builds homes for the homeless.

According to Larry, on November 6, 1999, he was introduced by a limousine driver named Jagir Multani—a man he knew—to a man he didn't know, a man he now knows to be Barack Obama. The two men had drinks, after which Larry asked Obama if he had drugs, and Obama indicated he did. The two of them then did drugs together in the limo. Then, according to Larry, "after snorting the first line, I used my right hand to rub Obama's left leg up to his crotch." With Obama's consent, he performed oral sex on Obama, interrupted only by Obama inhaling from a crack pipe.

The next day, November 7, Obama showed up at Larry's hotel room at the Comfort Inn & Suites in Gurnee, Illinois. Obama wanted an encore, according to Larry, so the two men once again did cocaine and had sex. Then Obama left and Larry never saw him again.

But he did see him on TV in 2004, addressing the Democratic National Convention. Larry was in Mexico at the time, and he recognized Obama as "the big eared guy who enjoyed smoking crack and getting head." And there he was, the very same guy, on the national stage! Larry watched in a trance. In 1999, of course, Obama had been a state senator. But by 2004, he was U.S. senator from Illinois, and already Democrats were touting him as a future presidential contender.

Between 2004 and 2008, when he first ran for president, Obama portrayed himself as a straightlaced guy, a political centrist, a unifier, a family man. This press-release puffery was supported by the media, whose coverage of Obama can only be described as messianic: Obama was Jesus Christ come back to earth! Larry could hardly believe it. He told me that his thought upon seeing this carefully constructed persona was simply, "What a fake!"

After Obama became a presidential candidate, Larry held a press conference on June 18, 2008, at the National Press Club, where he described what happened between him and Obama. Larry said he was a Democrat, and a man with a checkered past, but one who was also honest about himself. He called on Obama to be equally honest, to admit his drug use and come clean with the American people. Immediately following Larry's public statement, he was arrested by the D.C. police and taken away in handcuffs.

The arrest was supposedly based on an outstanding warrant from Delaware. Larry spent several days in prison before being transported to Delaware. But the matter was then dropped and Larry was released without being charged. The arrest, he says, was a political hit, to make sure that Larry was perceived as a criminal suspect lacking all credibility. And who ordered it? According to Sinclair, none other than Delaware's attorney general, Beau Biden, the son of Joe Biden.[9]

What we have at this point is a remarkable tale. But is it just a tale "told by an idiot, full of sound and fury, signifying nothing"? Larry's charge against Obama might seem thin and far-fetched, lacking corroboration, as they say, but Larry also disclosed in his press conference that, subsequent to his contacting the Obama campaign, he received several phone calls from a man named Donald Young. According to Larry, Young warned him to drop his public allegation against Obama because, otherwise, his life might be in danger.

Larry took this as a threat. Young didn't say who he was, but Larry found out that he was the choir director at Jeremiah Wright's church, the church Obama attended for two decades. Larry was convinced that the Obama people had put Young up to it. But little did he realize the urgency of Young's words. Several days later, Young called back and told Larry that he was not making idle threats. He, Young, had been having an affair with Obama, and he regarded his own life as imperiled. He was thinking of running off to Africa to become a teacher there.

On December 23, 2007, Donald Young was gunned down in his apartment in a supposedly random shooting. The Chicago police report says he was killed by "multiple gunshot wounds." The motive was supposedly robbery, but nothing of value was taken. The killer has never been found. Young was openly gay, and Larry contends that Young's affair with Obama was common knowledge at Wright's church, which had its own gay subculture, known as the Down Low Club or DLC. Although the church did its best to cover for Obama, how difficult would it have been for a good reporter to get members to talk?

So here was potential corroboration of Larry's story. And the best corroboration subsequently came from Young's own mother, Norma Jean Young. A former employee of the Chicago Police Department, Young accused the Chicago PD of placing low priority on finding out who killed her son. "There's more to the story," she said. "I do believe they are shielding somebody or protecting someone." Young added, "What was the cause of my son's death? . . . Donald and Obama were very close friends . . . I'm very suspicious that it may have been related to Obama."

These astounding accusations were not investigated or reported by a single American media outlet. Only one outlet carried it, a tabloid publication called *The Globe*. The *Globe* interview was published on July 17, 2010. Larry's press conference also received virtually no coverage. Nothing on the network news. Nothing in the *The New York Times* or *The Washington Post*. Nothing in the local newspaper, the *Chicago Tribune*. Nothing on NPR, CNN, MSNBC. Total blackout! To this day, Google censors a number of links that come up when you search for details of this case.

A couple of left-wing websites weighed in to dismiss Larry on the basis of his drug past, his record of writing bad checks and his previous aliases.[10] Larry even wrote a book in 2009 detailing his story; it was completely ignored, like a tree falling in a forest with no one around. No wonder that, in sharp contrast with Stormy Daniels, hardly anyone has heard of Larry Sinclair. He lives in obscurity; I hardly need to add that Larry does not have his own pornographic road show, and no town in Hollywood has declared a "Larry Sinclair Day."

Do I believe Larry? Or Donald Young's mom? I'm not sure. Since there is no recording of the incidents, there is no way to know about Larry's alleged two rendezvous with Obama, any more than there is a way to know whether what Stormy alleged about Trump actually happened. My point is this: if Stormy's allegation is big news—if the American people deserve to know, and to make up their own mind—then the same applies to Larry Sinclair and to Mrs. Young. If we had an objective news media, that's how they would see it. But of course we don't.

Now you might expect me to say, based on the contrasting coverage of Stormy Daniels and Larry Sinclair, that progressive media coverage reflects some sort of "double standard." This is the typical conservative complaint, but in a way it is naïve! Behind every double standard is a single standard waiting to be uncovered. The single standard is to do everything possible to discredit a key political opponent like Trump while doing whatever you can to cover up for a key political ally like Obama. "Protect our side—the side that seeks to move America in the direction of socialism—and destroy the other side." There's the consistent single standard that was applied here.

I've focused on one story, but that story stands for virtually every political story. Contrast the media hosannas when Obama successfully took out Bin Laden with the begrudging, hostile coverage when Trump took out the Iranian terrorist Soleimani. Incredibly, Soleimani was portrayed as a noble victim, Trump as a warmongering aggressor. Again, this is not so much a "double standard" as it is the media showing it sympathizes more with Islamic terrorists than it does with the current president of the United States. I could go on with examples, but I don't think I need to. The pattern here could not be more vivid and clear.

Fake news is all we can expect from the progressive media, and that for the most part is all we get. Thinking back, it's been this way for quite a while. The only difference is that they at least used to try to seem objective. CNN had *Crossfire*; *The New York Times* and other print media had some sort of distinction between the news and opinion sections. Now the pretense is gone; now they don't even try. The socialists in the media are all "out of the closet."

This media pimping for the socialist agenda is a serious problem that requires thought, resources and commitment on our part. It's not enough to deplore the outrages of the media. This is what we've been doing for decades and, Fox News Channel aside, we haven't done a whole lot beyond that. Long term, we have to create new outlets to reach our people, essentially an alternative universe of information, so we are not dependent on what they say. This means our own print media; our own networks; our own digital platforms. Essentially, we need to "secede" from the media.

Short term—and this is harder than it sounds—we have to work to reduce the power of fake news in our minds. In our minds! What this means is that we don't jump out of our chair when we see the latest outrage on CNN or in *The Washington Post*. Rather, we're indifferent. Or even better, we chuckle. We chuckle at seeing 18 CNN panelists who say the same thing, with a straight face. This isn't a news channel; it's Comedy Central! Remarkably, it's not the media that has power over us; we're the ones who have power over them, if we use it.

DEEP STATE THUGGERY

Now we turn from the progressive media to its sister institution, the Deep State. To use Orwell's terms, if the media represents the strongest arm of the socialist left's "outer party," then the Deep State represents the strongest arm of its "inner party." And the two work in concert. The Deep State routinely leaks to the media, and the media protects the Deep State from conservative and Republican efforts to expose the Deep State and curb its lawless abuses.

Both the media and the Deep State have a pose. The media's pose is objectivity: we are reporting the news fairly, without prejudice, without an ideological agenda. The Deep State's pose is neutrality. We, the institutions of the U.S. government—from the IRS to the DOJ to the FBI—are enforcing the laws in a neutral manner. We don't play favorites. Lady Justice is blind.

Ha, ha, ha. I saw this for myself, when I sat across from the prosecutorial team of the Southern District of New York. The front man here was Preet Bharara, aka Indian headwaiter. I give him that derogatory name because Bharara was a stooge, taking orders from Eric Holder at the Justice Department. And Holder was, by his own account, Obama's stooge or, as Holder himself put it, Obama's "wingman." Notice how Holder can candidly admit to doing Obama's bidding, while Trump's DOJ—according to the standard of the media—is supposed to be completely independent from the White House.

Did you, the Bharara team demanded of me, or did you not exceed the campaign finance limit? I admitted that I did—I gave $20,000 over the limit to a college friend of mine running for U.S. Senate in New York—and I added that I expected to receive the same penalty as anyone else who did the same thing. Not so fast, the Bharara goons said. We're going to get you on bank fraud. Bank fraud? Yes, they said, because you took your money out of your bank account. Wow! And, they added, we're going to get you on mail fraud. Mail fraud? Yes, they said, because you put your check in the mail. Wow, again.

My attorneys informed me that the U.S. government, at the insistence of the Obama administration, was using against me the same laws that were passed to go after ISIS and the mafia. In other words, if you can't get Al Capone for extortion and murder, get him for something—anything!—to get him off the street. Remarkably these laws were used to target me not because of what I did, but because I was an outspoken critic of the Obama administration. That's not my view; it's the FBI's view. I was red-flagged in my FBI file as a prominent opponent of the president.

No American has ever been prosecuted, let alone locked up, for doing what I did. The Bharara goon squad knew this, so they prepared a memo for the judge laying out a series of "comparable cases" and showing that, yes, in each of those cases, the defendant got jail time. But the Bharara team was engaged in outright lies. Not unintentional error, not exaggeration, but lying pure and simple.

Proof? It's given in a short appendix to this book.[11] Detail is important here, so if you want to see how the Deep State operates, under the cover of legalism, here it is in a single document. If you read the side-by-side chart, you'll see that none of the cases cited by the prosecution was remotely similar to mine; they typically involved repeat offenses, vastly greater sums of money and always a quid pro quo. By contrast with these cases, mine involved a first-time offense, a comparatively small amount of money and no corruption even alleged, since the candidate herself had no idea what I did.

We pointed out the lies to Judge Richard Berman. He acknowledged reading them. So he knew about them, but he pretended that nothing strange was going on. Berman is a Clinton appointee and, knowing that, the Bharara team presumed they could count on him. No wonder

Judge Berman rejected my claims of selective prosecution and selective punishment; he ultimately was the one carrying them out.

The Deep State deception was picked up, hook, line and sinker, by Anderson Cooper on CNN. Berating me on the air for saying that I was a victim of selective prosecution, Cooper declared that the very same Southern District of New York had prosecuted Democratic donor Jeffrey Thompson. So there! What Cooper didn't say—mirroring the Deep State's own tactic with the judge—was that Thompson got a penalty comparable to mine for a vastly greater offense.

Thompson violated both federal and state laws. He funneled $3.3 million in illegal contributions to a whole slew of Democratic candidates, 28 in all, including Obama and Hillary, partly with a view to gaining federal and local government contracts for his minority-owned accounting firm. For running this elaborate, corrupt scheme over many years, Thompson got six months in white-collar prison, a $10,000 fine and three years probation.[12]

Thompson's lenient sentence is actually typical. New York hotelier Sant Chatwal—also an Indian American—violated the campaign finance laws by using straw donors as fronts to give more than $180,000 above the limit to Hillary Clinton and other Democratic candidates. Chatwal, who was the founder of Indian Americans for Hillary, had a political motive in this case: he wanted Hillary to back a U.S.-India nuclear deal that Hillary had previously opposed.

Chatwal justified the straw donations as a necessary strategy to get politicians to do what he wanted. "That's the only way," he said in a secret recording made by federal officials, "to buy them." He was also convicted of witness tampering; the FBI recorded him trying to get witnesses to lie in court. "Never, never" admit to anything, Chatwal told them. "Cash has no proof." Even so, Chatwal got a fine, community service and three years' probation. No prison time.[13] I'm tempted to say "Unbelievable!" but knowing what I do now about the Deep State, my response is, "That's believable."

Rosie O'Donnell also exceeded the campaign finance limits, five times by her own account, with a series of Democratic candidates. I raised the Rosie case with Anderson Cooper on CNN, and he countered that Rosie had no intention of breaking the law. Yes, I said, she did. The proof is that Rosie spelled her name five different ways and used five different addresses. Why do this, unless you are trying to prevent computers from tracing them to the same person? Yet Rosie was not even charged.[14] I'm not saying she should have been—she, like me, had no corrupt intent—but if I was locked up for doing what I did, then Rosie should get the same treatment, shouldn't she?

Fortunately for me, the injustice in my case was corrected in late May 2018, when the president called. In his blunt, Trumpian way, he got right to the point. "Dinesh, you got screwed!" And Trump said he was going to pardon me the next day. I was elated; I could hardly believe it. I realized I was going to get my rights back—most importantly, my right to vote. I was also getting my American dream back; since my conviction, the left would gleefully call me "felon." I was in the process of becoming that rarest of creatures, an "ex-felon." And even more, I recognized the political implication. Trump was delivering a giant Up Yours to the Obama administration!

For Anderson Cooper, Trump's pardon was proof not that I was unfairly treated but that I had very powerful connections in high places. Is it not a fact, Dinesh, he asked on CNN, that it took a very powerful man, the president of the United States, to get you off the hook? Yes, I said, but it took another very powerful man, the former president of the United States, to get me on the hook. Cooper seemed very annoyed at this riposte, and I chuckled at his trademark quizzical expression, just as Trump had chuckled before he hung up the phone with me. Trump's last words to me were, "Don't tell anyone about your pardon, Dinesh, until I tweet about it in the morning."

SEAL IN A SEA OF SHARKS

For those who haven't been targeted by the Deep State, accounts like mine may seem somewhat surreal. That's because we've all been raised on a civics-book understanding of the American justice system. It's only when the full force of the U.S. government is trained against you—police cars, SWAT teams, helicopters circling overhead, a bailiff chanting "United States of America versus Dinesh D'Souza"—that you see how remote the civics-book America is from the gangsterized America of the left. Then, like Prince Hal in Shakespeare's *Henry V*, you become a different person who can truly say, "I have turned away my former self."

My wife, Debbie, is friends with Catherine Engelbrecht, founder of the Texas-based King Street Patriots as well as election watchdog group True the Vote. True the Vote is a national membership organization that investigates cases of voter fraud. Engelbrecht testified before Congress that prior to filing IRS forms to establish these two groups in 2010, her family and her small business had never been audited. As soon as she filed, however, "my family and I have been subjected to more than 15 instances of audit or inquiry by federal agencies."

First, her personal and business tax returns were investigated, with each audit going back several years. Then the Bureau of Alcohol, Tobacco and Firearms conducted its own inquiry and audit. Then the FBI came calling "on six separate occasions wanting to cull through membership manifests in conjunction with domestic terrorism cases."[15] Before she became politically involved: nothing. Since she became involved: a firestorm of federal inquiry and investigation. Concluson: Engelbrecht's crime was becoming involved in Tea Party politics and fighting against voter fraud.

My case was heard in 2013. Engelbrecht testified before Congress in 2014. So this nonsense has been going on for a while now, directed by the same thuggish Obama crew. But undoubtedly it reached a zenith in the period leading up to, and following, Trump's election. Trump's election was, to quote *New York Times* columnist David Brooks, "the shock of our lifetime." The left felt sure it had secured the election for Hillary. Even so, in the unlikely event that Trump won, they put in place an insurance policy.

That insurance policy was to create grounds for Trump's impeachment. The left's scheme to achieve this result began with the FISA misrepresentation, continued with the Mueller investigation and reached its ridiculous zenith with the Ukraine-related impeachment. The left's operating principle was recently articulated by John Dean, Nixon's former White House counsel, who resigned in disgrace and then pivoted left in order to restore his reputation.

"I think this president probably should have been impeached the day he walked in," Dean said in an interview with CNN. This same theme was echoed by socialist Democrat Rashida Tlaib, who was elected to Congress in 2018. Speaking to MoveOn.org activists just hours after she was sworn in, Tlaib vowed, "We're going to go in there and we're going to impeach the m*th*rf*ck*r."[16] Tlaib didn't back down even when a video of her remarks became public.

The initial mechanism for the socialist left to get rid of Trump was the Mueller investigation, launched—this is a measure of the power of the left—from within Trump's own Department of Justice. The Mueller investigation was intended to reverse the result of the 2016 election. That's what Mueller himself wanted, and Comey, and Rod Rosenstein—the whole Deep State crew.

Their joint effort failed, however, when Mueller was unable to show any collusion between Trump and Russia. Hence the Ukraine impeachment inquiry, which was directed not so much at removing Trump from office as at undercutting his prospects in the 2020 race. As leftist Democrat Al Green candidly stated in a TV interview, "If we don't impeach this president, he will get reelected."[17]

This whole anti-Trump campaign began with one man, a young Trump staffer named George Papadopoulos. My wife and I have gotten to know George, a dapper fellow, and his glamorous Italian wife Simona, who is both a model and a former policy staffer for the parliament of the European Union. Having read Papadopoulos' book, my wife, Debbie, said to him when they met, "I don't think you realized that you were a seal in a sea full of sharks." Papadopoulos laughed. It was a perfect analogy.

Papadopoulos wasn't even a huge Trumpster; he joined the Trump campaign because, somewhat against conventional wisdom, including mine, he thought Trump had a good chance to win. "To my way of thinking, Trump is like a stock," Papadopoulos wrote in his book. "In order to profit from it, I have to buy low—in other words, I feel I should offer my services to the campaign immediately."[18] The better Trump's official odds of winning, the harder it would become to get hired later.

Papadopoulos came on board as a Middle East policy analyst. He was based in London. To his astonishment, shortly after his appointment, he was introduced to a man named Joseph Mifsud, who seemed to have high-level global connections and who took an unusual interest in this obscure staffer. Mifsud informed Papadopoulos that the Russians had "dirt" on Hillary Clinton: "Thousands of emails." Papadopoulos had no idea what he was talking about. He also had no idea that Mifsud was a Deep State operative on behalf of the U.S. government and possibly other Western intelligence agencies.

Then Papadopoulos met Australian high commissioner Alexander Downer, who discussed U.S.-Australia relations with Papadopoulos and then mysteriously reported to his own government that Papadopoulos told him the Russians have a "surprise" for Hillary Clinton in the form of damaging emails she had written. Papadopoulos has no memory of telling Downer any of this. "None. Zero. Nada."[19] He also had no idea that Downer was close to the Clintons and, as Australia's foreign minister, engineered a $25 million donation to the Clinton Foundation.

Papadopoulos also received an email "out of the blue" from an American scholar teaching at Cambridge, Stefan Halper, requesting a meeting. Halper came with his research assistant, a sexy blond thirtysomething who called herself Azra Turk. Turk kept putting the moves on Papadopoulos, all the while asking him questions like, "Are we working with Russia?" Papadopoulos said nothing; to him, it felt like a scene out of a James Bond movie.

Then Halper fired a series of accusations against Papadopoulos. "I know you know about the emails. . . . Russia is helping you and your campaign, right? . . . You and your campaign are involved in hacking and working with Russia, right? . . . It seems you are a middleman for Trump and Russia." Basically, Halper was pushing for Papadopoulos to make admissions that, even if false, would sink the Trump presidency. He was infuriated when Papadopoulos did not comply.

Papadopoulos was then approached by Charles Tawil, whom he claims is an FBI operative posing as an Israeli businessman. Tawil denies this, but he admits handing Papadopoulos $10,000 in cash for work on a research project. Later Papadopoulos would be arrested by the FBI at the airport upon his arrival back in America. The media was in attendance. The FBI began to go through his bags. The headline they were looking for: TRUMP AIDE CAUGHT WITH $10,000 IN CASH. The optics could not be more incriminating.

Unfortunately for the Deep State setup crew, Papadopoulos wrote, "I gave the money to a lawyer in Greece." He left the cash behind, so they couldn't find it on him. The setup was a bust. But they arrested him all the same. "This is what happens," one of them said, "when you work for Trump." So what was Papadopoulos' crime? His crime was his affiliation with the Trump administration, which made him a target seal for the sharks to move in on.

Of course they had no intention to get him. His wife, Simona, told me they tried to get her to wear a wire so she could secretly record her then fiancé. "I refused," she said, "but they told me that George was finished, and that I could save myself by helping them." So they did seek to nab Papadopoulos, to arrest him and to charge him. In the end, however, they fully intended to let him go. And the price of letting him go, Papadopoulos realized after his arrest, was for him to blow the whistle on Trump. He had to confess that Trump colluded with Russia.

It didn't matter that Trump didn't collude with Russia. It didn't matter that if Trump had colluded with Russia, Papadopoulos—a young analyst assigned to Mediterranean and Middle East issues—would likely have no knowledge of it. All that the Deep State wanted was for Papadopoulos to say that Trump colluded with Russia. "If I had given them that," Papadopoulos told me, "it would have ended the Trump presidency, and I would have become one of the most famous people in the world."

To his credit, Papadopoulos refused to lie and give the Deep State what it wanted. But look at the extent to which the Deep State, and its allies in the media, were apparently willing to go. As Papadopoulos recounts, they set him up. That was Mifsud. He planted the information on Papadopoulos about the emails. Then Downer tried to extract the information—that they gave him!—and when Papadopoulos didn't play along, Downer claimed anyway that he did. Then they deployed Halper to clean up the Downer hit and try to get some kind of admission from Papadopoulos' own mouth. Finally, they deployed Tawil to stick Papadopoulos with a wad of cash, hoping to catch him red-handed when he entered the United States.

Let's sum up what these three cases—mine, Engelbrecht's and Papadopoulos'—tell us about the Deep State. In two of the cases, Engelbrecht's and mine, we were the target. The goal was to "take us out." Yet we were not the only target, because there was a broader objective. In both cases, the broader objective was to use us to send a message to others like us. "Don't screw with the left, because we have the power to destroy your life." That was the message.

In Papadopoulos' case, he was targeted, but he was not the actual target. Trump was the target, and Papadopoulos was their setup witness. They sought to use this completely innocent guy to fabricate a case against Trump. We cannot be naïve about the Deep State: this is who they are, and this is how they operate. They are unscrupulous thugs—thugs with badges—which makes them far more dangerous than ordinary criminals. Unless they are held to account, they will keep doing what they can to subvert our justice system and our political system.

WHEN TWO PLUS TWO MAKES FIVE

What is the point of all this aggression? What is the endgame of the socialist left? Never Trumper Jennifer Rubin—who has become an almost comically subservient apparatchik of the socialist left—puts it with her usual crudeness: "I think it's absolutely abhorrent that any institution of higher learning, any news organization, or any entertainment organization that has a news outlet would hire these people."

She means Trump supporters. She wants Trump supporters not only to exit the government, she wants them to be unemployable in the private sector. "It's not only Trump that has to lose," she says, "but that all his enablers have to lose. We have to collectively, in essence, burn down the Republican Party. We have to level them because if there are any survivors, if there are people who weather this storm, they will do it again."[20]

This is the voice of tyranny. It seeks to establish full control of the culture so that, using the instruments of government and the media, it can exercise tyrannical control over our lives. They don't just want to take our money; they want to turn us into sniveling devotees of their wickedness and corruption. If this seems like a far-out, fanciful picture, think of how close the left is to achieving its objective now.

They already control Hollywood and most of academia and the media. You might think that would be enough. But no! They also want the NFL. And the NBA. Think about it: a bunch of guys who bounce and run with a ball! Yet they want them too. They want the Boy Scouts, and they pretty much have them. They want to intimidate corporations into toeing their ideological line, even in matters that seem innocent or trivial. They want to force the Christian baker, Jack Phillips, to bake a cake for a homosexual wedding.

It doesn't matter to them that Phillips is a devout Christian, and that his objection to baking the wedding cake is a very narrow and principled one. His bakery Masterpiece Cakeshop is open to everyone, and gays, like anyone else, can buy cakes and other goodies there. Because Phillips has a moral objection to gay marriage, however, an objection rooted in his faith, he won't bake a wedding cake. He will happily refer gays to other bakeries that will oblige. This would seem like a solution that would satisfy everyone.

But not the activist left! For them, it's important to force Phillips to give in and go against the dictates of his conscience. That's what they mean by "nondiscrimination," a benign and even positive term that takes on a darker, coercive meaning in this context. So they file a complaint with the Colorado Civil Rights Commission, which rules against Phillips and imposes penalties designed to compel his conformity or drive him out of business.

Phillips sues, and the case goes all the way to the Supreme Court. Phillips wins! And one might think that at this point it's over—it was quite an ordeal that cost Phillips six years of his life, but finally he has prevailed, and religious freedom is secure, at least in this case. But no! A transgender attorney in Colorado, Autumn Scardina, comes waltzing into Phillips' bakery and demands he bake a cake to celebrate her transition from male to female. Phillips, once again, and on the same grounds, refuses. So she sues him! Phillips must go through the wringer once again.[21]

It's a form of terrorization, a historical specialty of the socialists. Sure, they want to ruin Phillips. But their wider objective is to show everyone in Colorado, and across the country, that this is what happens to you when you go against them. There is no point in resisting them because they will never stop. Few people are as tough as Phillips in their willingness to put everything on the line and refuse to submit even a second time. One of my heroes!

Corporations today operate under the strict surveillance of the left's censorship brigade. They live by Orwell's menacing slogan, BIG BROTHER IS WATCHING YOU. They recognize that Big Brother's enforcement is swift and ruthless, and very few have Jack Phillips' stomach for principled resistance. To take an example that is illuminating precisely because it is so trivial, consider the fashion retailer Forever 21, which featured on its website a white male model wearing a sweater with the phrase WAKANDA FOREVER. This was a reference to the movie *Black Panther*.

One critic tweeted, "Hey @Forever21, in what universe did you think it was OK to feature a white model in Wakanda gear. As a former #21 brand specialist for the company, I'm highly offended." Notice how the critic tags the company, in order to draw its attention, and draw the attention of other censorious leftists to the ideological deviation. He doesn't use the term "deviation," but he declares that he is "offended," which is code for, "Here's a clear ideological violation. Let's go get these guys on the charge of racism. Let's destroy their reputation."

Is it even necessary to point out the outcome? Forever 21 instantly deleted the tweet with the photo and in fact removed all images of the offending model from its website. The company tweeted, "Forever 21 takes feedback on our products and marketing extremely seriously. We celebrate all superheroes with many different models of various ethnicities and apologize if the photo in question was offensive in any way."[22] This sort of groveling before the icons of the left has become standard practice in corporate America. Some happily do it, and the rest are made to do it on pain of being branded as bigots.

The latest form of repression is digital censorship—censorship on digital platforms. This is the unkindest cut of all, because many conservatives have turned to digital platforms as an alternative to the narrowness of the mainstream media. Now they find themselves restricted, shadow banned and booted off those platforms. The pretext is "hate," even though in most cases the "hate" amounts to nothing more than vociferously resisting the hateful doctrines of the socialist left.

We are, again, in Orwell territory. Yet notice that the digital platforms are private. This is not government censorship but rather private companies acting to achieve the same repression that the state normally enforces. In Orwell's novels, the state is the primary villain. Orwell does, however, depict private individuals as informants. Someone tells, and that's how the state knows to go after you. That's the case here too. A journalist at Buzzfeed notifies YouTube or Twitter, and that's how you get permanently banned and become a digital unperson.

It's hard for me to believe that, thirty years after I came to America as an idealistic teenager, this is where we are headed. In college I read John Stuart Mill's *On Liberty*, which contains this thrilling declaration: "If all mankind minus one, were of one opinion, and only one person were of the contrary opinion, mankind would be no more justified in silencing that one person, than he, if he had the power, would be justified in silencing mankind."[23] We seem to have gone, in one generation, from the bracing atmosphere of Mill's *On Liberty* to the dark, dank atmosphere of Orwell's *1984*.

Hate week! The Ministry of Truth! The Thought Police! All of this—once the hallmark of faraway socialist regimes—is now familiar. It has become our world. I'm reminded of the great scene in *1984* where the protagonist Winston Smith is being interrogated by the agents of Big Brother. They want him to admit that two plus two equals five! Winston won't do it. Winston's position is that they have taken everything he has, they have destroyed his closest relationships, they have placed him under indefinite confinement, they have broken his dignity, so what does he have left?

Winston believes that he has only one thing left. He is free to say that two plus two equals four! And he is determined to hold on to that solitary form of freedom. And so they put him in a dark room, and deny him food and water, and subject him to all sorts of sensory deprivation. Since they know Winston is terrified of rats, they even unleash rats on him, so that the rats are swarming all over him and biting his face.

But mostly, it isn't the torture that wears him down; it's the interrogation process itself. "Their real weapon," Orwell writes, "was the merciless questioning that went on and on, hour after hour, tripping him up, laying traps for him, twisting everything that he said, convicting him at every step of lies and self-contradiction, until he began weeping as much from shame as from nervous fatigue."[24]

I'm reminded here of the Deep State "interview" of former national security adviser Michael Flynn, or of the Mueller team's interrogations of so many people whose only misdeed appears to have been their support for President Trump. The goal is not to uncover wrongdoing, since there is none, but to locate Statement A from an earlier interview that contradicts Statement B from a more recent one, so that you can charge the witness with the crime of making a false statement and compel them to say what you want them to say in exchange for prosecutorial leniency.

This is what Winston is also up against, and finally he gives in. Winston blurts out, helplessly, that two plus two equals five. So there! He has said it. Now are they satisfied? Now can he go? No, Winston, they tell him, you cannot go. We are not satisfied. Why? Because we know that in your mind you still believe that two plus two equals four. You are just *saying* five because you know that is what we want to hear. Our goal is not merely to gain your outward subjection but the conformity of your inner mind. We want to control that too!

This, then, is the ultimate objective of the socialist left in America: to brainwash us through propaganda and to terrify us into submission, so that we all become Winston, cowering and whimpering at first and ultimately giving in, not only on the outside but also on the inside, our ideals crushed, our dignity gone, finally embracing our abusers and captors by saying, in unison, "I love Big Brother." At this point, the left is content and our reeducation is complete.

MISTER TRUMP GOES TO WASHINGTON

It is against the magnitude and sheer evil of the socialist threat that we can, and must, understand Trump. Trump, it so happens, is not merely the quintessential capitalist in the manner I have highlighted in this book. He is also the political wartime general who is leading the charge for capitalism and against the socialists. His tactics are unorthodox—we've never had anyone like him before. So here we attempt to assess Trump in that second role.

It is commonly asserted on the left that Trump is responsible for the viciousness of American politics and the hatred and division that are now a staple feature of that politics. But Trump didn't cause the division. It would be more accurate to say that it caused him. The question we must ask is whether Trump's approach is effective in responding to the situation caused by the socialist left.

Trump is admittedly a very different figure from Reagan, and I say this as a former young Reaganite. Many on our side yearn for a return to the 1980s. The Never Trump phenomenon is, in part, a pining for the good old Reagan days. Reagan presumed the goodwill of the other side. He enjoyed sharing a joke with Democratic House Speaker Tip O'Neill, even with Sam Donaldson of ABC News, who, for those who don't recognize the name, was the Jim Acosta of an earlier day.

But Trump doesn't presume any such goodwill, because (as he himself remarked in his conversation with my family) he doesn't receive it. Moreover, Reagan focused on a few key priorities—combating the Soviet empire, cutting taxes—in the belief that you can only change the world in one or two ways, and he let the rest of it go, making jokes along the way. Chastised for ignoring the growth of government spending and the ensuing deficit, Reagan quipped that at $200 billion a year the deficit was "big enough to take care of itself."

Trump, by contrast, fights on every front. While rewriting the trade pact and nicking away at Obamacare and pushing through tax reform and slashing government regulation and saving the courts, Trump still finds time to swat Meryl Streep—bam!—and *Saturday Night Live*—bam!—and "failing" CNN—bam!—and the fake news *New York Times*—bam! Trump has one foot in the political fight and one in the culture war, and he seems to understand that the political fight takes place in just one corner of a larger cultural battleground.

Trump comes out of popular culture, and he has a very good feel for it. He's partly a comedian and an entertainer. His language is colloquial, even to the point of being coarse, but it is the kind of talk that people can understand and identify with, very different from the bureaucratic argot that is the standard discourse of both parties. Indeed, when Trump was accused of being unpresidential, he amusingly quipped that he was "twenty-first-century presidential."

As we saw earlier, Trump recognizes the power of social media. He literally sets the agenda for the national discourse from his Twitter account—sometimes with off-the-cuff tweets blasted out in the early hours of the morning. Trump uses his Twitter account to drive his opponents crazy, to keep them perpetually off balance, to stir their sputtering outrage.

He knows what he is doing. He's a mud wrestler, possibly the best mud wrestler in the world today. And a part of him clearly enjoys the fight, which is what it takes to be good at the sport. And while the left constantly accuses Trump of picking on this group or that group, he is in fact quite undiscriminating in his choice of targets. He is an equal-opportunity mud wrestler.

But is this man even a conservative? This was a fair question when first asked upon Trump entering the ring. Trump's background was politically ambiguous, and his record on pro-life and other issues was spotty at best. I used to wonder in the beginning, given that he donated to both parties, why didn't he run as a Democrat? How the left would have fawned over him; how they would have protected him. But he didn't, and now, virtually a full term into Trump's presidency, is there any doubt about where Trump stands? I don't think so. He is obviously the most conservative president since Reagan, and in some respects he's even more reliable than Reagan.

Like Reagan, Trump is an avid patriot. He loves his country. In the end, I believe, that's why he didn't run as a Democrat. He couldn't—he loves the country too much! In a eulogy for his political mentor, Henry Clay, Abraham Lincoln said, "He loved his country partly because it was his own country, but mostly because it was a free country." That's Trump! Lincoln added of Clay, "He burned with a zeal for its advancement, prosperity and glory, because he saw in such, the advancement, prosperity and glory of human liberty."[25] That's Trump again!

Trump is also, as Reagan was, a free market capitalist. The only caveat here is Trump's position on trade, but that too can be squared with free market principles. Trump, after all, backs tariffs not because he wants to curb trade among nations but because he wants to pressure other countries like China and France to take down their trade barriers. Trump's objective is not to have barriers but to remove all barriers and to have a level playing field for trade. One can agree or disagree with his strategy, but his purpose is more, not less, trade and freer, not more constricted, global trade.

Trump's trade policy can also be understood as a modest form of economic redistribution, not from the rich to the poor but from consumers to workers. Consumers, after all, have gotten the great windfall from the globalization, immigration and second communications revolution. It has been a revolution of better and cheaper products. But Trump knows that these same developments have severely hurt working-class people in manufacturing sectors, in the process wrecking whole communities! Even if it confounds strict libertarian principles, Trump insists—and he is right to insist—on some form of protection for those who have been hardest hit.

Finally, to the surprise of many conservatives and Republicans, Trump has proven to be very sound on the social issues, notably abortion. One pro-life activist said to me, "God must have a sense of humor. If we in the pro-life community got together to choose a leader to represent us, we would never have come up with Trump, or someone like Trump. But there he is, doing the Lord's work, stocking not just the Supreme Court but also the appellate courts with pro-life judges."

Trump has his weaknesses. In my view, he should have fired Comey on day one. Had he done that, there would have been no Mueller inquiry, and Trump would have controlled his Justice Department. But for whatever reason, Trump didn't do that, and he paid a high price for this negligence. As a consequence of it, wily Obama holdovers like Rod Rosenstein were in a position to retaliate against Comey's firing by launching the Mueller investigation while that idle figurehead, Jeff Sessions, watched in obtuse silence.

In a sense, Rosenstein figured out how to use Trump's own DOJ against him. Trump, in effect, was deprived of one of his most important cabinet agencies; any effort by Trump to tell the DOJ what to do could easily be construed by the Democrats as "obstructing justice."

This was the game successfully played by the left for most of Trump's term. And Trump almost paid with his presidency for his original mistake. Only recently did Trump finally secure his hold on the Justice Department through the appointment of William Barr.

Now, through John Durham's investigation, Trump for the first time has the chance to do to the left what it has been doing to him. We'll know he is succeeding when prominent figures on the left—from Clapper to Comey to Holder to Obama—wake up to police sirens, hear helicopters ahead and stumble out of bed to see automatic weapons trained on them, and men with handcuffs approaching them through the front door.

This is not only the best way, it's the only way to curb the excesses of the Deep State. Payback is the road back to a kinder, gentler politics, just as victory in the Civil War was the way to achieve a peaceful, post-slavery America. Some may be squeamish about the prospect of political revenge on the Deep State, just as many were squeamish about the approach of the Civil War, but I for one can't wait. Schadenfreude, I gotta say, is noble when it springs out of the aspiration to restore justice.

While Never Trumpers and others on the left express their contempt for Trump's character—they never tire of pointing out Trump's personal weaknesses—what I find interesting is how Trump's human flaws have nevertheless turned out to be political strengths. I no longer think that Trump has the Brobdingnagian ego that his critics attribute to him, but let's say he does. Let's say that he tells himself every day, like Muhammad Ali, "I am the greatest!" Such braggadocio would indeed be a human weakness.

But put yourself in Trump's place. The man is flayed on just about every media platform at every second of every day. Who can take this kind of abuse? A normal person would go into the fetal position and become a human wreck. Not Trump! Why not? Because the man's implacable self-assurance acts as his own personal wall. It creates for him a kind of insulation, so that Trump can ignore the shrieks of abuse and push confidently, resolutely ahead. We should be grateful for his conceit; that's how he manages to stay on track.

Another Trump weakness is the fact that he doesn't pick his fights; he attacks in all directions. If you attack Trump, no matter how irrelevant, inconsequential and picayune you are, he attacks you back. It's an emotional necessity with him. He has to do it; he cannot not do it. And this, I concede, is a weakness. Is it really necessary, all that invective and name-calling? It's not what we teach our children. We teach them to pick their fights, to exercise self-restraint.

Yet in a Republican Party that has nominated one Boy Scout after another—from George H. W. Bush to John McCain to Mitt Romney—and watched them get beaten to a pulp by unscrupulous, relentless opponents on the left, it's refreshing to have a fighter for a change. Even otherwise timorous Republicans, conservatives and Christians are uncharacteristically energized to have a leader who actually loves kicking people in the shins. Far from holding Trump back, we instinctively want to yell, "Kick him again!"

It's especially invigorating to see how effective Trump is in labeling his opponents. When he calls them names—"Crooked Hillary," "Crazy Bernie," "Sleepy Joe," "Mini Mike"—they stick. Notice that Trump's media opponents, who compose words for a living, have still not successfully pinned a damaging label on him. Their best labels—"Orange Man," "Mango Mussolini"—seem to indicate more their own frustration than anything especially descriptive or damaging about Trump.

Trump simply does not accept the parameters of acceptable discourse that the left has carved out, parameters that every previous Republican—even Reagan—dared not trespass. Consider the trademark conservative phrase: "the media elite" or the "liberal elite." Now here's Trump, at a 2018 campaign rally in Ohio: "They talk about the elite. The elite. Do you ever see the elite? They're not the elite, you are the elite." Here's Trump's point: Is some indignant professor of sociology at Bard College or malicious beat reporter for *The Baltimore Sun* really "elite"? Why should we admire angry, rootless people who live screwed-up lives?

Trump goes on to say that his supporters in the audience are the real elite. They are professionals, they run businesses, they own their own homes, they have functional families. In sum, they are "smarter" than the so-called elite, and they "make bigger incomes." Trump goes on to say, "I'm better than everything they have, including this," pointing to his head. "And I became president and they didn't. . . . And it's driving them crazy."[26] Trump wants to drive them crazy, because watching the self-appointed elite in apoplectic mode is both satisfying and entertaining.

Trump is the only Republican in the country who is unafraid—genuinely unafraid—of the media. While Reagan went over the heads of the media, Trump attacks the media head-on. Reagan was "above the fray," while Trump is "in the fray." Again, I view the difference as situational. Reagan was a peacetime general; he wasn't trying to neutralize the media, he merely sought a way to get his own message across. The media was just as powerful after Reagan as it had been before him. While the media couldn't hurt Reagan, they sure hurt his successors, the two Bushes, neither of whom had Reagan's way of circumventing the media.

Trump, by contrast, wants to hurt the progressive media, to expose them as frauds, to permanently reduce their credibility and influence. Even after Trump, CNN will still be fake news, and there's no way for *The New York Times* or *The Washington Post* to again become the hallowed institutions they once were. We're on to them now, and we can't unlearn what we know about their sleazy, dishonest operations. Future Republicans will benefit from the media carnage that Trump will leave in his wake.

If Trump loses in 2020, the left will treat his term as a regrettable blip, a moment in history when Americans lost their minds and then returned to their senses. There will be a comprehensive effort to sweep away everything connected to Trump, to wipe away not only the Trump "stain" but to discredit all of us who ever said anything positive about Trump. The left will try to ensure that Trumpsters are unemployable, unpublishable, reviled, ostracized—and all in the name of fighting "intolerance." If Trump goes, the MAGA concept goes with it.

But if Trump wins, then MAGA will be a reality by 2024. Reagan had two terms, and America was a different country in 1988 than it was in 1980. I know, because I lived through the change. And the Reagan Revolution lasted long past 1988; it got George H. W. Bush elected. Even Clinton was dragged by the Reagan tide for eight years. It's hardly an exaggeration to say that the Reagan revolution ended only in 2008 with Obama's election. Applying the same model, two terms for a man like Trump could change America for a quarter of a century.

We do at some point have to see beyond Trump. We won't always have him. We will have to get along without him. My hope is that he will bequeath us a Trumpified Republican Party, with old leaders who have learned from Trump or new leaders formed out of Trump's rib, so to speak. We can't go back to the usual, familial GOP invertebrate style; if we do, the other side will once again reduce us to rubble, and the Trump phenomenon will have been a brief and shining interregnum.

We're not going back. I'm not saying that the GOP needs Trump clones; I am saying we need a new generation of leaders who can assimilate the things that Trump does so effectively, fearlessly and gleefully. Trump has made it fun to beat the hell out of leftists and socialists, and even when Trump is gone, we must continue to enjoy the Trumpian experience of being a butt-kicking Republican, Christian, right-wing American capitalist.

ONWARD!

I'm going to close this book by spelling out what we must do, and to do that I must begin by complimenting the left. They set out a generation ago to transform America not just through politics but also through culture. And so they moved to Hollywood, and into the media, and took over the universities. They devoted themselves to teaching and organizing and activism.

And it worked! They didn't take over everything, but they largely took over the culture. And they created two Americas. This is the fact that we conservatives have so much trouble accepting. We continue to chant that this is one America, although we know in our hearts that that is no longer the case. So our fallback plan is to create our own space and hope and pray that both sides can live and let live.

We would be content to be left alone, but the left has no intention of leaving us alone. They want us to submit to them. They want our children. And they want the country—they are ruthlessly dedicated to its takeover. From a distance, I have to admire their commitment. We, by contrast, are committed to our family and our church and our neighborhood, but we don't have the same "all in" commitment to dominating the country that they do.

So we must develop it. This is not an option. It is a requirement for our moral and personal survival. We have to change our ways in order to make them change their ways. If we don't fight back, they will turn America into *1984*, and we will have no place to run to. What this means is that we have to contest their domination of the media, and academia, and Hollywood. We need to recapture some of that cultural space. We need to build our own megaphones.

We must use our influence. Most of us use a tiny fraction of the influence we have. We slip into the privacy of the voting booth and cast our ballot for Trump. Or we vote red down the line. But we don't tell our friends what we think. And we don't use our social media to share information with others. "I don't know, Dinesh, I only have 50 friends on Facebook." Yes, but each of them has 50 friends on Facebook. Don't be timid. Use your influence.

We must go after them like they go after us. This means holding them accountable and not backing down. There is no "let's move on" after they attempt a lethal strike. Contrary to some MAGA boasts, surviving lethal strikes is not #SoMuchWinning. We don't move on until we put the perpetrators into handcuffs. We're winning not when we barely live through lethal political shots; we're winning when we take lethal political shots at them.

They have unleashed their fury against us, just as they did a century and a half ago at Fort Sumter. Let's unleash our fury against them, as Lincoln did in response to Fort Sumter. The Republican Party, confused and somnolent before Lincoln, came together in full force once it took the full measure of the other side and decided that a line had been crossed. Our situation—not in a military but in a political sense—is quite similar. It's time for us to put on our battle fatigues.

When we do, and take the field, we will recognize our full strength. We underestimate that strength because, half the time, we aren't even ready to fight. We are in conciliatory, even surrender, mode. We are wearily ready to turn over the country to them. Not anymore! We know who they are, and we know what we're willing to do to protect ourselves and save our country. We become "one America" again by defeating them, just as they seek to become "one America" by destroying us. Our future doesn't depend on them; it depends almost entirely on us. In the words of Che Guevara, "Hasta la victoria siempre."

APPENDIX

UNITED STATES DISTRICT COURT
SOUTHERN DISTRICT OF NEW YORK

14 Cr. 34 (RMB)

UNITED STATES OF AMERICA

-against-

DINESH D'SOUZA,

Defendant.

REPLY SENTENCING MEMORANDUM ON
BEHALF OF DINESH D'SOUZA

BRAFMAN & ASSOCIATES, P.C.
Attorneys for Defendant
Dinesh D'Souza
767 Third Avenue, 26th Floor
New York, New York 10017
(212) 750-7800

BENJAMIN BRAFMAN
MARK M. BAKER
ALEX SPIRO
    Of Counsel

Gov's Referenced Case	Gov's Limited Description	Facts Omitted by the Government
A. United States v. Jenny Hou & Oliver Pan, 12 Cr. 153 (RJS) (S.D.N.Y.)	On May 2, 2013, Hou and Pan were found guilty by a jury of straw donor fraud in connection with donations made to a Democratic candidate for New York City Mayor. Pan, a fundraiser for the candidate, was responsible for eight donors totaling approximately $8,000 in matching funds. Hou served as the candidate's , campaign manager and also was convicted for lying to federal agents and obstruction of justice. On October 10, 2013, Judge Sullivan sentenced Hou to ten months in prison and Pan to three months in prison .	Both individuals in this case were integrally involved with the campaign. Both individuals went to trial on additional charges as well. Hou was also convicted of attempted wire fraud, obstruction of justice and making of false statements. Hou, according to the AUSA "chose to lie to FBI agents and withhold information from a grand jury." Pan was also convicted of conspiracy to commit wire fraud and attempt to commit wire fraud. Both were convicted of multiple felonies. It was also alleged by the Government that the candidate himself was intimately involved in the wrongdoing. In the present case, there was never any allegation that the candidate (Long) was even aware of the defendant's use of straw donors.
B. United States v. Jay Odom (N.D. Fla.)	On February 12, 2013, Odom pleaded guilty to one count of causing a presidential campaign to make a false statement to the FEC. Odom solicited ten donors who were employees of his business entities and their family members to each make the $2,300 maximum allowable contribution to a Presidential candidate's campaign committee and then used his personal funds to reimburse the contributions totaling $23,000. Odom was sentenced to six months in prison. (See Ex. B (Transcript of Sentencing)).	Odom, a "real estate developer who owned numerous companies," pleaded to a violation of 18 U.S.C. §1001(a)(2) for having made a "Materially False, Fictitious, and Fraudulent Statement to the Federal Election Commission." His conduct involved a presidential campaign and 10 donors. In contemporaneous state case in Florida, Odom had been charged with official misconduct by attempting to secure an appropriation, namely, the construction of a school under false pretenses in order to then transfer the school back to a private entity.
C. United States v. Joseph Bigica (D.N.J.)	On May 9, 2012, Bigica pleaded guilty to one count of conspiring to violate the FECA by using 19 straw donors, including family members, business associates and others, to make $98,600 in illegal contributions to the campaign committee of a federal candidate (and one count of failing to pay personal income taxes). Bigica reimbursed the straw donors using checks drawn on accounts in the name of his spouse or companies he controlled. Bigica was sentenced to 60 months in prison.	Bigica's conduct included the use of nearly 20 straw donors and nearly $100,000 in illegal contributions. His company provided services to a number of government entities. Bigica used checks from both companies he controlled and his wife to reimburse the donors. The conduct was part of an overall criminal scheme involving more than $2.5 million of tax fraud. In addition, Bigica was charged with failure to pay income tax.

Gov's Referenced Case	Gov's Limited Description	Facts Omitted by the Government
D. *United States v. Marybeth Feiss* (S.D. Fla.)	On February 17, 2012, Feiss pleaded guilty to one count of engaging in a conspiracy to violate the FECA. Feiss, an administrative assistant to an attorney, helped the attorney organize political events and assisted with the collection of campaign contributions made at those events. Feiss also made a $2,500 contribution to a Presidential candidate's campaign committee and the attorney then reimbursed her using money from his law firm. Feiss was sentenced to six months in prison.	Feiss worked for and with an attorney to help the attorney organize political events and assisted with the collection of campaign contributions made at those events. Feiss' firm attempted to influence the campaign in an effort to appoint specific individuals to political office to oversee the firm's business and the awarding of government contracts. After donations were made, the firm would reimburse the donors by disguising them as "bonuses" or "miscellaneous expenses." The total value of the fraud was over $800,000.
E. *United States v. Pierce O'Donnell*	On February 4, 2011, O'Donnell pleaded guilty to a misdemeanor count of making illegal conduit contributions. O'Donnell solicited ten employees of his law firm and at least one relative to make individual contributions of $2,000 each to a Presidential candidate's campaign committee, which he then reimbursed. O'Donnell was sentenced to two months in prison.	O'Donnell, an attorney, who had been *previously charged with a campaign violation*, solicited ten employees of his law firm and at least one relative to make individual contributions to a presidential campaign.

Gov's Referenced Case	Gov's Limited Description	Facts Omitted by the Government
F. *United States v. Christopher Tigani* (D. Del.)	On June 9, 2011, Tigani pleaded guilty to violating the FECA by soliciting employees of his company to make $219,800 in political contributions to candidates running for various federal and state offices. Tigani used company non-payroll checks to reimburse his employees for their straw donations. Tigani was sentenced to two years in prison.	Tigani solicited employees of his family's liquor business, N.K.S.Distributors, Inc., the exclusive distributor for Anheuser-Busch products in Delaware, to make over $200,000 in political contributions to candidates running for various federal and state offices. In addition to using company non-payroll checks to reimburse his employees for their straw donations, Tigani also used a company debit card to pay for what appeared to be personal expenses, including clothes, shoes, groceries and possibly personal restaurant bills. In addition to the campaign-finance violations, Tigani also pleaded to two counts of tax fraud. He had also volunteered his employees to work on campaigns, including making fund-raising calls, in addition to providing free beer and liquor for campaign events. He had even turned over his corporate offices for fundraising calls. All in all, following what appeared to have been favorable state land deals, the year-long FBI investigation revealed that Tigani, a friend of the then Delaware governor, had schemed to increase his political influence in matters that affected his family liquor business by making contributions to both state and federal campaigns that exceeded legal limits.

Gov's Referenced Case	Gov's Limited Description	Facts Omitted by the Government
G. United States v. George Tirado & Benjamin Hogan (D. Conn.)	On April 19, 2013, Tirado and Hogan each pleaded guilty to one count of engaging in a conspiracy to make false statements to the FBI and to impede the FEC's enforcement of federal campaign financial laws. Tirado, Hogan, and others engaged in a scheme to direct conduit contributions to a candidate for the U.S. House of Representatives. Tirado caused two illegal $2,500 conduit contributions and Hogan recruited three conduits and reimbursed those conduits in cash. Tirado was sentenced to 26 months in prison and Hogan was sentenced to 21 months in prison.	Both Tirado and Hogan plead guilty to one count of engaging in a conspiracy to make false statements to the FBI and to impede the FEC's enforcement of federal campaign financial laws. **Their criminal conduct had the corrupt purpose of intending to influence cigarette tax legislation by stopping a bill then pending before Congress. Both worked for a tobacco company that had unfavorable legal rulings recently issued precluding them from certain business interests.**

Gov's Referenced Case	Gov's Limited Description	Facts Omitted by the Government
H. United States v. F. Harvey Whittemore (D. Nev.)	In May 2013, Whittemore was found guilty by a jury on three counts, including violating the FECA by causing 29 straw donations to a federal candidate for a total of $133,400. Whittemore was sentenced to 24 months in prison. See Ex. A (Transcript of Sentencing)).	The Government fortunately attaches the 188 page sentencing transcript from the case upon which they rely so heavily and draw from at great length. Whittemore was a lobbyist and attorney. Whittemore used more than 10 donors totaling more than $100,000. **Whittemore lied to the FBI.** Whittemore went to trial and testified in his own defense after which the Government moved for a sentencing enhancement based on obstruction of justice. Whittemore was convicted of 3 felonies and his guideline calculation was level 22.

NOTES

PREFACE

1 John Milton, *Paradise Lost*, in Douglas Bush, ed., *The Portable Milton* (New York: Penguin, 1997), p. 457.

2 Joshua Muravchik, "Socialism as Epic Tragedy," May 16, 2019, nationalreview.com.

3 George Orwell, *1984* (New York: Signet Classics, 1977), p. 267.

4 Kristian Niemietz, *Socialism: The Failed Idea That Never Dies* (London: Institute of Economic Affairs, 2019), p. 304–6.

5 Ibid., p. 132, 189.

6 Cited by Rand Paul with Kelley Ashby Paul, *The Case Against Socialism* (New York: Broadside Books, 2019), p. 172.

7 Pankaj Mishra, "A Long & Undeclared Emergency," *New York Review of Books*, July 18, 2019, p. 35.

8 Owen Jones, "My Thoughts on Cuba," *Medium*, November 29, 2016, medium.com.

9 John Bunyan, *The Pilgrim's Progress* (Norwalk, CT: Easton Press, 1979), p. 13–14.

INTRODUCTION

1 Stacey Abrams, cited by Jonathan S. Tobin, "A Blue Wave of 'Undocumented Voters'?" October 17, 2018, nationalreview.com.

2 Joseph Schumpeter, *Capitalism, Socialism and Democracy* (New York: HarperPerennial, 2008), p. 167.

3 Matt Bruenig, "Nickel-and-dime socialism," February 11, 2017, medium.com.

4 Bhaskar Sunkara, "Socialism's Future May Be Its Past," *New York Times*, June 26, 2007, nytimes.com; Owen Jones, "My Thoughts on Cuba," *Medium*,

November 29, 2016, medium.com; Ugo Okere, cited by Charles C. W. Cooke, "Socialism Is Not Democratic," May 16, 2019, nationalreview.com.

5   DSA Constitution & Bylaws, as amended by the 2017 National Convention, Democratic Socialists of America, dsausa.org; tweet by Ilhan Omar, August 8, 2018, @IlhanMN; Alexandria Ocasio-Cortez, cited by Robert Westbrook, "Socialism and the Democracy Deficit," *New Republic*, May 20, 2019, newrepublic.com.

6   Mehdi Hasan, "Why Is Nancy Pelosi So Afraid of Socialism?" July 6, 2018, theintercept.com; Peter Hasson, "Nancy Pelosi says Democrats don't support socialism," April 15, 2019, dailycaller.com.

7   Billy House, "Pelosi Says She and Ocasio-Cortez Don't Have 'That Many Differences,'" July 26, 2019, bloomberg.com.

8   Mike Brest, "Cory Booker: 'I Am Not a Socialist,'" March 18, 2019, dailycaller.com; Rachel Frazin, "Kamala Harris: 'I am not a democratic socialist,'" February 19, 2019, thehill.com; John Harwood, "Democratic Sen. Elizabeth Warren: 'I am a capitalist'—but markets need to work for more than just the rich," July 24, 2018, cnbc.com; Joseph Lawler, "Warren spurns 'socialism' in favor of 'capitalism with serious rules,'" January 30, 2019, washingtonexaminer.com; Emily Bazelon, "Elizabeth Warren Is Completely Serious," *New York Times*, June 17, 2019, nytimes.com.

9   Jonathan Easley, "2020 Democrats spar over socialism ahead of first debate," June 26, 2019, thehill.com.

10 Hannah Bleau, "Elizabeth Warren promises day one executive order on fossil fuel leases, pledges to ban fracking," September 6, 2019, breitbart .com.

11 Hannah Bleau, "Joe Biden promises environmentalist: 'Look into my eyes; I guarantee you, we are going to end fossil fuel,'" September 7, 2019, breitbart .com; Justin Caruso, "End of Discussion: Bernie Sanders Says We're Going to Stop Using Coal, Gasoline," August 22, 2019, dailycaller.com; "Transcript: Mayor de Blasio Announces New York City's Green New Deal," April 22, 2019, www1.nyc.gov.

12 Osita Nwanevu, "A Decisive Year for the Sunrise Movement and the Green New Deal," May 14, 2019, newyorker.com; Sam Dorman, "AOC appears to claim Miami will be gone 'in a few years' because of climate change," September 13, 2019, foxnews.com; Astra Taylor, "Reclaiming Our Future," May 17, 2019, newrepublic.com.

13 Amanda Woods, "Obamas Buy Martha's Vineyard Estate from Celtics Owner Wycliffe Grousbeck," December 6, 2019, nypost.com.

14 Nathan Hultman, "We're almost out of time: The alarming IPCC climate

report and what to do next," October 16, 2018, brookings.edu; Joseph Stiglitz, "Corporate greed is accelerating climate change," April 21, 2019, cnn .com.

15 Jack Crowe, "AOC's Chief of Staff Admits the Green New Deal Is Not About Climate Change," July 12, 2019, nationalreview.com.

16 Joseph Stiglitz, *The Price of Inequality* (New York: W. W. Norton, 2012), p. 143.

17 Bazelon, "Elizabeth Warren Is Completely Serious"; Colin Wilhelm, "Warren to propose substantial new wealth tax, would raise 1 percent of GDP a year," January 24, 2019, washingtonexaminer.com.

18 David Dayen, "How to Cure Corporate America's Selfishness," *New Republic*, August 15, 2018, newrepublic.com.

19 John Jay College of Criminal Justice, "Congresswoman Alexandria Ocasio-Cortez Captivates the Audience at John Jay College," April 23, 2019, jjcuny.edu.

20 J. David Goodman and William Neuman, "Mayor de Blasio Says Wealth Is 'in the Wrong Hands,' Pledges to Redistribute It," *New York Times*, January 10, 2019, nytimes.com; Joe Setyon, "Bill de Blasio: 'We Will Seize Their Buildings and We Will Put Them in the Hands of a Community Nonprofit,'" January 10, 2019, reason.com.

21 Schumpeter, *Capitalism, Socialism and Democracy*, p. 61.

22 Jeremy Rifkin, *The End of Work* (New York: G. P. Putnam's Sons, 1996); Derek Thompson, "A World Without Work," *Atlantic*, July–August 2015, theatlantic .com.

23 Katharine Schwab, "Alexandria Ocasio-Cortez: We should be excited about automation," March 19, 2010, fastcompany.com.

24 Tweet by PragerU, April 29, 2019, @prageru; Gallup survey, cited by Peter Slevin, "The Many, Tangled American Definitions of Socialism," *New Yorker*, June 14, 2019, newyorker.com.

25 Simon Van Zuylen-Wood, "When Did Everyone Become a Socialist?" *New York*, March 4, 2019, nymag.com.

26 Jarrett Stepman, "I Went to a Socialism Conference. Here Are My 6 Observations," July 15, 2019, dailysignal.com.

27 Grace Segers, "Schumer announces support for bill to form committee on reparations," July 16, 2019, cbsnews.com; Peter Hasson, "Every Democratic 2020 Frontrunner Supports Bill Forcing Male Athletes Into Girls' Sports," June 18, 2019, dailycaller.com.

28 Karl Marx, cited by James R. Rogers, "Is Identity Politics a Capitalist Plot?" March 1, 2019, lawliberty.org.

29 Christine Rosen, "The War of the Socialisms," *Commentary*, February 12, 2019, commentarymagazine.com.

30 Peter Svab, "Sanders Field Organizer Advocates Violent Revolution, Gulags for Trump Supporters, Liberals, in Undercover Videos," January 14, 2020, theepochtimes.com; Zachary Stieber, "Second Bernie Staffer Praises Gulags," January 21, 2020, theepochtimes.com.

CHAPTER 1: THE INVENTION OF INVENTION

1 William Jennings Bryan, cited by Daniel J. Boorstin, *The Americans: The Democratic Experience* (New York: Vintage, 1974), p. 557.

2 Friedrich Engels, cited by Irving Howe, *Selected Writings 1950–1990* (New York: Harcourt Brace Jovanovich, 1990), p. 383–84.

3 Werner Sombart, *Why Is There No Socialism in the United States?* (White Plains, NY: IAS Press, 1976), p. 106.

4 Howard Zinn, *A People's History of the United States* (New York: HarperPerennial, 2005), p. 10.

5 Adam Shaw, "Top 2020 Democrats Under Fire for 'Collective Bashing of America' After Cuomo Gaffe," August 18, 2018, foxnews.com; Ian Schwartz, "Eric Holder to Trump: 'Exactly When Did You Think America Was Great?'" March 27, 2019, realclearpolitics.com.

6 For a summary of this debate, see Herman Belz, "Selling the Framers Short," *Claremont Review of Books*, February 24, 2014, claremont.org.

7 Thorstein Veblen, *The Theory of the Leisure Class* (New York: Penguin, 1994), p. v, vi, 137.

8 Jack Schwartz, "How Socialism Made America Great," July 1, 2019, thedailybeast.com.

9 Richard Thompson Ford, "Neo-Socialism and the Rise of the Machines," *American Interest*, July 18, 2019, the-american-interest.com.

10 *Encyclopædia Britannica*, "Gilded Age," britannica.com.

11 George Orwell, *1984* (New York: Signet, 1977), p. 75.

12 "Extract from John F. Kennedy's Remarks at a Dinner Honoring Nobel Prize Winners of the Western Hemisphere," April 29, 1962, monticello.org.

13 Benjamin Franklin, *The Autobiography of Benjamin Franklin* (New York: Touchstone, 2004); see also Ralph Lerner, "Franklin, Spectator," in Ralph Lerner, *The Thinking Revolutionary* (Ithaca, NY: Cornell University Press, 1987), p. 42–52.

14 Tim Murphy, "How Bernie Sanders Learned to Be a Real Politician," *Mother*

Jones, May 26, 2015, motherjones.com; Tim Murphy "You Might Very Well Be the Cause of Cancer: Read Bernie Sanders' 1970s-Era Essays," *Mother Jones*, July 5, 2015, motherjones.com; Sarah Lyall, "Bernie Sanders's Revolutionary Roots Were Nurtured in '60s Vermont," *New York Times*, July 3, 2015, nytimes.com; Blake Seitz, "Bernie Sanders Was Asked to Leave Hippie Commune for Shirking, Book Claims," April 19, 2016, freebeacon.com.

15 Eric Foner, "How Bernie Sanders Should Talk About Democratic Socialism," *Nation*, October 21, 2015, thenation.com.

16 Astra Taylor, "Reclaiming the Future," *New Republic*, May 17, 2019, newrepublic.com.

17 "Constitution in Crisis," *Harper's*, October 2019, p. 25–32.

18 Abraham Lincoln, "Lecture on Discoveries and Inventions," Jacksonville, Illinois, February 11, 1859, in Abraham Lincoln, *Selected Speeches and Writings* (New York: Vintage, 1992); Michael Novak, *The Fire of Invention* (Lanham: Rowman & Littlefield, 1997), p. 53–59.

19 Adam Smith, *The Wealth of Nations* (Chicago: University of Chicago Press, 1976), Vol. 1, p. 362–63.

20 Albert O. Hirschman, *The Passions and the Interests* (Princeton, NJ: Princeton University Press, 1977), p. 32, 73, 132–33; Montesquieu, *The Spirit of the Laws* (Cambridge: Cambridge University Press, 1989), p. 389–90.

21 James Otis, cited by John Richard Alden, *George Washington: A Biography*, p. 101, books.google.com; cited by Matthew Spalding, *We Still Hold These Truths* (Wilmington: ISI Press, 2012), p. 67.

22 John Dickinson, cited by Bernard Bailyn, *The Ideological Origins of the American Revolution* (Cambridge, MA: Harvard University Press, 1992), p. 101.

23 Ibid., p. 120.

24 Alexander Hamilton, James Madison, John Jay, *The Federalist* (New York: Barnes & Noble, 2006), Book 10, p. 53; Book 12, p. 65.

25 Thomas Jefferson, *Writings of Thomas Jefferson* (Washington, D.C.: Thomas Jefferson Memorial Association, 1904), p. 466.

26 William James, cited by Andrew Reeve, *Property* (London: Macmillan, 1986), p. 298–99.

27 Hamilton, Madison, Jay, *The Federalist*, Book 10, p. 56.

28 Abraham Lincoln, cited by Eric Foner, *Free Soil, Free Labor, Free Men* (New York: Oxford University Press, 1970), p. 20, 30.

29 Thomas Jefferson, *Notes on the State of Virginia* (New York: W. W. Norton, 1982), p. 120; Hamilton, Madison, Jay, *The Federalist*, Book 10, p. 54.

30 Gordon Wood, *The Idea of America* (New York: Penguin, 2011), p. 294.

31 Joseph Story, cited by F. A. Hayek, *The Constitution of Liberty* (Chicago: University of Chicago Press, 2011), p. 277.

32 Frederick Douglass, "What the Black Man Wants," 1865, teachingamericanhistory.org.

33 Frederick Douglass, "Self-Made Men," 1872, monadnock.net.

34 H. W. Brands, *Masters of Enterprise* (New York: The Free Press, 1999), p. 19.

35 Burton W. Folsom Jr., *The Myth of the Robber Barons* (Herndon, VA: Young America's Foundation, 1991).

36 David McCullough, *The Wright Brothers* (New York: Simon & Schuster, 2015).

CHAPTER 2: THE DREAM AND THE NIGHTMARE

1 William Shakespeare, *Julius Caesar* (New York: Washington Square Press, 1959), Act III, Scene 2, p. 56.

2 Mohammed Younis, "Four in 10 Americans Embrace Some Form of Socialism," May 10, 2019, news.gallup.com; Olivia B. Waxman, "What Is Democratic Socialism?" *Time*, October 24, 2018, time.com.

3 Frank Newport, "Democrats More Positive About Socialism Than Capitalism," August 13, 2018, news.gallup.com.

4 Nathan Robinson, *Why You Should Be a Socialist* (New York: All Points Books, 2019), p. 11; Gabriel Debenedetti, "Sanders invokes FDR to defend democracy socialism," November 19, 2015, politico.com.

5 Robert Reich, "The Same Old Scare Tactic About Socialism," June 11, 2019, prospect.org; Jamelle Bouie, "Why Bernie Sanders Isn't Afraid of 'Socialism,'" *New York Times*, June 17, 2019, nytimes.com.

6 Sean Wilentz, "Fighting Words," *Democracy Journal*, Spring 2018, democracyjournal.org.

7 Jack Schwartz, "How Socialism Made America Great," July 1, 2019, thedailybeast.com.

8 Paul Hollander, *Political Pilgrims* (Lanham, MD: University Press of America, 1990).

9 Charles C. W. Cooke, "Socialism Is Not Democratic," May 16, 2019, nationalreview.com.

10 Joseph Schumpeter, *Capitalism, Socialism and Democracy* (New York: HarperPerennial, 2008), p. 263.

11 Bernard Bailyn, *The Ideological Origins of the American Revolution* (Cambridge, MA: Harvard University Press, 1992), p. 55–56.

12 Nisha Stickles and Barbara Corbellini Duarte, "Exclusive: Alexandria Ocasio-Cortez explains what democratic socialism means to her," March 4, 2019, businessinsider.com; Astra Taylor, "Reclaiming the Future," May 17, 2019, newrepublic.com; Waxman, "What Is Democratic Socialism?"

13 Paul Krugman, "Trump Versus the Socialist Menace," *New York Times*, February 7, 2019, nytimes.com.

14 Joseph Simonson, "Bernie Sanders: Soviet socialism 'not my thing' but 'Denmark and Sweden do very well,'" April 6, 2019, washingtonexaminer.com; Josh Rigin, "Bernie Sanders's foreign policy is a risk for Democrats against Trump," *Washington Post*, February 3, 2020, washingtonpost.com; Sam Dorman, "Details of Sanders' Soviet 'honeymoon' exposed, as entourage member recalls shock at Bernie's America-bashing," May 3, 2019, foxnews .com; Michael Kranish, "Inside Bernie Sanders's 1988 10-day 'honeymoon' in the Soviet Union," *Washington Post*, May 3, 2019, washingtonpost.com; Joseph Simonson, "Bernie Sanders praised communist Cuba and the Soviet Union in the 1980s," June 6, 2019, washingtonexaminer.com; Jonathan Chait, "Bernie's Pro-Sandinista Past Is a Problem, and His Response Is Not Good," May 27, 2019, nymag.com; Paul Sperry, "Don't be fooled by Bernie Sanders— he's a diehard communist," January 16, 2016, nypost.com; Helen Raleigh, "Bernie Sanders once said breadlines are good—I grew up in Communist China and I can tell you they're not," February 22, 2019, foxnews.com; Miriam Elder, "Bernie Sanders' Trip to the Soviet Union Exposes Socialism's Blind Spots," July 11, 2019, buzzfeednews.com.

15 Javier C. Hernandez, "A Mayoral Hopeful Now, de Blasio Was Once a Young Leftist," *New York Times*, September 22, 2013, nytimes.com; John Cage, "Bill de Blasio forced to defend his honeymoon to Cuba on *The View*," August 2, 2019, washingtonexaminer.com; William Neuman, "De Blasio's Guevara Lesson," June 28, 2019, nytimes.com.

16 Ronald Radosh, "De Blasio's Nicaragua Fling," September 30, 2013, nydailynews.com; Eric Levitz, "In Appeal to Hard Left, Bloomberg Praises Chinese Communism," *New York*, December 2, 2019, nymag.com.

17 John P. Diggins, *Mussolini and Fascism* (Princeton, NJ: Princeton University Press, 1972), p. 279.

18 W. E. B. Du Bois, "Russia, 1926," in David Levering Lewis, ed., *W. E. B. Du Bois: A Reader* (New York: Henry Holt, 1995), p. 582; Werner Sollors, "W. E. B. Du Bois in Nazi Germany," *Chronicle of Higher Education*, November 12, 1999, chronicle.com; Philip S. Foner, ed., *W.E.B. Du Bois Speaks* (New York: Pathfinder, 1988), p. 286, 319.

19 Charles F. Bryan, "Behind the Wheel," Virginia Historical Society, June 29, 2016, richmond.com.

20 Cited by Walter Isaacson, *Steve Jobs* (New York: Simon & Schuster, 2011), p. 567.

21 Henry Ford, cited by H. W. Brands, *Masters of Enterprise* (New York: The Free Press, 1999), p. 96.

22 Jill Lepore, "Eugene V. Debs and the Endurance of Socialism," *New Yorker*, February 11, 2019, newyorker.com.

23 Bhaskar Sunkara, *The Socialist Manifesto* (New York: Basic Books, 2019), p. 175.

24 Woodrow Wilson, cited by Burton Folsom Jr., *New Deal or Raw Deal?* (New York: Threshold Editions, 2009), p. 255.

25 Woodrow Wilson, "What Is Progress?" 1913, teachingamericanhistory.org.

26 Edward Alsworth Ross, *Social Control* (New York: Macmillan, 1918), p. 74, 82.

27 Ira Katznelson, *Fear Itself* (New York: Liveright Publishing, 2013), p. 145.

28 Cass R. Sunstein, *The Second Bill of Rights* (New York: Basic Books, 2004), p. 1.

29 Franklin D. Roosevelt, "State of the Union Message to Congress," January 11, 1944, fdrlibrary.marist.edu.

30 Frank Freidel, *Franklin D. Roosevelt* (Boston: Little, Brown, 1990), p. 150.

31 Thomas Piketty, *Capital in the Twenty-First Century* (Cambridge, MA: Harvard University Press, 2014), p. 473; Folsom, *New Deal or Raw Deal?*, p. 145, 250.

32 Folsom, *New Deal or Raw Deal?*, p. 165.

33 Robert Dallek, *Franklin D. Roosevelt* (New York: Viking, 2017), p. 278; Howard Ball, *Hugo L. Black* (New York: Oxford University Press, 1996), p. 98–99.

34 Josh Lederman, "Inside Pete Buttigieg's plan to overhaul the Supreme Court," June 3, 2019, nbcnews.com; Ronn Blitzer, "Senate Dems deliver stunning warning to Supreme Court: 'Heal' or face restructuring," August 13, 2019, foxnews.com; Quint Forgey, "Ginsburg opposes 2020 Democrats' proposals to expand Supreme Court," July 24, 2019, politico.com.

CHAPTER 3: ALIEN NATION

1 Lewis Carroll, "The Walrus and the Carpenter," jabberwocky.com.

2 Cited by Miguel Salazar, "Do America's Socialists Have a Race Problem?" December 20, 2018, newrepublic.com; tweet by Elizabeth Warren, November 7, 2019, @ewarren; Anthony Leonardi, "Warren Promises to Fill Half of Her Cabinet with Women and Nonbinary People," January 22, 2020, washingtonexaminer.com.

3 Doug Henwood, "The Socialist Network," May 16, 2019, newrepublic.com.

4 Stacey Y. Abrams, "E Pluribus Unum?" *Foreign Affairs*, March–April 2019, foreignaffairs.com.

5   Maggie Haberman, "Fordham piece called Warren Harvard Law's 'first woman of color,'" May 15, 2012, politico.com; MJ Lee and Daniella Diaz, "Elizabeth Warren releases plan to aid Native Americans ahead of closely watched conference," August 16, 2019, cnn.com.

6   Kenneth Garger, "Kirsten Gillibrand wants to explain white privilege to 'white women in the suburbs,'" July 14, 2019, nypost.com.

7   Alex Henderson, "'This isn't 1980': Filmmaker Michael Moore reminds Democratic leaders who their base really is," August 1, 2019, alternet.org.

8   Benedict Anderson, *Imagined Communities* (London: Verso, 2016), p. 6–7, 144.

9   Rod Dreher, "The Woke Menace," February 7, 2019, theamericanconservative.com.

10 *San Diego Reader*, October 21, 2010; Angela Davis, cited by Paul Hollander, *From Benito Mussolini to Hugo Chavez* (Cambridge: Cambridge University Press, 2016), p. 37.

11 Karl Kautsky, cited by Michael Harrington, *Socialism: Past and Future* (New York: Arcade Publishing, 2011), p. 49.

12 Elizabeth Wilson, *Bohemians* (New Brunswick, NJ: Rutgers University Press, 2000), p. 10, 75.

13 Herbert Marcuse, *An Essay on Liberation* (Boston: Beacon Press, 1969), p. 81, 87.

14 Andrew Feenberg and William Leiss, eds., *The Essential Marcuse* (Boston: Beacon Press, 2007), p. 246–47.

15 Ibid., p. 236.

16 Herbert Marcuse, *Eros and Civilization* (Boston: Beacon Press, 1974), p. 201, 211.

17 Osita Nwanevu, "A Decision Year for the Sunrise Movement and the Green New Deal," May 14, 2019, newyorker.com.

18 Gregg Re, "Green New Deal would cost up to $93 trillion, or $600 G per household, study says," February 25, 2019, foxnews.com.

19 Ellie Bufkin, "Climate activist celebrities arrive at 'Google Camp' by yachts, helicopters and private jets," July 31, 2019, washingtonexaminer.com.

20 CBS News, "One of earth's fastest-shrinking glaciers is growing again," March 28, 2019, cbsnews.com; Shelby Lin Erdman, "Major Greenland glacier growing again, surprising scientists, after years of ice loss," March 25, 2019, boston25news.com.

21 "Largest glaciers in Iceland growing for first time in decades," December 5,

2018, iceagenow.info; Cap Allon, "Icelandic Glaciers are expanding for the first time in decades," December 6, 2018, electroverse.net.

22 Susan J. Crockford, "State of the Polar Bear Report 2018," thegwpf.org.

23 Amanda Prestigiacomo, "Ocasio-Cortez: I Was Joking About the World Ending in 12 Years, and You're an Idiot if You Believed Me," May 13, 2019, dailywire.com.

24 "The NASA/Hansen Climate Model Predictions vs. Reality," Figure 4.2 in Alex Epstein, *The Moral Case for Fossil Fuels* (New York: Penguin, 2014), p. 102.

25 Ibid., p. 6, 8; Charles Mann, "The Book That Incited a Worldwide Fear of Overpopulation," *Smithsonian*, January 2018, smithsonianmag.com; Julian Simon, *The Ultimate Resource 2* (Princeton, NJ: Princeton University Press, 1996), p. 35.

26 Richard Morrison, "Betting on the Future: 25 Years Later," Competitive Enterprise Institute, September 29, 2015, cei.org.

27 See, e.g., John Fleck and William Connolley, "The Global Cooling Mole," March 7, 2008, realclimate.org.

28 John Gribbin, "Cause and Effects of Global Cooling," *Nature* 254 (1975).

29 Lowell Ponte, *The Cooling* (Englewood Cliffs, NJ: Prentice-Hall, 1976), p. xi, xv–xvi, 240, 247.

30 Natasha Fernández-Silber, "Why We're Socialists, Not 'Progressives,'" July 1, 2019, jacobinmag.com.

31 Pamela Kyle Crossley, "Walls Don't Work," *Foreign Policy*, January 3, 2019, foreignpolicy.com.

32 Nick Givas, "Tlaib doubles down on AOC's concentration camp comments, claims border agents believe it's a 'broken system,'" July 7, 2019, foxnews.com.

33 Zolan Kanno-Youngs, "'We Are All Immigrants,' N.Y. Gov. Andrew Cuomo Says During Speech at Harlem Church," *Wall Street Journal,* November 20, 2016, wsj.com; Michael Shear and Ron Nixon, "More Immigrants Face Deportation Under New Rules," *New York Times*, February 22, 2017, nytimes .com.

34 Suketu Mehta, *This Land Is Our Land* (New York: Farrar, Straus and Giroux, 2019), p. 22, 197, 209, 215.

35 Deroy Murdock, "Yes, We've Nabbed Terrorists on the Southern Border," January 10, 2019, nationalreview.com.

36 Hollie McKay, "ISIS plotted to send westerners to US through Mexico border: report," June 6, 2019, foxnews.com.

37 Hollie McKay, "How Minneapolis' Somali community became the terrorist recruitment capital of the US," February 16, 2019, foxnews.com.

38 Mohammad Tawhidi, "Ilhan Omar Calls for the Protection of a Notorious Terrorist Organization," August 29, 2019, timesofisrael.com.

39 Esme Murphy, "Terror Suspect Released to Halfway House Kept Box Cutter Under Bed," July 6, 2015, minnesota.cbslocal.com.

40 Nick Givas, "In resurfaced interview, Ilhan Omar answers question on 'jihadist terrorist' by saying Americans should be 'more fearful of white men,'" July 24, 2019, foxnews.com.

41 Gertrude Himmelfarb, *One Nation, Two Cultures* (New York: Alfred A. Knopf, 1999), p. 6.

42 Peter Hasson, "Here's a List of Hoax 'Hate Crimes' in the Trump Era," February 18, 2019, dailycaller.com.

43 Fred Siegel, "Young and 'Oppressed' in America," August 20, 2019, city-journal.org.

44 Paul Bedard, "Book: Kavanaugh accuser's attack 'motivated' by defending Roe v. Wade," September 3, 2019, washingtonexaminer.com.

45 Kevin Breuninger, "Kavanaugh accuser Julie Swetnick alleges he was 'very aggressive,' but her latest interview raises new questions," October 1, 2018, cnbc.com.

46 Jamie Dupree, "Senate panel says woman admits fake accusation against Kavanaugh," *Atlanta Journal Constitution*, November 2, 2018, ajc.com.

47 Marcie Bianco, "Miley Cyrus' split with Liam Hemsworth isn't just celebrity gossip—it's a blow to the patriarchy," August 16, 2019, nbcnews.com.

48 Shulamith Firestone, "The Dialectic of Sex," introductory chapter, marxists.org.

49 Mike Miksche, "Teaching Young Dogs Old Tricks," February 5, 2019, slate.com.

50 Dawn Ennis, "No, Mario Lopez," August 1, 2019, thedailybeast.com; Chase Strangio, "Mario Lopez's comments about transgender kids aren't just dumb. They're dangerous," August 1, 2019, nbcnews.com; Sandra Gonzalez, "Mario Lopez apologizes for 'ignorant' comments about parenting and gender identity," July 31, 2019, cnn.com.

CHAPTER 4: VENEZUELA, SI; SWEDEN, NO

1 Bill Ayers, address at World Education Forum, Caracas, 2006, billayers.org.

2 Andrea Rondón Garcia, "What 'Made in Socialism' Means to Venezuelans," July 27, 2015, panampost.com.

3 Paul Krugman, "The Venezuela Calumny," January 29, 2019, nytimes.com;

Paul Krugman, "Trump Versus the Socialist Menace," February 7, 2019, nytimes.com; Roger Cohen, "Socialism and the 2020 Election," *New York Times*, March 8, 2019, nytimes.com; Dean Obeidallah, "Joseph Stiglitz defines economic terms for 2020: 'The swamp has never been murkier,'" April 27, 2019, salon.com.

4 Olivia B. Waxman, "What Is Democratic Socialism?" *Time*, October 24, 2018, time.com; Bhaskar Sunkara, *The Socialist Manifesto* (New York: Basic Books, 2019), p. 105–6.

5 Matt Bruenig, "Norway Is Far More Socialist Than Venezuela," January 27, 2019, peoplespolicyproject.org.

6 Kaylee Greenlee, "Sorry, AOC and Bernie Sanders: Scandinavia Is No Socialist Paradise," July 27, 2019, nationalinterest.org; Rev. Ben Johnson, "What Alexandria Ocasio-Cortez gets wrong about Europe," January 8, 2019, blog .acton.org.

7 Jeffrey Dorfman, "Sorry Bernie . . . But Nordic Countries Are Not Socialist," July 8, 2018, forbes.com; Corey Iacono, "The Myth of Scandinavian Socialism," February 25, 2016, fee.org; John Stossel, "Sweden Isn't Socialist," January 2, 2019, reason.com.

8 Matthew Yglesias, "Denmark's prime minister says Bernie Sanders is wrong to call his country socialist," October 31, 2015, vox.com.

9 Matt Bruenig, "Another Thing Trump's Anti-Socialist Report Gets Wrong," October 25, 2018, jacobinmag.com.

10 Alister Doyle and Simon Johnson, "Not in My Backyard?" February 16, 2016, reuters.com.

11 Joel Kotkin, *Tribes* (New York: Random House, 1993), p. 6.

12 Ibn Khaldun, *The Muqaddimah* (Princeton, NJ: Princeton University Press, 1967), p. 99, 126.

13 "Our Documents: Franklin Roosevelt's Address Announcing the Second New Deal," October 31, 1936, fdrlibrary.marist.edu.

14 Thomas Kaplan, "Elizabeth Warren Calls Trump a White Supremacist," August 9, 2019, nytimes.com; Eric Bradner, Sarah Mucha and Jeff Zeleny, "Joe Biden says Trump 'has fanned the flames of white supremacy in this nation,'" August 7, 2019, cnn.com; Julio Rosas, "AOC: Racists were key part of Trump's coalition of voters," August 15, 2019, washingtonexaminer.com.

15 Toni Morrison, "Making America White Again," November 14, 2016, newyorker.com.

16 Julio Rosas, "Beto O'Rourke: 'This country was founded on white supremacy,'" July 10, 2019, washingtonexaminer.com.

17 Nikole Hannah-Jones, "1619 Project," *New York Times Magazine*, August 4, 2019, nytimes.com.

18 George Fredrickson, *Racism* (Princeton, NJ: Princeton University Press, 2002), p. 79, 81.

19 Robert Kaiser, "Why Can't We Be More Like Finland?" *Seattle Times*, September 25, 2005.

20 Martin Selsoe Sorensen, "Denmark Plans to Isolate Unwanted Migrants on a Small Island," December 3, 2018, nytimes.com.

21 Peter S. Goodman, "The Nordic Model May Be the Best Cushion Against Capitalism. Can It Survive Immigration?" July 11, 2019, nytimes.com; Ida Auken, "We Danes aren't living the 'American Dream.' And we still aren't socialist," February 22, 2020, washingtonpost.com.

22 Ayers, address at World Education Forum, Caracas, Venezuela, November 2006.

23 Paul Hollander, *From Benito Mussolini to Hugo Chavez* (Cambridge: Cambridge University Press, 2016), p. 256–57; Kiraz Janicke, "Joseph Stiglitz, in Caracas, Praises Venezuela's Economic Policies," October 11, 2007, venezuelanalysis.com; Dan Hannan, "In Venezuela, the destructive force of socialism is at work," July 10, 2017, washingtonexaminer.com; Fox News, "Carter praises Chavez for 'improving the lives of millions,'" December 20, 2015, foxnews.com; tweet by Michael Moore, March 5, 2013, @MMFlint; Ben Child, "Sean Penn, Michael Moore and Oliver Stone pay tribute to Hugo Chavez," March 6, 2013, theguardian.com; Chris Carlson, "Supermodel Naomi Campbell 'Amazed' at Venezuelan Social Programs," November 1, 2007, venezuelanalysis.com; Naomi Campbell, "When Naomi Campbell interviewed Hugo Chavez," November 10, 2013, originally published in the February 2008 issue of British *GQ*, gq-magazine.co.uk.

24 Sara Carter, "Rashida Tlaib Calls for $20 Per Hour Minimum Wage," July 23, 2019, saracarter.com; Joe Setyon, "Bill de Blasio Proposes Mandated Paid Vacations Because 'New Yorkers Need a Break,'" January 9, 2019, reason.com.

25 See, e.g., Annie Lowrey, "The City That's Giving People Money," May 24, 2019, theatlantic.com.

26 Joi Ito, "The Paradox of Universal Basic Income," *Wired*, March 29, 2018, wired.com.

27 Ibid.; Jon Henley, "Finland to end basic income trial after two years," *Guardian*, April 23, 2018, theguardian.com.

28 Tweet by Andrew Yang, November 27, 2019, @AndrewYang; Tonya Riley,

"What Andrew Yang's Universal Basic Income Would Actually Look Like," April 23, 2019, motherjones.com.

29 Ella Nilsen, "Elizabeth Warren has the biggest free college plan yet," April 22, 2019, vox.com; Adam Harris, "What Sets Bernie Sanders's Student-Debt Plan Apart," June 24, 2019, theatlantic.com.

30 Brittany M. Hughes, "Med Student to '60 Minutes': Free Tuition Would Help Me Focus on Learning Instead of Having to Pay for It," April 8, 2019, mrctv.org.

31 John Gage, "I want them to back off—Whoopi Goldberg Rips Democrats supporting single-payer healthcare," September 13, 2019, washingtonexaminer .com.

32 John Delaney, cited by Charles Blahous, "The Fundamental Divide Revealed in the Democrats' Debates," August 2, 2019, economics21.org.

33 Tweet by Bernie Sanders, March 6, 2019, @berniesanders.

34 Nima Sanandaji, "So Long, Swedish Welfare State?" September 5, 2018, foreignpolicy.com; Kevin Pham, "'Socialist' Nordic Countries Are Actually Moving Toward Private Health Care," June 13, 2019, dailysignal.com.

35 Kyle Pomerleau, "How Scandinavian Countries Pay for Their Government Spending," June 10, 2015, taxfoundation.org.

36 Dorfman, "Sorry Bernie."

37 Anu Partanen, *The Nordic Theory of Everything* (New York: Harper, 2017), p. 276, 287.

38 Matt Bruenig, "Nickel-and-dime socialism," February 11, 2017, medium.com.

39 "Rudolf Meidner on the Meidner Plan," persistenceofpoverty.blogspot.com.

40 Andreas Møller Mulvad and Rune Moller Stahl, "What Makes Scandinavia Different?" August 4, 2015, jacobinmag.com.

41 Nikolas Kozloff, "Hugo Chavez and the Politics of Race," October 14, 2005, counterpunch.org.

42 Amy Chua, *Political Tribes* (New York: Penguin Press, 2018), p. 128.

43 Keith Johnson, "How Venezuela Struck It Poor," July 16, 2018, foreignpolicy .com.

44 Chua, *Political Tribes*, p. 133–34.

45 Bill Ayers, "Venezuela and the Evil Empire," March 7, 2019, billayers.org.

46 Marie Arana, *Bolivar: American Liberator* (New York: Simon & Schuster, 2014).

47 Nick Fagge, "The Rich Kids of Venezuela," February 5, 2019, dailymail.co.uk;

"Children of Venezuela's elite including ex-leader Hugo Chavez's daughter flaunt wealth," February 6, 2019, news.com.au.

48 Alasdair Baverstock and Peter Foster, "Venezuela: the wealth of Chavez family exposed," April 14, 2013, telegraph.co.uk; Peter D'Amato, "Being the ex-President's daughter pays off: Hugo Chavez's ambassador daughter is Venezuela's richest woman," August 10, 2015, dailymail.co.uk.

CHAPTER 5: JUST DESERTS

1   Adam Smith, *The Theory of Moral Sentiments* (Indianapolis, IN: Liberty Fund, 1982), p. 25.

2   Tess Bonn, "Sanders: China has done more to address extreme poverty 'than any country in the history of civilization,'" August 27, 2019, thehill.com.

3   Ira Stoll, "Are Democrats Now the Party of the Rich?" November 12, 2018, reason.com.

4   John Harwood, "Capitalism is in crisis—and business leaders know it," September 4, 2019, cnbc.com; Nick Hanauer, "The Pitchforks Are Coming . . . for Us Plutocrats," July–August 2014, politico.com.

5   Alyssa Taylor, "Ocasio-Cortez calls capitalism an 'irredeemable' system," March 11, 2019, foxbusiness.com.

6   Joseph Stiglitz, *Freefall* (New York: W. W. Norton, 2010), p. xxi; Joseph Stiglitz, *The Price of Inequality* (New York: W. W. Norton, 2012), p. xii.

7   Tweet by Ilhan Omar, October 29, 2019, @IlhanMN.

8   Nathan Robinson, *Why You Should Be a Socialist* (New York: All Points Books, 2019), p. 7. Fox News, "Obama to Business Owners: 'You Didn't Build That,'" July 16, 2012, foxnews.com; Lucy Madison, "Elizabeth Warren, 'There Is Nobody in This Country Who Got Rich on His Own,'" CBS News, September 22, 2011, cbsnews.com.

9   Evie Fordham, "AOC: 'No one ever makes a billion dollars. You take a billion dollars,'" January 21, 2020, foxbusiness.com.

10 Tweet by Bernie Sanders, May 18 2019, @berniesanders.

11 Michael Walzer, *Spheres of Justice* (New York: Basic Books, 1983), p. 108.

12 John Rawls, *A Theory of Justice* (Cambridge: Harvard University Press, 1971), p. 15, 72, 74; Ed Quish, "John Rawls, Socialist?" *Jacobin*, August 22, 2018, jacobinmag.com; William Edmundson, "The Philosophical Case for Socialism," *Prospect*, October 19, 2018, prospectmagazine.co.uk.

13 Kim Kelly, "What 'Capitalism' Is and How It Affects People," April 11, 2016, teenvogue.com.

14 Rutger Bregman, "No, wealth isn't created at the top. It is merely devoured there," March 30, 2017, theguardian.com.

15 Charles Mathewes and Evan Sandsmark, "Being rich wrecks your soul. We used to know that," July 28, 2017, washingtonpost.com; Tylor Standley, "Virtue Can't Redeem Capitalism," January 15, 2019, sojo.net.

16 Aristotle, *Politics* (New York: Barnes & Noble, 2005), Book 3, p. 68.

17 Amartya Sen, *The Idea of Justice* (Cambridge, MA: Harvard University Press, 2009), p. 12–15.

18 Rawls, *Theory of Justice*, p. 3.

19 Adam Smith, *The Wealth of Nations* (Chicago: University of Chicago Press, 1976), Vol. 1, p. 18.

20 F. A. Hayek, *The Constitution of Liberty* (Chicago: University of Chicago Press, 2011), p. 157.

21 Joseph A. Wulfsohn, "Michael Moore says he doubts Elizabeth Warren really considers herself a 'capitalist,'" September 14, 2019, msn.com; Irving Howe, *A Margin of Hope* (New York: Harcourt Brace Jovanovich, 1982), p. 346.

22 "First African Enrolled in Hawaii Studied Two Years by Mail," *Ka Leo O Hawaii*, October 8, 1959.

23 Donald Trump, *The Art of the Deal* (New York: Ballantine Books, 2015), p. 47, 65.

24 Joseph Schumpeter, *The Entrepreneur* (Palo Alto, CA: Stanford University Press, 2011), p. 71.

25 Trump, *Art of the Deal*, p. 120–21.

26 Schumpeter, *Entrepreneur*, p. 122.

27 Trump, *Art of the Deal*, p. 121.

28 Schumpeter, *Entrepreneur*, p. 7.

29 Trump, *Art of the Deal*, p. 48.

30 Schumpeter, *Entrepreneur*, p. 5, 64.

31 Trump, *Art of the Deal*, p. 137–38.

32 Ibid., p. 182, 184.

33 Schumpeter, *Entrepreneur*, p. 207.

34 Donald Trump, *The Art of the Comeback* (New York: Times Books, 1997), p. 11.

35 Dylan Matthews, "Zero-Sum Trump," January 19, 2017, vox.com.

36 Ludwig von Mises, "Socialism," in Mark Hendrickson, ed., *The Morality of*

Capitalism (Irvington-on-Hudson: Foundation for Economic Education, 1996), p. 129.

37 Rene Ritchie, "The Secret History of iPhone," January 22, 2019, imore.com.

38 David Brancaccio, "The true origin story behind McDonald's," National Public Radio, February 9, 2017, marketplace.org; H. W. Brands, *Masters of Enterprise* (New York: The Free Press, 1999), p. 213.

39 Glenn Rifkin, "The Greatest Marketer You May Not Know," February 13, 2017, kornferry.com.

40 Jason Del Rey, "The making of Amazon Prime, the internet's most successful and devastating membership program," May 3, 2019, vox.com.

41 Robert Nozick, *Anarchy, State, and Utopia* (New York: Basic Books, 2013), p. 151, 160–61.

42 Rawls, *Theory of Justice*, p. 102.

43 Joe Weisenthal, "We Love What Warren Buffett Says About Life, Luck and Winning the 'Ovarian Lottery,'" December 10, 2013, businessinsider.com.

44 Milton Friedman, *Capitalism and Freedom* (Chicago: University of Chicago Press, 1974), p. 165.

45 Tweet by Rand Paul, August 2, 2019, @RandPaul.

46 Katherine Hignett, "Bill Gates Pledges $1 Billion to Fight Malaria as Experts Fear Resurgence," April 20, 2018, newsweek.com; Bill Gates, "Mosquito Wars," August 15, 2017, gatesnotes.com.

47 Jeffrey Gettleman, "Meant to Keep Malaria Out, Mosquito Nets Are Used to Haul Fish In," January 24, 2015, nytimes.com.

48 Abby Phillip, "Liberal filmmaker Michael Moore's conservative neighbors gawk, revel in his messy divorce," *Washington Post*, July 22, 2014, washingtonpost.com.

49 Michael Kruse, "The Secret of Bernie's Millions," Politico, May 24, 2019, politico.com; PoliZette staff, "Bernie Just Revealed His Full-Throated Embrace of Capitalism," April 15, 2019, lifezette.com.

50 Michela Tindera, "How Elizabeth Warren Built a $12 Million Fortune," August 20, 2019, forbes.com.

51 Hillary Hoffower, "The Obamas are worth 30 times more than when they entered the White House in 2008—here's how they spend their millions," January 17, 2019, businessinsider.com; Maureen Callahan, "Michelle Obama's Money-Making Hypocrisy Is Laughable," November 14, 2018, nypost.com.

52 Peter Schweizer and Jacob McLeod, "6 Facts about Hunter Biden's Business Dealings in China," October 10, 2019, nypost.com; Peter Schweizer, "How

Five Members of Joe Biden's Family Got Rich Through His Connections,"
January 18, 2020, nypost.com.

53 Ben Schreckinger, "Biden Inc.," Politico, August 2, 2019, politico.com; Matt
Viser, "Once the poorest senator, 'Middle Class Joe' Biden has reaped millions
in income since leaving the vice presidency," *Washington Post*, June 25, 2019,
washingtonpost.com.

CHAPTER 6: THE ART OF WAR

1 Abraham Lincoln, *Selected Speeches and Writings* (New York: Vintage Books,
1992), p. xxiv.

2 Abraham Lincoln, cited by Harry V. Jaffa, *A New Birth of Freedom* (Lanham,
MD: Rowman & Littlefield, 2004), p. 245.

3 Lord Charnwood, *Abraham Lincoln* (Mineola, NY: Dover Publications, 1997),
p. 167–68.

4 David M. Potter, *The Impending Crisis* (New York: HarperPerennial, 1976),
p. 560.

5 George Orwell, *1984* (New York: Signet Classics, 1977), p. 208–9.

6 Jill Filipovic, "Stormy Daniels, Feminist Hero," August 24, 2018, nytimes.com.

7 Lily Burana, "The Stormy Daniels (and Melania Too) Effect," August 24, 2018,
huffpost.com.

8 Michael Balsamo, "California's West Hollywood declares 'Stormy Daniels
Day,'" May 24, 2018, apnews.com.

9 Some of the information in the preceding account comes from Lawrence W.
Sinclair, *Barack Obama & Larry Sinclair* (Fort Walton Beach, FL: Sinclair
Publishing, 2009).

10 See, e.g., Ben Smith, "Sinclair's Rap Sheet," June 8, 2008, politico.com.

11 "Reply Sentencing Memorandum on Behalf of Dinesh D'Souza," *United States
of America vs. Dinesh D'Souza*, United States District Court, Southern District
of New York, 14 Cr. 34 (RMB), 2014. This document is excerpted in the
appendix to this book.

12 United States Attorney's Office, District of Columbia, "Jeffrey Thompson
Sentenced for Conspiring to Violate District of Columbia Campaign Finance
Law," August 15, 2016.

13 Stephanie Clifford and Russ Buettner, "Clinton Backer Pleads Guilty in a
Straw Donor Scheme," April 17, 2014, nytimes.com; Stephanie Clifford,
"Hotelier Avoids Prison for Violating Campaign Finance Laws," *New York
Times*, December 18, 2014.

14 Anna Sanders, "Rosie O'Donnell's campaign donations to Dems went over legal limit," May 5, 2018, nypost.com.

15 Statement of Catherine Engelbrecht, "Hearing on Oversight and Government Reform," U.S. House of Representatives, February 6, 2014.

16 Chuck Ross, "John Dean: Trump Should Have Been Impeached as Soon as He Took Office," November 16, 2019, dailycaller.com; Ryan Bort, "Rep. Rashida Tlaib Calls Trump a 'M*th*rf*ck*r' While Promising Impeachment," *Rolling Stone*, January 4, 2019.

17 Tim Hains, "Rep. Al Green: 'I'm Concerned If We Don't Impeach This President, He Will Get Re-Elected,'" May 6, 2019, realclearpolitics.com.

18 George Papadopoulos, *Deep State Target* (New York: Diversion Books, 2019), p. 25.

19 Ibid., p. 76.

20 Tim Hains, "Jennifer Rubin: Only Way to Purge GOP of Trump Is to 'Burn Down the Republican Party' with 'No Survivors,'" August 27, 2019, realclearpolitics.com.

21 Hank Berrien, "Colorado Christian Baker in Court Again. This Time It's Over 'Gender Transition' Cake," December 20, 2018, dailywire.com.

22 Kathleen Joyce, "Forever 21 Apologizes for Using White Man to Model 'Black Panther'-Inspired Sweater," December 19, 2018, foxnews.com.

23 John Stuart Mill, *On Liberty* (Cambridge: Cambridge University Press, 1989), p. 20.

24 Orwell, *1984*, p. 241.

25 Lincoln, *Selected Speeches and Writings* (New York: Library of America, 2009), p. 87.

26 CBS News, "Trump says supporters are the 'real elite' at campaign rally in Ohio," August 4, 2018, cbsnews.com.

INDEX

Abrams, Stacey, 96
academia, 17, 71, 176, 224, 225, 227, 245, 256
Adams, John, 69
Affluent Society, The (Galbraith), 100
Affordable Care Act (Obamacare), 13, 18, 157, 249
Albania, 3
alienation, 28–29, 105, 117
Amazon, 202–204
American Civil War, 37, 52, 57–58, 60, 70, 84, 98, 145, 220, 252
American dream, 7, 28–30, 35–36, 70, 239
American Revolution, 15, 36, 45
 causes of, 48–51
 as rejection of monarchy, 1, 63–64
 success of, 70
 winners and losers, 70–71
American socialism. *See* identity socialism
Anderson, Benedict, 97–98
Angola, 3
Animal Farm (Orwell), 2, 4
Antifa, 95, 108, 133, 170, 171, 226–227
Aristotle, 181
Asian Indians, 119–123, 141, 149, 165.
 See also India
Augustine, 9
Auken, Ida, 149
automation, 24, 117, 210–211
Ayers, Bill, 100, 150, 170, 171

al-Baghdadi, Abu Bakr, 221
Bailyn, Bernard, 69
Beard, Charles, 38–39, 40, 42, 73
Belafonte, Harry, 150

Benin, 3
Berman, Richard, 237–238
Bezos, Jeff, 202–203
Bharara, Preet, 236–237
Bianco, Marcie, 130
Biden, Frank, 215–216
Biden, Hunter, 215–216
Biden, James, 215–216
Biden, Joe
 climate change policy, 18
 and Equality Act, 27
 family of, 215–216
 healthcare policy, 157
 and identity politics, 97
 property and wealth, 215, 217
 and socialism, 16, 17
 on Trump, Donald, 144
Bill and Melinda Gates Foundation, 212–213
bin Laden, Osama, 221, 235
Black, Hugo, 93
Black Lives Matter, 95
Bloomberg, Michael, 73
Bolívar, Simón, 136, 166, 170
Bolivia, 3
Bolshevik Revolution, 3, 70, 83
Booker, Cory
 and Equality Act, 27
 and Green New Deal, 109
 and identity politics, 97
 and reparations, 27
 and socialism, 16, 17
 tuition-free college policy, 156
Bouie, Jamelle, 66
Box, Jason, 112

Brands, H. W., 60
Bregman, Rutger, 180
Brooks, David, 240
Brooks, Preston, 227
Brooks, Rosa, 46
Brown, Robert, 38
Bruenig, Matt, 12, 137, 139, 162
Bryson, Reid, 115
Buffett, Warren, 108, 156, 175, 208
Bunyan, Paul, 8
Burana, Lily, 230
Bush, George H. W., 226, 253, 254
Bush, George W., 254
Buttigieg, Pete, 97
    and Equality Act, 27
    and Supreme Court expansion, 94
    tax policy, 21
    on Universal Basic Income, 153

Cambodia, 3
Campbell, Naomi, 151–152
capitalism
    and China, 6–7
    and democracy, 200
    and identity socialism, 22–25
    Marx, Karl, on, 2, 188–191, 197
    and Ocasio-Cortez, Alexandria, 22,
        23–25, 176, 178
    Schumpeter, Joseph, on, 11–12, 23–25
    and Trump, Donald, 190–191
    and Warren, Elizabeth, 16, 22
    See also entrepreneurial capitalism
Capitalism and Freedom (Friedman), 209–210
Carnegie, Andrew, 212
Carter, Jimmy, 151, 224
Castro, Fidel, 14, 67, 74, 76, 135
Chakrabarti, Saikat, 20
Chamberlain, Wilt, 206–208
Chatwal, Sant, 238
China
    and capitalism, 6–7
    Cultural Revolution, 3, 6, 77–78
    Deng Xiaoping, 6
    economy, 4
    Great Leap Forward, 6
    Mao Zedong, 3, 6, 67, 70, 73, 78
Chomsky, Noam, 151
Christian, Shirley, 76
Chua, Amy, 165–166

Clapper, James, 225, 252
climate change, 107, 139, 167–168, 171
    Green New Deal, 18–20, 26, 87–88, 89,
        109–114, 116
    Sunrise Movement, 19, 109
Clinton, Bill, 97, 205, 214, 217, 224–225,
    237, 254
Clinton, Hillary, 225, 238
    affordable college policy, 18
    immigration policy, 117
    presidential election of 2016, 96, 156,
        174–175, 228, 240, 242
    and Trump, Donald, 253
Clinton Foundation, 242
Cohen, Roger, 136
collectivism, 14–17, 67, 106
Collins, Edward K., 60
Comey, James, 225, 241, 251–252
communications revolution, 202, 205
communism
    and China, 6–7
    and Gramsci, Antonio, 102
    Marx, Karl, on, 68, 111
    and Roosevelt, Franklin D., 67, 73
    and sister ideologies, 67
    socialism as economic program of, 3
    and Soviet Union, 4
    and traditional family, 27
    and tribal identification, 142
Communist Party USA, 101
Constitution, U.S., 37, 38, 45–46
    Bill of Rights, 46, 48, 53–54, 88
    Civil War amendments, 70
    and majority rule, 53–54
Cooke, Charles C. W., 68
Cooper, Anderson, 229, 238–239
Crockford, Susan, 113
Croly, Herbert, 73, 85
Cuba, 3, 4, 138
    Castro, Fidel, 14, 67, 74, 76, 135
    and de Blasio, Bill, 75–76
    Hollander, Paul, on, 67, 77, 79
    nationalization of industry, 12, 138
    and Sanders, Bernie, 73, 74
Cuban revolution, 74–76
Cultural Revolution (China), 3, 6, 77–78
Cuomo, Andrew, 37, 120
Cyrus, Miley, 130
Czechoslovakia, 3

Dalio, Ray, 175
Dallek, Robert, 78, 93
Daniels, Stormy, 229–231, 234–235
Darwin, Charles, 84–85
Davis, Angela, 100–101
Dawkins, Richard, 80
de Blasio, Bill, 73
    climate change policy, 19
    and Cuba, 75–76
    on democratic socialism, 22–23
    and entitlement mentality, 22–23
    and Nicaragua, 75
    proposed compulsory paid vacations, 152
Dean, John, 240–241
Debs, Eugene, 33, 45, 79, 82–83
Delaney, John, 157–158
democracy
    and America's founding, 51–55
    and capitalism, 200
    definition of, 51
    and entrepreneurs, 31, 200
    and French Revolution, 70
    and identity socialism, 13–15, 17, 96,
        185–187
    and Wilson, Woodrow, 81
democratic socialism
    and America's founding, 44–45
    de Blasio, Bill, on, 22–23
    and equity, 210
    and healthcare policy, 159
    and immigration policy, 119
    and India, 5
    label of, 15
    and majority rule, 51, 52, 55, 185
    moral claim of, 176, 185
    and Ocasio-Cortez, Alexandria, 72–73
    and Omar, Ilhan, 14
    Roosevelt, Franklin D., on, 65
    and Scandinavia, 136–137
    and Venezuela, 163–164
Democratic Socialists of America, 96
    membership growth, 65
    and Ocasio-Cortez, Alexandria, 14
    and Tlaib, Rashida, 14
    2019 conference, 26
Deng Xiaoping, 6
Denmark. See Scandinavia
Dewey, John, 85
Diamondstone, Peter, 43

Dickinson, John, 48
Dorfman, Jeffrey, 138, 161
Douglas, Stephen A., 52, 226
Douglass, Frederick, 36, 45, 56–58, 227
Downer, Alexander, 242, 243
Du Bois, W. E. B., 73, 78–79
Duran, John, 230
Duranty, Walter, 77

East Germany, 3, 4–5
Economic Interpretation of the Constitution of
    the United States, An (Beard), 38
Ehrlich, Paul, 115
Electoral College, 55, 87
Engelbrecht, Catherine, 240, 244
Engels, Friedrich, 33–34, 190
entitlement mentality, 13, 22–23, 30–31,
    50, 66, 88, 91, 153, 155
entrepreneurial capitalism, 173–176
    and automation, 210–211
    and empathy, 204
    fair share or just deserts argument against,
        177–181
    greed and selfishness argument against,
        180
    inequality argument against, 176–177
    justice argument against, 180–182
    and luck, 205–211
    and Marxist critique, 187–190
    and philanthropy, 212–213
    progressive and socialist wealth, 213–217
    and revolution, 199–200, 205
    and self-interest, 182–187
    Smith, Adam, on, 184, 186
    supply-side entrepreneurs, 198–201
    and Trump, Donald, 190–198

fake news, 227–229, 231–236
fascism
    Hollander, Paul, on, 78
    and Mussolini, Benito, 78
    National Socialism, 3, 67, 73, 78, 101,
        103
    and neo-Nazism, 72
    and Roosevelt, Franklin D., 73
    and sister ideologies, 67
    socialism as economic program of, 3
Federal Reserve Board, 86
Federalist, The, 49, 51, 146

feminism, 14, 26–27, 95, 106, 108, 128–130
Fernández-Silber, Natasha, 116
feudalism, 1–2, 27, 103
Finland, 137, 138, 139, 147, 149, 152,
      153, 155, 158–161
Firestone, Shulamith, 130
Foner, Eric, 45
Forbes, Alexander, 92
Ford, Christine Blasey, 128–129
Ford, Henry, 81–82
Franklin, Benjamin, 40–44, 55, 59
Franks, Mary Anne, 46
Fredrickson, George, 145
French Revolution, 45, 48
Freud, Sigmund, 107
Friedman, Milton, 154, 209–210
Fulton, Robert, 59–60

Gabbard, Tulsi, 17
Galbraith, John Kenneth, 100
Gandhi, Mohandas, 5, 7
Gates, Bill, 52, 108, 212
Gates Foundation, 212–213
gender issues, 26–28, 96, 106–107
   feminism, 14, 26–27, 95, 106, 108,
      128–130
   as tactic of the left, 126–133
   transgender people and movement, 26,
      28, 96, 107, 126, 131–133, 245
   See also sexual orientation and sexuality
Ghana, 3
Gilded Age, 39–40, 200
   robber barons, 39, 59–62
Gillibrand, Kirsten
   and Green New Deal, 109
   and Supreme Court expansion, 94
Ginsburg, Ruth Bader, 94
Glover, Danny, 150
Goldberg, Whoopi, 157
Gorbachev, Mikhail, 4
Gore, Al, 111
Gramsci, Antonio, 102, 106
Green, Al, 241
Green New Deal, 18–20, 26, 87–88, 89,
      109–114, 116
Guevara, Che, 76, 256

Hamilton, Alexander, 49
Hannah-Jones, Nikole, 145

Hansen, James, 114
Harding, Warren G., 79
Harris, Kamala, 136
   and Equality Act, 27
   and Green New Deal, 109
   and identity politics, 97
   livable incomes proposal, 154
   and socialism, 16
   and Supreme Court expansion, 94
   tuition-free college policy, 156
"Harrison Bergeron" (Vonnegut), 179
Hayek, Friedrich, 2, 175, 184
   The Constitution of Liberty, 184
   The Road to Serfdom, 2
healthcare
   Affordable Care Act (Obamacare), 13,
      18, 157, 249
   Medicaid, 96, 99
   Medicare, 99
   Medicare for All, 18, 20, 25, 152,
      157–159
   and Scandinavia, 158–159
Heidegger, Martin, 100, 102–103, 105
Henriksen, Martin, 148
Hickenlooper, John, 16–17
Hill, James J., 60–61
Hirschman, Albert O., 47, 48
history from below, 36–40
Hitler, Adolf, 70, 78–79, 103, 209
Holder, Eric, 37, 236, 252
Hollander, Paul, 67, 77–79
Hollywood, 17, 108, 110, 151, 171, 208,
      215, 225, 227, 230, 234, 245, 255–256
Hoover, Margaret, 77
Howe, Irving, 185
Hultman, Nathan, 20
human trafficking, 2
Hume, David, 46
Hungary, 3

Iceland, 113, 136, 138
identity politics
   and dissent, 133
   and education, 171
   and identity socialism, 11
   and indifference, 37
   and physical handicap, 56
   and Roosevelt, Franklin D., 93
   and Scandinavian countries, 146, 148

and 2020 Democratic presidential
  candidates, 96–97
and Venezuela, 164–166
and Wilson, Woodrow, 86
identity socialism (American socialism),
  25–32
  agenda of race and sex, 126–133
  and American founding, 56, 58
  and capitalism, 22–25
  central moral claim of, 14
  and class socialism, 100
  and collectivism, 14–17
  cultural issues, 25–29
  and Debs, Eugene, 82
  definition of, 25
  and dissent, 29
  economic issues, 11–25
  and entitlement mentality, 22–23
  goals of, 27–29, 98–99
  and Green New Deal, 109–116
  and illegal immigration, 28, 116–125
  international models for, 135–152
  and intersectionality, 28
  and Marcuse, Herbert, 100–109
  and Roosevelt, Franklin D., 65–67
  Scandinavian socialism compared with,
    135–163
  and sister ideologies, 67–69
  and social division, 27–28, 144
  and socialist temptation, 29–32
  and taxation, 20–21, 155
  Venezuelan socialism compared with,
    163–172
  and victimology, 37, 140
  and work, 24–25
India, 5–6, 7, 12–13, 29, 34, 119–123
industrial revolution, 59, 173–174
Inslee, Jay, 20
intersectionality, 28, 107
ISIS, 123–125, 237
Isser, Mindy, 26
Isserman, Maurice, 73
Italy, 67, 73, 78, 101

Jackson Lee, Sheila, 27
Jacobin, 13, 26, 45, 65, 116, 162–163
James, William, 50
Jefferson, Thomas, 40, 49, 52, 55, 56–57,
  211

Jobs, Steve, 179, 199
Johnson, Lyndon B., 99
Jones, Owen, 8, 14
judicial review, 45, 54

Kaiser, Robert, 147
Katz, Debra, 129
Katznelson, Ira, 86, 93
Kautsky, Karl, 101
Kavanaugh, Brett, 128–130
Kazin, Michael, 136
Kennedy, John F., 21, 40
Keynes, John Maynard, 92, 126
Ibn Khaldun, 141–142
King, Martin Luther, Jr., 98
King, Stephen, 206–208
Kotkin, Joel, 141, 142
Kroc, Ray, 200–201, 205, 212
Krugman, Paul, 73, 135–136
Ku Klux Klan, 86, 93, 145
Kuznetsov, Vadim, 73

La Follette, Robert, 83
Lamarck, Jean-Baptiste, 85
Lamont, Corliss, 73, 77
Lamont, Ned, 175
Langley, Samuel, 61
Laos, 3
Lenin, Vladimir, 68
  Du Bois, W. E. B., on, 78
  and Gramsci, Antonio, 101–102, 103
  and history of socialism, 2
  on revolution, 101–102
  What Is To Be Done?, 101–102
Lewis, Sophie, 27
Lincoln, Abraham, 98
  on Clay, Henry, 250
  Farewell Address (February 11, 1861),
    223–224, 226
  first inaugural address (1861), 53
  lecture on discoveries and inventions
    (1859), 46–47, 48
  on majority rule, 53
  on popular consent, 53, 185
  and Republican Convention of 1860,
    219–220
  on self-made man, 36
  on slavery, 52, 56–57, 220
  wartime strategy, 227, 256

Lindsey, Hal, 114
Little Red Book (Mao), 6
Lombardi, Vince, 205
Lopez, Mario, 132–133

Madison, James, 4, 49, 51, 52–53, 115,
    146–147
Maduro, Nicolás, 68, 136, 164, 171–172
majority rule, 51–55, 185
    and Bill of Rights, 53–54
    and checks and balances, 54–55
    and distribution of power, 55
    and federalism, 54
    and judicial review, 54
    and representative government, 54
    and separation of powers, 54
    and U.S. Constitution, 53
Mali, 3
Maraniss, David, 205
Marcuse, Herbert, 100–109, 116, 133, 146
Markey, Ed, 109
Marx, Karl
    on America, 33–34
    on capitalism, 2, 188–191, 197
    and Chavez, Hugo, 135
    Critique of Hegel's "Philosophy of Right,"
        27
    definition of socialism, 12
    and Manicheanism, 143
    and Marcuse, Herbert, 101–102, 104,
        105–107
    on role of class in socialism, 96, 111
    on social division, 27
    on transformation of human nature, 68
Marxism
    and alienation, 29
    and revolution, 101–102
    and traditional family, 27, 142
    transposition of categories, 105–107
Mathewes, Charles, 180
Matthews, Dylan, 197
McCarthyism, 73
McCullough, David, 61–62
McDonald, Forrest, 38
McDonald's, 200–201, 205–206
Medicaid, 96, 99
Medicare, 99
Medicare for All, 18, 20, 25, 152, 157–159
Mehta, Suketu, 119–122

Meidner, Rudolf, 161–162
Melin, Carl, 148–149
#MeToo, 96, 128–130
Mill, John Stuart, 247
Mishra, Pankaj, 7
monarchy, 1–2, 22, 53, 63–64, 70, 185
Montesquieu, 48
Moore, Michael, 97, 151, 185, 213, 214
Morita, Akio, 202
Morrison, Toni, 144
Mozambique, 3
Mueller, Robert, 225, 240–241, 248, 251
Muravchik, Joshua, 3
Murger, Henri, 104
Mussolini, Benito, 78, 101

National Socialism (fascism), 3, 67, 73, 78,
    101, 103
nationalized industry, 6, 12–13, 66, 166
Nazism, 3, 78, 86, 100, 103, 109–110, 119
neo-Nazism, 72, 131, 137
Never Trumpers, 222, 227, 244, 249, 252
New Deal, 20, 65–66, 73, 78, 88, 89,
    93–94, 98, 99, 143
Newton, Isaac, 84
Ngo, Andy, 127, 133
Nicaragua, 3, 67, 74–76, 77
Nicaraguan revolution, 76
Nietzsche, Friedrich, 31, 137
1984 (Orwell), 2, 3–4, 40, 78, 225, 236,
    246, 247–248, 256
North Korea, 3, 4–5, 6, 73, 138
Norway. *See* Scandinavia
Nozick, Robert, 206–207

Obama, Barack, 225, 232–237, 238
    Affordable Care Act, 13, 18, 157, 249
    and Buffett, Warren, 208
    Chavez, Hugo, on, 165
    community organizer, 79
    and end of Reagan Revolution, 254
    and expansion of government, 13
    fair share and equality policies, 177–178,
        189
    and Holder, Eric, 236
    immigration policy, 117
    and killing of Osama bin Laden, 221,
        235
    net worth of, 214–215, 217

purchase of Martha's Vineyard property, 19–20, 215
"remaking of America," 29
and Trump, Donald, 239
voter demographics, 97
Obama, Barack, Sr., 186
Obama, Michelle, 19–20, 214–215, 217
Ocasio-Cortez, Alexandria
and capitalism, 22, 23–25, 176, 178
on the end of work, 24
and entitlement mentality, 22, 23
and Green New Deal, 19, 109, 110, 113, 114
and illegal immigration, 118
resignation of chief of staff, 20
and socialism, 1, 14, 15–17, 72–73, 87–88, 137–138
and Sunrise Movement, 19
on Trump coalition, 144
O'Donnell, Rosie, 238–239
Okere, Ugo, 14
Omar, Ilhan, 1, 14, 15–16, 17, 89, 118, 124–125, 149, 176–177, 189
O'Rourke, Beto, 17, 94, 96–97, 123, 144, 169
Orwell, George
Animal Farm, 2, 4
on Big Brother, 225, 246, 247
1984, 2, 3–4, 40, 78, 225, 236, 246, 247–248, 256
on outer and inner parties, 236
on private individuals as informants, 247–248
Otis, James, 48

Paine, Thomas, 45
Papadopoulos, George, 241–244
Partanen, Anu, 161
Passions and the Interests, The (Hirschman), 47
Paul, Rand, 211
Pelosi, Nancy, 15–16, 17, 228
Penn, Sean, 151
People's History of the United States, A (Zinn), 37
People's Republic of China. See China
Pilgrim's Progress, The (Bunyan), 8
Plato, 31
Poland, 3
Political Pilgrims (Hollander), 67, 77–79

Ponte, Lowell, 115–116
Ponzi, Charles, 89–90
popular sovereignty, 52
Potter, Beatrix, 198–199
Prakash, Varshini, 19
Pritzker, Jay, 175

railroad industry, 59–61, 173
Rand, Ayn, 175, 184
Rasmussen, Lars Løkke, 139, 148
Rawls, John, 179–180, 182, 185, 208–209
Reagan, Ronald, 21, 75, 221, 223, 226
and Cold War, 224
and Marcuse, Herbert, 101, 108
Trump, Donald, compared with, 249–250, 253–254
Reagan Revolution, 254
reeducation, 29, 108, 132–133, 248
Reich, Robert, 66
reparations
for colonialism, 121
for slavery, 27, 97, 126
reproductive justice, 26
Rifkin, Jeremy, 24
RINOs (Republicans in name only), 228
robber barons, 39, 59–62
Robinson, Nathan, 65, 177
Rockefeller, John D., 212
Romania, 3
Roosevelt, Franklin D.
and class warfare, 143–144, 146
on democratic socialism, 65
make-work programs, 92
and Mussolini, Benito, 78
New Deal, 20, 65–66, 73, 78, 89, 93–94, 98, 99, 143
and race, 93, 99
Sanders, Bernie on, 65, 67
Second Bill of Rights, 88–89, 91, 143
and Social Security, 66, 89–90, 91, 93, 99
and socialism, 45, 65–67, 88–94, 95–96, 99
and Supreme Court, 66, 93–94
tax policy, 91–92
and unemployment insurance, 66, 99
Roosevelt, Teddy, 82, 83
Rosenstein, Rod, 241, 251
Ross, Edward Alsworth, 85–86
Rubin, Jennifer, 244

Sanders, Bernie, 42–45
  and Burlington-Yaroslavl sister city
    arrangement, 74
  on China, 173
  climate change policy, 18
  and Cuba, 73–74
  and Debs, Eugene, 82
  definition of socialism, 87
  and Diamondstone, Peter, 43
  and Equality Act, 27
  fair share and equality views, 178
  Franklin, Benjamin, compared with, 42
  free-college policies, 18, 152, 156
  and Green New Deal, 109
  healthcare policy, 157–159
  and identity politics, 27–28, 97
  and Nicaragua, 74–75
  Project Veritas investigation of, 29
  property and wealth of, 213–214
  proposed worker ownership, 21
  on Roosevelt, Franklin D., 65–67
  and socialism, 1, 12, 15, 16, 17, 18
  and socialist nations, 73–75
  tax policy, 21, 159, 161
  and Trump, Donald, 253
  and Venezuela, 137
Sandsmark, Evan, 180
Scandinavia
  Denmark, 136–140, 148–149, 158,
    160–162, 171
  healthcare, 158–159
  market economy, 139–140
  Meidner Plan, 161–162
  Norway, 136–141, 146–149, 152, 158,
    160–162, 167, 171
  privatization, 162
  "Sven Socialism," 137–138, 139, 162
  Sweden, 12, 136–138, 146, 148–149,
    152, 158, 160–162, 171
  taxes, 159–163
  tribes and race, 146–149
  unification socialism of, 139–143
  welfare state model, 152–153
  See also Finland; Iceland
Schumer, Chuck, 27, 228
Schumpeter, Joseph, 23–25
  Capitalism, Socialism and Democracy,
    11–12
  on creative destruction, 32

The Entrepreneur, 190–193, 194, 196
  on will of the people, 69
Schwartz, Jack, 39, 66
Scott, Rodney, 120–121
Sedition Act, 79
Seidman, Louis Michael, 46
self-invention, 36, 58
self-made man, 36, 45, 55–58, 62
Sen, Amartya, 181–182
Seward, William H., 219–220
sex trafficking, 2
sexual freedom and repression, 42–43
sexual orientation and sexuality
  and founding fathers, 55
  and intersectionality, 28, 106–107
  Marcuse, Herbert, on, 106–108
  and religion, 97
  and socialism, 28, 95, 98–99, 144, 224,
    245
  as tactic of the left, 126, 130, 132
  See also gender issues
Shakespeare, William
  Henry V, 240
  Julius Caesar, 63–64
Sinclair, Larry, 231–235
slavery
  American Civil War, 37, 52, 57–58, 60,
    70, 84, 98, 145, 220, 252
  and ancient Greece, 51
  Douglass, Frederick, on, 56–58
  and Founding Fathers, 56–57
  Fredrickson, George, on, 145
  Lincoln, Abraham, on, 52, 56–57, 220
  O'Rourke, Beto, on, 144
  and reparations, 27, 97, 126
  socialism compared to, 2
  and Soviet Union, 2, 3, 27
Smith, Adam, 6, 47, 48, 84, 175
  and Lincoln, Abraham, 46
  The Theory of Moral Sentiments,
    183–184
  The Wealth of Nations, 46, 84, 183–184,
    204
Smith, Al, 66
Smollett, Jussie, 127–128
Social Security, 66, 89–90, 91, 93, 99
socialism
  critiques of, 7–8
  definitions of, 11–14, 87–88

early history of, 141–143
as economic failure, 3–4
and labels, 16–20
national socialist experiments, 3
public opinion on, 64
"real socialism," 7, 68
Schumpeter, Joseph, on, 11–12
slavery compared to, 2
temptation of, 8–9
test case of East and West Germany, 4–5
test case of North and South Korea, 5
and totalitarianism, 3–4
See also identity socialism; Scandinavia;
   Venezuela
Soleimani, Qasem, 235
Solzhenitsyn, Alexandr
   The Gulag Archipelago, 2, 75
   imprisonment, 75
   One Day in the Life of Ivan Denisovich, 2
Somalia, 123–125
Sombart, Werner, 33–34
Souls of Black Folk, The (Du Bois), 78
South Korea, 4–5
Soviet Union, 68, 137
   Bolshevik Revolution, 3, 70, 83
   collapse of, 4
   five-year plans, 5
   Hollander, Paul, on, 67, 77–79
   nationalization of industry, 12
   and Reagan, Ronald, 249
   and Sanders, Bernie, 67, 73–74
   and Solzhenitsyn, Aleksandr, 75
   Stalin, Joseph, 29, 73, 75, 77, 133
   totalitarianism and violence in, 3
   and Wilson, Woodrow, 86
Spirit of the Laws (Montesquieu), 48
Stahl, Lesley, 157
Stalin, Joseph, 29, 73, 75, 77, 133
Standley, Tylor, 180
Stepman, Jarrett, 26
Stiglitz, Joseph, 20, 21, 136, 150, 176
Story, Joseph, 54
Stossel, John, 138
Sunkara, Bhaskar, 13, 83, 136–137
Sunrise Movement, 19, 109
Sunstein, Cass, 89
Supreme Court
   Gibbons v. Ogden, 59–60
   judicial review, 54

*Masterpiece Cakeshop v. Colorado Civil
   Rights Commission,* 245–246
nomination of Brett Kavanaugh, 128
proposed expansion of, 93–94
Roe v. Wade, 226
and Roosevelt, Franklin D., 66, 93–94
Svendsen, Gert Tinggaard, 140
Sweden. *See* Scandinavia

Tanzania, 3
Tarbell, Ida, 78
taxes
   and Buttigieg, Pete, 21
   and identity socialism, 20–21, 155
   and Roosevelt, Franklin D., 91–92
   and Sanders, Bernie, 21, 159, 161
   and Scandinavia, 159–163
   top marginal rate, 21, 91–92, 160
   wealth tax, 21, 162
Taylor, Astra, 19, 45, 73
technological revolution, 173–174, 199
terrorism, 28, 123–125, 221, 235, 240
Theory of the Leisure Class, The (Veblen), 39
This Land Is Our Land (Mehta), 119–122
Thomas, Norman, 66, 83
Tlaib, Rashida, 1, 14, 15–16, 17, 89, 118,
   149, 152, 241
transgender people and movement, 26, 28,
   96, 107, 126, 131–133, 245
Trump, Donald
   The Apprentice, 198
   The Art of the Comeback, 197
   The Art of the Deal, 191
   business career of, 191–198
   and capitalism, 190–191
   and Daniels, Stormy, 229–231, 234–235
   donors and fundraising, 174–175
   D'Souza's first meeting with, 220–223
   energy policy, 13
   immigration policy, 118, 120, 122, 123
   impeachment, 216, 221–222, 240–241
   Krugman, Paul, on, 73, 136
   "Make America Great Again" slogan, 34
   Mueller investigation, 225, 240–241,
      248, 251
   and North Korea, 6
   O'Rourke, Beto, on, 144
   pardon of D'Souza, 239
   politics of, 248–255

Trump (*continued*)
    Reagan, Ronald, compared with,
        249–250, 253–254
    on socialism, 34
    and spectacle, 195–198
    State of the Union address (2019), 34
    supporters, 127, 144, 225, 244
    voter demographics, 97
    Warren, Elizabeth, on, 144
Trump, Donald, Jr., 229
Trump Derangement Syndrome, 226
Trump International Hotel (Washington,
    D.C.), 187
Twain, Mark, 40

unemployment insurance, 18, 66, 87, 99
Universal Basic Income, 18, 152, 153–156

Vanderbilt, Cornelius, 59–60, 62, 192
Veblen, Thorstein, 39
Venezuela, 3, 4, 73, 120, 221
    attacks on entrepreneurs and wealth,
        166–168
    Bolívar, Simón, 166, 170
    Bolivarian Revolution, 136
    Chavez, Hugo, 135–136, 150–151,
        163–169, 172, 206, 217
    Chavistas (ruling class), 68, 164–171
    class and race, 163–167
    colectivos (armed militias), 170
    conformity, 170
    gun confiscation, 169–170
    identity politics, 164–166
    land confiscation, 168
    Maduro, Nicolás, 68, 136, 164, 171–172
    Misión Cultura, 166
    oil industry, 150–151, 164–168
    Petróleos de Venezuela (PDVSA),
        167–168
    rigging the system in favor of social
        regime, 168–169
    socialists themes, 164–172
    wealth from politics, 171–172
Venezuelan revolution, 150–151
Vietnam, 3
Vietnam War, 105–106, 109

Villard, Henry, 60–61
Voegelin, Eric, 68
von Mises, Ludwig, 198–199
Vonnegut, Kurt, 179

Wallace, Henry, 83
Walzer, Michael, 178–179, 205
Warren, Elizabeth
    ancestry controversy, 97, 214
    and capitalism, 16
    and Equality Act, 27
    fair share policies, 161, 162, 177, 178,
        189
    on fracking, 18
    and Green New Deal, 109
    healthcare policies, 157, 158
    and identity socialism, 27, 96
    proposed Accountable Capitalism Act, 22
    proposed wealth tax, 21, 162
    and socialism, 12, 16, 17
    on student debt forgiveness, 18
    and Supreme Court expansion, 94
    on Trump, Donald, 144
    and wealth, 217
Washington, George, 40, 48, 63–64, 65,
    170, 219
Weissgerber, Martin, 29
West, Cornel, 150
Westing, Corrie, 26–27
Wilde, Oscar, 70–71
Wilentz, Sean, 66
Williamson, Marianne, 97
Wilson, Elizabeth, 104
Wilson, Woodrow, 79–87, 93
Wood, Gordon, 53
Wright, Jeremiah, 233–234
Wright, Wilbur and Orville, 61–62

Yang, Andrew, 18, 153–156
Young, Donald, 233–235
Yugoslavia, 3

Zambia, 3
Zimbabwe, 3, 4, 138
Zinn, Howard, 37
Zuckerberg, Mark, 108, 175